Orchestra

OF

EXILES

Orchestra

OF
EXILES

JOSH ARONSON
& DENISE GEORGE

BERKLEY BOOKS, NEW YORK

BERKLEY

An imprint of Penguin Random House LLC
375 Hudson Street, New York, New York 10014

This book is an original publication of Penguin Random House LLC.

Library of Congress Cataloging-in-Publication Data

Names: Aronson, Josh. | George, Denise.
Title: Orchestra of exiles : the story of Bronislaw Huberman, the Israel
Philharmonic, and the one thousand Jews he saved from Nazi horrors / Josh
Aronson & Denise George.
Description: First edition. | New York : Berkley 2016.
Identifiers: LCCN 2015036463 | ISBN 9780425281215
Subjects: LCSH: Huberman, Bronislaw. | Violinists—Biography. | Tizmoret
ha-Erets-Yiâsre®elit. | LCGFT: Biographies.
Classification: LCC ML418.H82 A85 2016 | DDC 787.2092—dc23
LC record available at https://lccn.loc.gov/2015036463

First edition: April 2016

PRINTED IN THE UNITED STATES OF AMERICA

10 9 8 7 6 5 4 3 2 1

Jacket design by Rita Frangie.
Jacket photo of Bronislaw Huberman © Studio Lipnitzki / Roger Viollet.
Text design by Laura K. Corless.
Title page art © Alenavlad / Shutterstock.

Most Berkley Books are available at special quantity discounts for bulk purchases for
sales promotions, premiums, fund-raising, or educational use. Special books, or book
excerpts, can also be created to fit specific needs. For details, write: SpecialMarkets@
penguinrandomhouse.com.

Penguin
Random
House

We wish to dedicate this book
to the millions of Jews who suffered
and perished during the Holocaust,
and to Bronislaw Huberman.

DISCLAIMER

Every event in this book is true; happened the way it is told; all characters are historical. Some dialogue has been created.

CONTENTS

PRELUDE

*One cannot read very much about the Holocaust without being
struck . . . by the indications of diabolical inspiration for what
happened. It appears in the extraordinary cruelty of the Nazis, in
the philosophy of their leaders, in their explicit hatred of God and
of religion, in their determination to wipe out Christianity as well
as Judaism, in their open embrace of paganism and occultism, in
their sexual perversity, and in their satanic, cultic practices.*

Roy H. Schoeman, author of *Salvation Is from the Jews*[1]

By the early 1920s, the Great War in Europe has ended, but its devastating
results remain. People are starving. Crying children run barefoot down
debris-strewn streets. Families are homeless, cold, and destitute. A blanket
of dark disillusionment shrouds Europe, suffocating dreams and smothering hopes. Despondent veterans, still wearing bloodstained, lice-infested
uniforms, stand dispassionately on street corners, staring deadpan into
space, dangling their arms by their sides in utter defeat and holding within
their hearts no hope of finding a job, or even a crust of bread.

In Munich, Germany, the slight, pale man with brown hair parted to
one side stands on a platform, his head erect, his steel-blue eyes fixed on
the faces of hungry crowds. Loud, and with great drama, he shouts words
of hate and words of hope to hundreds of German people who so desperately
want his promises to come true.

"Once I really am in power," he bellows, his voice strange and hypnotic,
"my first and foremost task will be the annihilation of the Jews. As soon
as I have the power to do so, I will have gallows built in rows at the Marien-
platz in Munich . . . as many as traffic allows. Then the Jews will be hanged

indiscriminately, and they will remain hanging until they stink. They will hang there as long as the principles of hygiene permit."

He pauses, and continues: "As soon as they have been untied, the next batch will be strung up, and so on down the line, until the last Jew in Munich has been exterminated. Other cities will follow suit, precisely in this fashion, until all Germany has been completely cleansed of Jews."[2]

When Adolf Hitler finishes his speech, some Germans applaud wildly, cheering and calling out with supportive enthusiasm. They seem ready for a new government, fresh leaders who will restore respect and prosperity to their war-humiliated fatherland. Others remain deathly quiet, as if worried about their family members should this man become Germany's leader.

In Berlin, 1934, young Horst Salomon shouts, lifts his hands above his head, and taps his feet in an excited dance. His mother bursts into his room, seeming alarmed by his sudden enthusiastic roar.

"Horst!" she shouts. "What has happened?! Why are you making so much noise?"

The muscular Jewish man waves a letter and picks up his mother, laughing and swinging her around until she orders him to stop.

"Put me down, Horst! You're making me dizzy!" she cries, laughing. "Tell me what's going on!"

"Mother! I've just heard I will be participating in the weight-lifting competition here in Berlin during the 1936 Summer Olympic Games! The International Olympic Committee has awarded the Summer Games to our city!"

"Oh, Horst!" she cries. "This is wonderful! It's what you've always wanted!"

"Watch out, Josef Manger!" Horst shouts. "I'm going for gold!"

One year later, Horst ties his French horn to his motorcycle and dashes to the Berlin concert hall, running inside and joining the rehearsal already in progress. When the practice ends, the conductor, Wilhelm Furtwängler, approaches him.

"Son," he says softly. "Please be on time for our next rehearsal. The Berlin Philharmonic needs you from the beginning."

"Yes, Maestro," Horst says, smiling.

Horst and Maestro Furtwängler have become good friends through the orchestra's family of musicians. They meet often for coffee in a nearby Berlin café. At one meeting, Furtwängler seems downcast.

"Horst, Germany is changing," he says, shaking his head. "Nineteen thirty-five is bringing terrible changes to our fatherland."

He takes a deep breath. "Not long ago, when I heard rumors that Joseph Goebbels planned to fire Jewish musicians from Germany's orchestras, I faced a difficult decision. Should I stay in Germany, or should I leave? I met with Goebbels, telling him that removing Germany's superb Jewish musicians is not in the Fatherland's best interests. I asked him to promise me he wouldn't fire the Jewish musicians in the Berlin Philharmonic. Goebbels assured me he would show leniency toward certain *key* Jewish players, if I committed to stay as the Berlin Philharmonic's conductor. I stayed. But now I am questioning my decision, no longer sure I can protect my Jewish musicians."

In 1935, Lorand Fenyves, a sixteen-year-old, gifted Jewish musician, studying at Budapest's Liszt Academy with violinist Jenő Hubay, leaves his class late and walks down the school's long hallway. With the exception of the school's janitor, who mops the floor, Lorand is alone in the hallway.

Turning toward the front door, Lorand smiles at the janitor. He is eager to get home, wanting to describe the day's class to his older sister, Alice, also a violinist.

Suddenly he hears a thunderous noise around the corner several yards ahead of him. Men scream: "Where are the filthy Jews, the Jewish garbage?" He hears plaster fall and break, and glass shatter. Lorand stops, drops his violin case, and slams his back against the wall, hoping he hasn't been seen.

As the pandemonium comes closer, his heart races, and his hands form tight fists. He knows he cannot fight so many.

As if from nowhere, he feels a strong hand grab his shoulder and throw him into a nearby bathroom. He tumbles to the floor.

"Lock the door! Stay quiet!" a man tells him. "Hungarian Nazis! Do not come out!"

Slamming the door and locking it, Lorand scampers to a corner. In the space between the floor and door, Lorand sees the janitor's shoes, the old man standing outside as if guarding the room.

"Get out of here, you hoodlums!" he hears the janitor shout.

"Out of our way, old man!" the intruders scream. "We want Jews!"

"There are no Jews here! Now get out!" the janitor shouts.

Lorand hears a thud, and a pitiful whimper. He jumps to his feet, rushing to unlock the door, wanting desperately to help the janitor.

"Do not come out!" the janitor screams, as if predicting Lorand's compassionate response.

Fists pound the door, the wood vibrating with every hit. The door panels shake, threatening to shatter. Angry men's voices curse, calling out: "Unlock the door, you filthy Jew! We know you're in there!"

"Do not come out!" the janitor screams again.

Lorand stays inside, terrified of the mob screaming for Jewish blood, protected by the locked door, but yearning to help the old man.

The commotion lasts a long time; each second seems an eternity to Lorand. His body trembles as he waits for them to break down the door and burst in. After a long while, however, the swearing, threats, and pounding stop. Lorand hears the sounds of retreating boots, and then silence.

"Lorand, it's safe now. The thugs are gone," the janitor calls to him.

Lorand leaves the room, kneels beside the old man, and helps him to his feet.

"I'm not hurt," the janitor says. "Just get out of here before they come back!"

"But . . ." Lorand says. "Your head is bleeding. Let me take you to the doctor."

"No!" he shouts. "Go home! Hurry!"

When Lorand arrives home, his hands still tremble. He tells his sister about the dangerous encounter.

"Our family isn't safe in Budapest anymore!" he cries. "We must leave Hungary. I fear the violence will just get worse."

In April 1936, the bloody uprising in several cities in Palestine mushrooms, bringing savagery from both Muslim, Jewish, and Christian Palestinian leaders and clerics, as they capture and kill each other.

The uncontrollable violence boils hotter, spilling into the scorching Palestinian summer, destroying homesteads and devouring people, Arab, Jew, and Christian. When Britain sees no hint of a cease-fire in sight, the government threatens to halt immigration to Palestine, thus handing out death sentences to Jews still trapped inside Hitler's European hellhole.

Part 1

A SON IS BORN

But the hearts of small children are delicate organs. A cruel beginning in this world can twist them into curious shapes. The heart of a hurt child can shrink so that forever afterward it is hard and pitted as the seed of a peach. . . .

Carson McCullers[1]

CHAPTER 1

The Boy

Childhood should be carefree, playing in the sun; not living a nightmare in the darkness of the soul.

Dave Pelzer, *A Child Called "It"*[1]

On December 19, 1882, in the small city of Częstochowa, Silesia, Poland, Alexandra Huberman takes a deep, labored breath and places her hand low on her bulging belly. She closes her eyes against the pain, each contraction becoming more severe and frequent.

"Jacob, the child is coming," she tells her husband. She walks to the next room and stretches out on the thin mattress. In bouts of pain, Alexandra grasps the hand of the midwife, and waits for the birth of her first child.

Jacob does not follow her, but sits in silence in the parlor of their small, shabby home. Alexandra prays to birth a boy, not for herself, but for her husband, Jacob, who wants a son with long, strong fingers who can play the violin. She knows that only a boy will appease her husband. She grimaces at the thought of birthing a daughter.

As Alexandra waits, she stares at the ceiling and walls, the chipped paint, the stained and peeling wallpaper. Before she married Jacob, she knew he had little means and not much financial potential. But Alexandra believed marriage would prove a better option for her, a poor Polish teenager in the late 1800s. She knew that choosing *not* to marry would mean *no* possibility of income and no legitimate children.

Alexandra hates Jacob's quick temper. Within weeks of the wedding, she learned the full scope of her husband's outbursts. She dares not oppose him, but instead obeys his demands, her fear of him growing each year. By the time she conceived, any feelings of love for Jacob had died. Terror now replaces tenderness, intimacy has become dread. Alexandra buries her fragile heart in a deep, dark hole, having learned to live without affection and struggling to find new ways to defuse Jacob's rage.

With the exception of their Polish upbringing and Jewish heritage, Alexandra and Jacob have little in common. Jacob taught school when they married, making little money, but putting food on their table, and providing them with shelter in Częstochowa, a small town south of Łódź. His employers fired him after one of his violent flare-ups. No other school dared hire him. Working as a lowly lawyer's clerk, he now earns barely enough to maintain life and home.

Alexandra winces when she feels another contraction.

"Please be a boy," she mumbles. "A son might possibly tame Jacob's wrath, and perhaps make him a decent father."

After another contraction, the midwife prepares for the birth. She raises Alexandra's legs, placing a pillow beneath them and covering her with a sheet to preserve her modesty.

"I am grateful to have you here," she tells the midwife.

"I'm glad Jacob allowed me to come," the midwife responds. "A woman should not give birth alone, especially for the first time."

Jacob had, at first, refused the midwife's assistance.

"Women expecting babies should know what to do," he said. "Instinct should teach them. We do not need help from hired outsiders."

But for the first time, Alexandra had spoken up, trying to reason with him.

"I fear giving birth, Jacob. Something could go wrong—puerperal fever or milk leg or convulsions. I don't want to be alone."

"Silly woman!" he had said.

Jacob changed his mind, however, allowing Alexandra her midwife—but one who expected no payment.

Jacob becomes the father of a healthy boy, but shows no delight in him, even refusing to hold the infant.

"We will name him 'Bronislaw,'" Jacob says as he examines the infant's fingers. "Yes," he says, "this child has the fingers of a violinist. He will become the musician I have always yearned to be."

After Jacob leaves the room, Alexandra nurses her newborn, smiling and running her hands across the baby's soft skin.

"Perhaps, little one," she whispers, "I can love you enough for both Jacob and me."

Bronislaw learns early how to tiptoe around his father's temper. He avoids any behavior that risks bringing his father's fury, and seldom smiles or speaks. He loves his mother but fears his father.

A few days before Bronislaw's fourth birthday, he asks: "Mama, do you think Papa will buy me an accordion for my birthday?"

Alexandra smiles. "I'll ask him, son."

"No, Bronislaw," his father tells him. "You'll play the violin."

On his birthday, Bronislaw receives a used violin and bow. He looks at his father with disappointment, but says nothing.

"You will come to like it in time," Jacob says, as if sensing the boy's letdown. "And if you don't, you'll still learn to play it."

Jacob places the violin under the youngster's chin and the bow in his tiny hand, and instructs him on the appropriate way to hold both.

Over the next few years, Jacob becomes the father of two more sons. Within minutes of each boy's birth, Jacob checks the child's fingers.

"No. No. Bronislaw is the only one with a violinist's fingers," he says.

CHAPTER 2

A Childhood Denied

*How did I become a musician, a violinist? . . . My father was a
passionate admirer of music, but self-taught, and it worried him
all his life that the circumstances of his youth had not allowed him
to be a musician. Thus, he hoped to find his own personal ambitions
realized in his son.*

Bronislaw Huberman[1]

Bronislaw, a small child with dark shoulder-length hair and sad brown eyes,
holds the violin under his chin. He has practiced for hours.

"I am weary, Papa," he cries. "My fingers hurt. Please let me rest."

"No! You have a gift, and you must work hard to become a great violinist," Jacob says. "One day, with my help, you'll be famous. Keep practicing.
All violinists have blisters on their fingertips! In time, they'll become
calluses and won't hurt as much."

The child's spontaneous, frightened cries bring Jacob's fury.

"I will not tolerate tears!" he shouts. "You will practice until I tell you
to stop!"

The child pushes his long bangs out of his eyes, wipes his nose on his
sleeve, and repositions the violin under his chin.

"Soon," Jacob says, "you will be ready to perform in public, and you
can earn money for our family. Then we can stop living like poor peasants."

Bronislaw's musical abilities bloom. He shows a natural mechanical
ability with his arms, hands, and fingers, coupled with a mysterious talent
to make music. With the boy's innate gifts, and his father's demands push-

ing him to practice, Bronislaw soon advances far beyond what his father can teach him.

Late one evening, as he lies in his bed in the next room, Bronislaw overhears his parents talking.

"Alexandra, the child is a prodigy! We must send him to Warsaw for a musical education. If he is to flourish, he needs professional guidance."

"But, Jacob, he's only seven years old, still a baby! Please don't take him away."

"It's for his good, and ours, too," Jacob says. "I will take him to the conservatory in Warsaw. I refuse to allow his early years to be wasted—as mine were by my father! In no time, our son will be ready to give concerts and make money."

"But, Jacob," Alexandra pleads. "Children are dying from the influenza. I've heard the epidemic is spreading to Europe's major cities. It's too dangerous for him to travel."

"Do not cross me, woman!" Jacob shouts. "Bronislaw's musical education is more important than the remote chance of illness! He must begin these lessons immediately!"

Bronislaw has heard enough. He pulls the blanket over his face, closes his eyes, and tries to sleep. But he can't. His parents' conversation has unnerved him, making him sick to his stomach.

CHAPTER 3

Leaving Home

Huberman's tone was invariably pure and fine-grained, his left hand absolutely sure in the most complicated passage work, and his bow arm extremely steady and flexible.

Noel Strauss[1]

Several months later, Jacob fills his pocket with the family's last rubles. Alexandra places her son's clothes in a bag and packs two meager lunches. Together, father and son travel by train to Warsaw, soon arriving at the Warsaw Conservatory. Jacob has arranged for Bronislaw to audition for professors Mieczyslaw Michalowisz and Maurycy Rosen, two exceptional teachers.

"Stand up straight, Bronislaw! Put your hands by your side and do not speak. When I tell you to play, do so perfectly, as I have taught you!" Jacob tells him.

When Jacob meets the two professors, he introduces himself and his son. The boy stares at the floor, his hair falling forward and covering most of his face.

"Hold your head up, Bronislaw!" Papa tells him.

Without speaking or smiling, the child with the pale face, dressed in worn knickers, tunic, and scuffed shoes, raises his head, looks up at the two men who tower above him, and he puts out his hand.

"The boy is shy," Papa tells them. "He does not meet or interact well with people. But my son is a prodigy! He must be allowed to study here."

The professor, Michalowisz, glances at Rosen, who nods his approval.

"Yes, Mr. Huberman," Michalowisz says. "Let us hear Bronislaw play. Then we will judge whether we will teach him."

Jacob sees Professor Rosen raise his eyes to the ceiling and overhears him mumble to Michalowisz: "Another prodigy? How many more of these so-called prodigies must we endure?"

Jacob ignores the comment. "Play your violin, Bronislaw."

The boy positions the instrument under his chin, holding the bow firmly in his right hand, and begins to play.

As Bronislaw plays, Jacob watches each professor's face begin to change from nonchalance, to surprise, to enthusiasm. He notices how each leans forward in his chair, drops open his mouth, and seems surprisingly impressed by the child's talent. When Bronislaw finishes, the professors sit in silence, as if unable to fathom the performance of the frail, timid child.

"Extraordinary!" Professor Rosen exclaims. "The boy's playing is phenomenal!"

Jacob smiles. "Will you teach him?"

"Yes, of course!" Rosen says.

"We can enroll him right away," Professor Michalowisz says. "Mr. Huberman, your son is truly talented—a prodigy, just as you say."

For the next several months, Jacob escorts his son daily to the conservatory. He worries little about the Russian influenza epidemic raging across Europe during the fall and winter of 1889. But Jacob soon tires of Michalowisz and Rosen, and arranges for Bronislaw to study with Isidor Lotto at the Warsaw Conservatory. Professor Lotto works Bronislaw hard, readying him for his first stage appearance.

On the afternoon of the boy's first concert, Jacob washes his son's long hair, combing the bangs and sides close around his face. In front of a large audience, Bronislaw stands on the stage at the Warsaw Institute of Music, and plays Louis Spohr's Second Violin Concerto with piano accompaniment.

Jacob stands to the side of the stage, eyeballing the boy's every move.

"He plays so incredibly well," Isidor Lotto tells Jacob after the concert. "But he's such a serious and nervous child. Does he never smile?"

Jacob ignores Lotto's question. After three months of study with Professor Lotto, Jacob takes Bronislaw out of the Warsaw Conservatory.

"Bronislaw," he says, "your study time in Warsaw is over. You have had the privilege of studying with Professors Michalowisz, Rosen, and Lotto. Now the time has come for you to perform on the stages of Europe. I will arrange the tours and accompany you."

O n the evening of April 20, 1889, in Braunau Am Inn, a small Austrian village four hundred miles southwest of Częstochowa, Klara Pölzl gives birth to her fourth baby—the only child who lives.

Her husband and uncle, Alois Schicklgruber, a civil servant almost three decades her senior, names the child Adolf, baptizing him as a Roman Catholic.[2]

"I will call him 'Adi,'" Klara tells her husband.

For the next five years, Klara lavishes her young son, Adi Hitler, with full-time attention and affection.[3,4]

CHAPTER 4

Concerts for Cash

As soon as it was recognized that I had talent, [my father] gave up working in order to build up my career. I was only ten years old at the time, and there were two younger brothers, but the whole financial support of the family fell on me.

Bronislaw Huberman[1]

In 1892, the small boy, holding a violin and bow, walks out onto a large European concert stage. His head lowered, he glances up and sees hundreds of people sitting before him, waiting for him to play. He takes a deep breath, and notices his father standing behind the stage.

"You must play perfectly!" his father tells him.

The child focuses on his father's face as he pulls the bow across the strings, his left hand masterfully pressing the taut lines with blistered fingertips. When he finishes, he takes a slight bow. The audience responds with thunderous applause. With a smile on his face, Bronislaw runs backstage to his father.

"Bronislaw," Papa tells him. "You did not do your best. You can play better than that. Your art deserves more effort. Your audience deserves more."

"I'm sorry, Papa," Bronislaw whispers, the smile gone from his face. "I'll try harder next time."

❦

After watching the audience's enthusiastic response to Bronislaw's performance, Jacob wastes no time arranging for his son to play more concerts on Europe's stages.

"Wake up and get dressed, Bronislaw," Jacob tells him early one morning. "You must practice for tonight's concert."

"I'm tired, Papa," the boy whines. "Please let me sleep a little longer."

"No, Bronislaw, get up and practice."

"Yes, Papa," the boy says.

One evening in October 1892, the well-known Russian pianist, composer, and conductor Anton Rubinstein attends one of his concerts.

Jacob looks out over the crowd and spots the famous founder of the St. Petersburg Conservatory.

"Bronislaw, play perfectly!" Jacob says. "Anton Rubinstein is here to hear you. He can help us get ahead in your career."

When Bronislaw finishes, Jacob rushes to greet Rubinstein.

"I am Bronislaw's father," he tells him, holding his chin high. "What did you think of my son's performance?"

"Sir," Rubinstein exclaims, "only a genius plays like that! You must take the boy to study with Joseph Joachim in Berlin."

"I will consider it," Jacob tells him.

Late that night, Jacob rises from bed, counting again the money Bronislaw has earned. He remembers Rubinstein's affirming comment, and before dawn, he makes a decision.

I will quit my job, and take Bronislaw all over Europe to perform and make money. And I will ask Professor Joseph Joachim to teach him.

Bronislaw is pleased when Papa takes him home to Częstochowa. But at dinner one night, Jacob announces: "Alexandra, Bronislaw and I will be going to Berlin. I've decided to quit my job."

Jacob places a basket on the table. "Every ruble we earn will go into this basket. When we have enough money, I will take Bronislaw to Berlin to study with Joseph Joachim."

During the next weeks, Bronislaw plays concerts in Częstochowa. After one performance, a well-dressed, five-year-old boy approaches him.

"I like how you play," the child tells him.

"Thanks," Bronislaw says. "What's your name? Do you play the violin, too?"

"I'm Arthur . . . Arthur Ru-bin-stein," he says slowly with deliberate clarity. "And, no, I'm not 'lated to *Anton* Ru-bin-stein."

Arthur digs in his pocket and pulls out a small printed card: *Arthur Rubinstein, the Great Piano Virtuoso. No Relation.*[2]

"How old are you, Arthur?"

"Five," he says, holding up five fingers. "I play the piano."

"Where do you live?"

"In Łódź."

"What does your father do?"

"He works, but mostly he reads the Talmud."

"Want to come to my house and play sometime?" Bronislaw asks.

"Sure! I'll ask my mother."

Arthur's mother, Felicia Heyman Rubinstein, brings her son to visit Bronislaw's home several times after the boys' first meeting.

"The boys are becoming good friends," she tells Jacob. "They have much in common, especially their love of music."

"Yes," Jacob responds. "Both boys are musical prodigies. How far has Arthur progressed? He is still quite young."

"Arthur is progressing well," she says. "He's making significant advances. I have spoken with Joseph Joachim about recommending a piano teacher in Berlin."[3]

"For both our sons, music must be a priority," Jacob says. "As budding artists, Arthur and Bronislaw should practice harder and enjoy fewer playtimes."

"Mr. Huberman, but I don't see how brief times of fun interfere with their practice. Surely, young boys are entitled to have some fun."

"*Entitled?* An interesting word, Mrs. Rubinstein. You make decisions about Arthur, but Bronislaw will learn that sacrificing playtime proves a small price to pay for the serious pursuit of art—*l'art pour l'art.* Don't you agree?"

Felicia hesitates, pressing her lips together.

"No, sir, I do not. Art should never be viewed only for the sake of art! Art's purpose is bigger, bringing joy and encouragement to the giver and hearer. Joy and encouragement should be a part of every child's life, not relentless practicing and performing! Thank you for Bronislaw's playdate with Arthur, Mr. Huberman. Please let me know if, and when, it is convenient to bring Arthur again."

CHAPTER 5

The Teacher

I state with pleasure that the nine-year-old Huberman from Warsaw possesses a truly remarkable musical talent. In all my life I have hardly ever encountered such a promising, precocious musical development on the violin.

Joseph Joachim, 1891

In January 1892, ten-year-old Bronislaw finds a few rare minutes of solitude when Jacob leaves the house, tending to some bank business. The boy feels grateful for the respite from practice. Since his father quit his job, he spends more time with Bronislaw, demanding he practice for hours each day, and arranging concerts in Częstochowa.

The boy counts the rubles in the basket on the kitchen table.

I'm glad they're adding up so slow. I don't want to leave home.

Bronislaw sits beside the parlor window, watching for his father. He holds his violin, alert and ready to practice should his father come home unexpectedly.

Papa won't like it if I'm not practicing.

Home life has changed since Bronislaw returned from Warsaw. His father's demands are harsher. His two brothers cause noisy chaos around the clock, keeping him from rest or sleep. When he practices, they interrupt him, causing him anxiety, disrupting his concentration, and upsetting his delicate stomach.

Bronislaw notices his mother's behavior is also changing while the family saves its rubles. She seems withdrawn, spending more time each day alone in bed.

"One day," she tells Bronislaw, "I will leave your father and marry a rich duke. We will have servants, and lots of money to buy food and whatever we want! We will live in a palace on the French Riviera."

Her smile disappears, and her face turns ashen. "Maybe one day my dream will come true, son, for I have certainly made a mess of my life and marriage."

"I want you to be happy, Mama."

"Bronislaw," she says, wiping tears from her eyes, "you and I are both burdened with all the cares and sorrows of a family, yet without any of the joys a family can bring. I'm sorry, son. I am not able to change it."

Sometimes late at night, Bronislaw overhears his mother crying and his parents arguing.

"Jacob, stop pushing Bronislaw so hard," he hears his mother say.

"I am not pushing him! I am simply providing opportunities my father never provided for me!"

"Jacob, with all our money going into that basket," his mother complains, "I cannot provide decent meals for our family!"

"Then we will sell our furniture!" Papa shouts.

Week after week, Bronislaw watches the basket of rubles become fuller. Papa makes good on his threat, and sells much of the family's furniture. When the rubles add up to four hundred, Bronislaw and Papa head to Berlin.

"When do you plan to return, Jacob?" Alexandra asks.

"When our rubles run out, or when Bronislaw starts earning more money. Not until then," Jacob says.

One spring morning in 1892, Jacob buys two one-way train tickets to Berlin. After a trip of six hundred and fifty kilometers, they arrive in Berlin, the city of museums, universities, theaters, and concert halls. Jacob welcomes being in the bustling German capital, home to a million people, thriving with industry, politics, culture, and new financial opportunities.

"Son, we have finally made it to Berlin!" he says. "Bronislaw, what happens here in Berlin will forever change our lives!"

CHAPTER 6

The Brief Education of Bronislaw Huberman

I was for the most part self-taught, for at twelve years old, I had my last lesson. As I was not conceited enough to imagine myself a finished artist, I do not feel that I am repudiating a debt of gratitude to my teachers when I say this. In teaching myself, I early learned the curse which is bestowed upon us instrumentalists: "In the sweat of thy brow shalt thou gain thy technique."

Bronislaw Huberman[1]

When Jacob visits Joseph Joachim at his studio in Berlin, requesting Bronislaw's audition, the teacher refuses him.

"My son is a prodigy," Jacob tells Joachim. "He has an extraordinary stretch and long, strong fingers, and has been studying the violin for four years in Warsaw with Professors Michalowisz, Rosen, and Isidor Lotto. Bronislaw has given several public concerts, playing Spohr's Second Violin Concerto, as well as others. After one concert, Anton Rubinstein said: 'Only a genius plays like—'"

"I am totally sick of *'enfants prodiges'* who want to audition!" Joachim interrupts him. "I will not hear him!"

"But . . . we have money to pay you and . . ."

The teacher again refuses, closing the door.

"I have heard the rumors about the Maestro Joachim," Jacob tells Bronislaw. "Joachim does not like child prodigies. We must trick him into hearing you."

Jacob sends Joachim a telegram, pretending to be a barrister needing to talk about an urgent legal matter. Joachim accepts his invitation to meet. Jacob disguises himself, hides Bronislaw behind his back, and knocks on Joachim's studio door.

The maestro doesn't seem to recognize Jacob. He invites him inside. But when Joachim sees the boy holding a violin, he becomes furious.

"You!" he shouts. "The *'enfant prodige'—ah non, ah non!*" and motions for them to leave. "I have had more than enough of them! I do not want to know any more! Go away, go away!"

"Sir," Jacob begs, holding his hand over his heart. "Please hear my boy. I have brought him hundreds of miles, and at a great sacrifice to meet you."

The maestro closes his eyes, puts his hand to his forehead, shakes his head, and roars: "Play!"

Startled, Bronislaw's hands shake as he begins to play.

But soon, as always, the music pulls him inside and his nervousness falls away. When Bronislaw finishes, Joachim jumps up and embraces the boy.

"Yes!" he shouts. "Bronislaw, *you* will study with me! Thank you, Mr. Huberman, for bringing your son to me!"

"You . . . you are . . . ah . . . welcome, sir," Jacob says.

Jacob is shocked. He knows Bronislaw plays well, but to him, Joachim's words sound like the words of a god!

"Excuse me. Wait here," Joachim tells Jacob. He leaves the room, reappearing in a few minutes with a note in his hand.

"This is what I think of your son, Mr. Huberman," Joachim says, handing Jacob the paper to read.

After reading the note, Jacob asks: "Do you really think my son possesses a 'truly remarkable musical talent'? Then, sir, how soon can you begin teaching him?"

"Right away!" the maestro responds.

CHAPTER 7

The Great Joachim

For Joseph Joachim, the unparalleled interpreter of the classics,
I have only the most affectionate reverence . . . eight months with
Joachim in Berlin were sufficient to "tame the exuberance of
my Slavic temperament" without making me lose my natural
originality.

Bronislaw Huberman

For most of 1892, Bronislaw and his father arrive early for lessons with Joseph Joachim. But almost each day, they are met by Joachim's assistant, Karl Markees.

"The maestro is away," Markees always explains. "He asks me to teach Bronislaw today."

For eight months, and to Jacob's chagrin, Bronislaw studies most days with Markees instead of Joachim. Papa also arranges for Bronislaw to study with Charles Gregorovitch, a gifted virtuoso, a pupil of Joachim and Henryk Wieniawski.

"I like Mr. Gregorovitch," Bronislaw tells his father. "He's taught me a lot. But I've learned all I can from him. And I'm learning nothing from Mr. Markees."

"Then we must leave," Jacob says. "I will arrange lessons in Frankfurt with the German violinist Hugo Heerman. He, too, was a student of Joachim. Perhaps you can also study at the Paris Conservatory with Martin Marsick."[1]

Bronislaw and Jacob travel to Frankfurt, and Bronislaw studies with

Professor Hugo Heerman for six weeks. Then Jacob takes his son to Paris, studying for three weeks with Professor Martin Marsick. After that, Bronislaw's formal education comes to an abrupt halt.

"Bronislaw, we have spent all our rubles," Papa tells him. "Your education is finished, and you must now become your own teacher. I will arrange concerts so you can earn some money. After all, son, we have to eat every day."

During 1893, out of sheer determination, Jacob is able to arrange concerts in Holland, Belgium, Paris, London, Brussels, Berlin, Austria, Romania, and the United States. During the boy's performances, Jacob stands in the wings, partially hidden by the curtain, watching and criticizing Bronislaw's every move, and pressuring him to play perfectly.

"You can play better than that!" Jacob berates him after most concerts. "Our family's welfare depends on the cash from your performances!"

"But, Papa, I'm tired," Bronislaw whines. "I need to rest."

"You can rest when we have all the money we need," Jacob says.

"But I miss Mama. And I want to see my friend Arthur."

"We have no time for family, friends, and boyish nonsense, Bronislaw. Art and music are a privilege reserved for just a few. You have extraordinary opportunities to perfect your art, and we will take full advantage of them."

CHAPTER 8

The Aging Diva

Her voice is a technical marvel, her staccatos are marvels of accuracy, her legato is impressively smooth and pure, her voice lifts and glides with an exceptional virtuosity, her chromatic scale is deliciously sweet, and her trill is wonderful and solid.

Music critic Rodolfo Celletti on Adelina Patti[1]

World-famous opera singer Adelina Patti makes a deliberate entrance into the European concert hall where twelve-year-old Bronislaw will perform that evening. She wants to hear the boy prodigy everyone is talking about. As expected, spontaneous applause welcomes her when she walks in. She bows to her admirers, taking a seat and waiting for the performance.

A woman beside her smiles. "Miss Patti, I so enjoy your singing. And you are still so beautiful."

"You are most kind," Patti responds. "Looking beautiful is important to me."

As she waits, Adelina Patti thinks back over her long, successful career. She recalls her American tour in 1862, singing at the White House in Washington, D.C., for President and Mrs. Abraham Lincoln. Their young son Willie had just died of typhoid, and they were in mourning. She remembers how the Lincolns cried throughout her performance, requesting an encore of the newly written song she sang, "Home, Sweet Home."

She thinks about the performances that have taken her to Europe, Russia, the United States, South America, and many exotic places. She has enjoyed her career, but she knows the time has come to end it. She no longer wants to travel, and her voice is wearing out. She will miss the applause, the accolades, and, of course, the money.

Patti sees the small twelve-year-old violinist shuffle onto the stage. She watches him pause, face the audience, tune his violin, and then begin to play. She is enthralled with the boy, fully captivated by the young musician. When the concert ends, she stands, applauding, and making her way backstage to Bronislaw.

"Child!" she exclaims, embracing Bronislaw tightly to her ample breast, almost smothering him. "You play like an angel! You must come play at my farewell concert in January in Vienna. I shall be so sad if you say you cannot!"

Bronislaw steps back and gasps a deep breath.

"Yes, Miss Patti, Bronislaw will be honored to play!" Jacob says quickly.

"Then, Mr. Huberman! It is settled! I will have the arrangements made!"

In Vienna, on January 12, 1895, on behalf of Miss Patti, Jacob gently pushes his son onto the concert stage.

"Bronislaw, play perfectly," he orders. "Don't mess up this opportunity. Important people are here tonight!"

The boy picks up his violin, nods to the accompanying pianist, and plays the first movement of Mendelssohn's Concerto. Jacob waits to hear the audience's reaction when Bronislaw finishes.

Even before the boy takes a halfhearted bow, the crowd leaps to its feet, applauding with thunder. They shout for an encore. It, too, receives loud, long applause.

Miss Patti, listening backstage, hears the crowd's clapping, their calls for third and fourth encores. She whispers to the master of ceremonies.

"If that boy plays one more encore, I will leave this hall!" she threatens. "*I* deserve that response, not a twelve-year-old child!"

"You will have to admit, Miss Patti," he says, "the boy's performance is sensational."

"I will admit no such thing!" Patti says. "I am annoyed by this sideshow! Remove him from the stage at once!"

After Bronislaw is escorted from the stage, Adelina Patti, dressed in a long jeweled gown and elbow-high gloves, her light brown hair piled high on her head in a fashionable bun, walks onto the stage and is greeted by loud, welcoming applause. She bows slowly, and motions for the audience's silence. As the orchestra plays, she sings as beautifully as possible, but her voice is shaky, no longer young and strong. When she finishes, her listeners applaud respectfully, but only a few in the audience stand.

As she bows for the final time, the master of ceremonies walks onto the stage and motions for Bronislaw to come stand beside them. He puts his arm around the boy's shoulders.

"Tonight, we have come to say farewell to a *setting* star," he says, nodding toward Miss Patti. The audience applauds with refined courtesy. Miss Patti takes several dramatic bows.

"But tonight we have the great joy of greeting a brand-new *rising* star!" he shouts, his arms spread toward the young Huberman.

The audience springs to its feet, applauding wildly and calling for yet another encore.

This one concert has just ignited our career, son!" Jacob exclaims. Grabbing Bronislaw's hand, he rushes into the crowd, attempting to greet every celebrity he thinks can boost his son's fame.

That evening, invitations pour in from maestros and presenters who attended the concert, and were astounded by Bronislaw's performance. Jacob accepts each request, guaranteeing Bronislaw's appearance.

"January twenty-ninth of next year in Vienna's Musikverein Hall," a conductor tells him, "I invite you to play the Brahms Concerto with me. Will you agree to it?"

"Yes! Of course!" Jacob says instantly. "The boy will be delighted."

When father and son return to the hotel room, Jacob, still wearing his overcoat, counts the money Bronislaw has earned that evening.

"Because of you, Bronislaw," Jacob says, "we will become very rich!"

Hearing no response, he calls: "Did you hear me, son?"

Jacob turns his head, glancing at the bed. The twelve-year-old, still dressed in his concert clothes and shoes, lies flat on his stomach, sound asleep.

CHAPTER 9

The Gift

*A delicious play of curves and colors—the noble sphinx-like head
from which it rolls down or unfolds itself . . . that amber color
deepening to a rich, an almost reddish brown towards the center
where the sound-life pulsates strongest, quickest! . . . And behold
the fine fiber of the wood shining through the varnish like delicate
roses through my fingernails. What can be finer?*

Violinist, professor, and author Paul Stoeving (1861–1948),
describing an Antonio Stradivari violin[1]

Franz Joseph, Emperor of Austria and King of Hungary, and his wife,
Elisabeth, the Duchess of Bavaria, sit in a Paris concert hall in 1895, listening to thirteen-year-old Bronislaw Huberman play the violin. Over the
years, the emperor has earned the reputation of being distant and *unap-
proachable*. Trying hard to change people's opinions, Joseph is careful to
return the nods of those around him.

"I believe young Huberman plays even more beautifully tonight than
when we first heard him," the emperor whispers to his wife.

"Yes," she agrees. "He plays exquisitely."

Emperor Franz Joseph looks impressive wearing his custom-made military uniform, complete with a chestful of badges and medals. The white-
whiskered leader has served the Habsburg monarch faithfully since 1848,
the year his father, Archduke Franz Karl, renounced his right to the crown.[2]
On his lap, the emperor holds a large, long box.

After the concert, accompanied by his father, Bronislaw greets his audience, accepting graciously their compliments and praises, but feeling overwhelmed by the crowds.

"Papa," he whispers, his face blushing, "must I speak to all these people? There are so many of them! Can we please leave now?"

"No, Bronislaw. We must meet all the people. They can help us. Raise your head, smile, and extend your hand to all who speak to you."

Before Bronislaw and Jacob leave the concert hall, a uniformed messenger approaches them.

"Sir," the messenger tells Jacob, "the Emperor Franz Joseph and his wife, the duchess, wish to meet your son. Follow me please."

He escorts Jacob and Bronislaw to a small elegant room.

"Your concert tonight was phenomenal!" the emperor tells the boy.

"Thank—"

But before Bronislaw can thank him, Jacob steps forward and bows.

"Emperor Joseph, Duchess, I am honored to meet you!" Jacob tells them. "This is your second occasion to hear my son play, isn't it?"

"Yes, it is. And we look forward to hearing him a third and fourth time," the duchess says, placing her hand gently on Bronislaw's shoulder.

"Bronislaw, dear, you play beautifully. I certainly enjoyed your—"

"He is a child prodigy!" Jacob interrupts. "You could help him reach the success he deserves, if you will!"

"Excuse me, Mr. Huberman," the duchess says, her eyes narrowed and glued on Jacob's face. "I was speaking to your son, not to you."

"Thanks," Bronislaw responds. "I'm . . . I'm glad you like my playing."

"Young Mr. Huberman," the emperor says, handing the box to Bronislaw, "I have a special gift for you."

Jacob thrusts out his hand, taking hold of the box. "I take care of all monies and gifts my son receives," he says.

Joseph raises his eyebrows, stares at Jacob, and then jerks the gift from his hand.

"Well, sir, I am sure you do," he says. "But I am giving this gift to your son, not to you. I want *him* to accept it, not you or anyone else!"

The messenger steps forward, pushes out his chest, and in a loud voice addresses Jacob. "Stand back, sir!"

"I . . . I apologize. Please forgive me, Your . . . ah . . . Highness," Jacob says, his voice trembling.

"The box is for *me*, sir?" the boy asks.

"Yes, son." Joseph places it in Bronislaw's hands.

"Thank you, sir!" Bronislaw says, removing the lid and peeking inside.

"It's beautiful!" he exclaims, his face lighting up. "I've never seen such a fine violin! And . . . and . . . you're giving it to *me*?"

"A boy of your talent needs a violin like this," Joseph tells him. "Take good care of it, son. The most famous craftsman of all time, Antonio Stradivari, made this violin long ago in his workshop in Cremona. It is very rare."

"May I play it?" Bronislaw asks, his voice alive with excitement.

"It will be our pleasure to hear you play it!" the duchess says. "Bronislaw, notice how Antonio's violin has a lower arch than most made in Cremona in that day. It also has a much more powerful sound. Antonio paid great attention to both the violin's aesthetic and acoustical qualities. And this particular violin was once owned by the prominent English violinist George Alfred Gibson."

Bronislaw lifts the violin and bow carefully from the box, running his fingertips gently across the fingerboard, bridge, pegs, and strings. Like the boy's eyes, the violin's varnish sparkles. He positions the Stradivarius under his chin, pulls the bow across the strings, and makes a sound of unparalleled beauty.

"It is indescribably pleasing, is it not?" the duchess asks. "Like the voice of an angel. Look at the elegant curve of the scroll," she says, lightly touching the violin. "He carved so intricately the f-holes. A Stradivarius sounds like no other in the world. It is the aged wood he chose for it, the special varnish he created, and the matchless technique with which he fashioned all of his instruments."

Bronislaw smiles, nods his head in appreciation, and continues to play.

"Bronislaw, this violin is a masterpiece, and young man, you are certainly its rightful owner."

With happiness written on his face, Bronislaw plays until Jacob tells him to stop.

"That is enough, Bronislaw," Jacob says. "It is getting late, and I must speak with the emperor."

"Sir," Jacob tells Franz Joseph, moving within inches of the emperor's face, "as I said before, you could be a great help to my son's budding success, if only—"

The duchess steps forward, waving Jacob away like a fly with a flip of her bejeweled hand. She turns to her husband, whispering loud enough for all to hear: "What a buffoon! How dare this uncultured peasant ask a favor of us!"

She looks down at Bronislaw with smiling eyes: "This violin is a treasure. Play it proudly, son."

"Thank you . . . thank you so very much!" Bronislaw says.

The emperor pats the boy's back. "Bronislaw, we should like to keep in contact with you, attend more of your concerts, and help you in any way we can. You honor us with your beautiful music. You will bring joy to all who hear you play this special violin."

They bend down, embracing and kissing the boy before they leave. When they ignore Jacob's outstretched hand, he starts to dart after them. The emperor's aide grabs Jacob's arm, stopping him.

"Stand back! The Emperor Franz Joseph and Duchess Elisabeth are leaving now," he orders. "They have said all they have to say to you."

Late that evening, Bronislaw and his father return to their hotel room. The boy takes the violin from its case, strokes its smooth, honeyed wood, and clutches it to his heart.

"I love this violin, Papa!" he says. "I'm so happy they gave it to me!"

"The emperor and duchess were quite rude to me!" Jacob says, spitting on the floor. "They insulted me, and refused to shake my hand!"

Jacob grabs the Gibson Stradivarius from Bronislaw's hands, flipping it front to back, eyeballing it. "I wonder how much money we could get for it?"

"Oh no, please no," Bronislaw beseeches him, reaching out and gently taking the violin from his father. "I could never part with it, Papa! Never!"

"Shut up, boy! We need the money more than you need this expensive violin. I will find a buyer in the morning."

"No! Papa! You will *not* sell my violin!" the boy shouts, stomping his foot. "I forbid it! It belongs to *me*, not to you!" shouts Bronislaw in a powerful, protective voice, opposing his father for the first time in his life.

Inching away, Bronislaw holds the violin tight in his arms. "You'll have to kill me to get my violin!"

CHAPTER 10

The Old Composer

*The classical composer par excellence of the present day, who free
from any provincialism of expression or national dialect . . . writes
for the whole world and for all time—a giant, lofty and unap-
proachable—Johannes Brahms.*

Edward Elgar, 1886, describing Johannes Brahms[1]

Settled in his seat on the evening of January 29, 1896, Johannes Brahms
waits impatiently to hear the child violinist perform his concerto in Vienna's Musikverein Hall. Old and sick, Brahms doesn't want to be here.
But his best friend, Joseph Joachim, urged him to attend and hear Bronislaw
Huberman play. Brahms has agreed to come, even though, like Joachim,
he dislikes child prodigies, especially hating the immature technical wizards
who murder his works.

The old composer checks his pocket watch, taps his fingers on the
armrest, and thinks back to his own early beginnings in his hometown of
Hamburg. Tonight he feels unusually fatigued. Placing his hand on his
painful right side, he looks at the friends and colleagues sitting around him:
Gustav Mahler, Anton Bruckner, Hans Richter, Eduard Hanslick, Karl
Goldmark, Johann Strauss, and other luminaries of Vienna's music world.

When Bronislaw steps onto the stage, Brahms smiles, noticing peach
fuzz on the teenager's face. When Brahms hears the first few notes of his
Concerto played on the Gibson Stradivarius, he sits up straight, leans forward, and listens closely. Twenty minutes later, he is completely riveted to

the music, tears forming in his eyes as he listens to the boy play the Andante of his second movement.

After the Finale, wiping his face with a handkerchief, Brahms rushes to the green room to meet the young violinist. The child stands in the center of a packed crowd. Like the Red Sea dividing for Moses, the people part to make a passage for the great composer to approach the boy. Brahms embraces him, complimenting Bronislaw on his performance and repeatedly stroking the child's rosy cheeks.

"You played my concerto beautifully, son. I am quite impressed with you!" he exclaims.

"Thank you, sir," Bronislaw says. "But I'm disappointed the audience applauded after the Cadenza. Their applause broke into my playing of the Cantilena!"

Brahms throws back his head, laughing out loud.

"Well, Bronislaw! You should not have played it so beautifully! One of these days, I will compose a fantasy for you . . . that is, if I have any fantasy left!"

"A *fantasy*? I will look forward to playing it, sir," Bronislaw says.

A serious look comes across Johannes Brahms's face, and his heart feels strangely warmed.

Drawing his wrinkled face and full white beard up to Bronislaw's ear, the composer whispers: "Son, with your youth and wonderful talent, you will surely become one of the most celebrated musicians of our time. I hope I live long enough to see the man, the great musician, you will certainly become."

Brahms presses a small card into the boy's hand.

"Honor the gift you have been given, Bronislaw. I pray for you a long productive life of good health, so that you may make an important and lasting contribution to music . . . *l'art pour l'art* . . . for art's sake."[2]

When the young violinist and his father return to the hotel, Bronislaw looks at the card the maestro placed in his hands. Penned at the top is a row of hand-drawn musical notes—the first four bars of the Brahms concerto. Below them is a personal message, expressing pleasure in, and gratitude for, the boy's performance.

That night, Bronislaw sleeps with the note tucked firmly in his hand.

B ronislaw plays ten sold-out concerts in Vienna during 1896. He treasures his beloved Gibson Stradivarius, remembering the emperor's encouraging words and playing the violin with pride.

Telegrams pour in with invitations to perform in Europe, Russia, South America, England, and the United States. Jacob eagerly accepts them all.

In the winter and spring of 1897, Bronislaw travels to many places in the world, his father always close by his side. Jacob receives all the money the teenager earns, and coaxes him constantly to play better, better, better. Bronislaw becomes physically and emotionally drained, growing increasingly frustrated and resentful as Jacob's demands intensify. He wonders why he can never please Papa.

O n April 3, 1897, Bronislaw hears the heartbreaking news: Johannes Brahms is dead.

"He has died from liver cancer at sixty-three years of age," Jacob tells him. "He was certainly a great help to us, Bronislaw."

A deep sadness fills the boy's heart.

For a long time after learning of Brahms's passing, Bronislaw reflects on the concert he played for the famous composer at the Musikverein Hall in Vienna, and how Johannes Brahms embraced and hugged him, stroking his cheeks with large wrinkled hands.

CHAPTER 11

The Gathering

Anyone who wants to work in behalf of the Jews needs . . . a strong stomach.

Theodor Herzl, 1899, from the essay "The Family Affliction"[1]

Theodor Herzl paces the floor of his Viennese home in the summer of 1897. The Budapest-born visionary has a mission in mind. He yearns to create a permanent place in Palestine so that Jews can build, settle, work, rear their families, and be safe and free from the world's ever-growing anti-Semitism. The year before, Herzl published a controversial pamphlet titled "The Jewish State," strongly urging the restoration of the Jewish state and encouraging the world's Jews to embrace it with a sense of pride and joy. He holds the first Zionist Congress on August 29, in the concert hall of the Basel Municipal Casino in Basel, Switzerland.

As he waits for the delegates to arrive, he recalls the many times he himself encountered episodes of anti-Semitism. As a student at the University of Vienna in 1882, he tried hard to assimilate into the society, like so many other Jews in that city. But he constantly ran into strong resistance from the Viennese.

Perhaps our ambitious young men, to whom every road of advancement is now closed, and for whom the Jewish state throws open a bright prospect of freedom, happiness, and honor, will see to it that this idea is spread.[2]

Herzl feels encouraged when two hundred people, from seventeen countries, arrive at the congress in Basel, the beautiful old city that rests on the Rhine.

"The main item on our agenda," Herzl tells them, "is the establishment of the World Zionist Organization and the declaration of Zionism's goals."

The audience, dressed formally in tails and white ties, listens attentively as Herzl continues:

"We must strive to build our Jewish homeland. We must reject assimilation and conversion as solutions to the problem of anti-Semitism. The aim of Zionism is to create for the Jewish people a home in Eretz-Israel secured by law."

"Can we include 'secured by *international* law' within this statement?" delegate Leo Motzkin suggests.

"Certainly," Herzl says.

"Jewish farmers, artisans, and manufacturers need a settlement in Eretz-Israel. We must, by local and international law, organize and unite the whole of Jewry and strengthen Jewish national sentiment and consciousness. We must work with the consent of government, where necessary, in order to reach the goals of Zionism."

The audience applauds heartily.

"As you well know, not long ago," he says, "Captain Alfred Dreyfus, the Jewish officer in the French army, was unjustly accused of treason. Anti-Semitism was the cause of that verdict. I, myself, have heard the mobs in France shout 'death to the Jews,' and it is terrifying. The essence of the Jewish problem is not individual, but national. The Jews are one people. Our plight can be transformed into a positive force by the establishment of a Jewish state. In my opinion, the only solution to violent anti-Semitism is the mass immigration of Jews to a land they can call their own!"

Two hundred people jump to their feet, shouting their agreement and support.

"Let us begin today collecting funds from Jews around the world, working toward the practical realization of this important goal!" he says. "Let us become for the entire globe a 'light unto the nations.'"

Before the congress ends, Theodor Herzl is elected president of the World Zionist Organization, the political arm of the Jewish people.[3]

CHAPTER 12

Dilemmas and Decisions

When I was sixteen, I came to the conclusion that an artist cannot be important if he fails as a human being.

Bronislaw Huberman

Late one night in 1898, after a particularly grueling concert in Berlin, Jacob tells his son:

"At sixteen years old, Bronislaw, you are already a famous violinist! I have scheduled you for concerts around the world for the next five years."

"Papa, there are so many things about music I don't know. May I take a break from concerts and go back to school?"

Jacob frowns.

"Do you understand what you are asking me, boy? The financial well-being of our family rests on your shoulders! You cannot stop now! If I cancel your concerts, we will lose money. You don't want your family to go hungry, do you?"

"No, Papa. But I'm tired. I can't sleep. I don't feel well. Please let me stop for a while."

"You cannot stop, Bronislaw! I will not allow it! If you step out of circulation—even for a short time, you will be forgotten, and your career will end. Do you want to take that risk? Do you wish to become a non-working musician, unknown and unimportant—a poor peasant?"

"No, Papa. But without more musical education, I fear I will fail as a human being. An artist can't be important if he fails as a human being. Papa, I *must* stop!"

Jacob focuses his eyes on Bronislaw, and takes a hard look at his son. He sees a skinny boy with drooping, rounded shoulders. He places his hand beneath Bronislaw's chin, lifting his son's head to examine his face. Bronislaw's complexion is paler than usual, with heavy black circles beneath his eyes.

"Do you feel sick, Bronislaw?" he asks, putting the back of his hand to his son's forehead, checking for fever.

"I have felt sick for a long time, Papa. I *must* stop and rest!"

Worrying that Bronislaw will become too ill to perform again, he nods his head.

"I will allow you to take a brief break, Bronislaw. You can go back home to rest and study music. But only for a short time, until you feel better and look healthier."

Before the old century passes and the new one begins, seventeen-year-old Bronislaw arranges a meeting in Berlin with Arthur Rubinstein, now twelve years old. For the past two years, Arthur has been studying in Berlin. Upon meeting, the two friends hug.

"I hear you're doing well here in Berlin, Arthur! I've read some wonderful reviews from your piano concerts!"

"I like living here," Arthur says. "Enjoy giving concerts, too. Mother put me in Professor Joachim's care. He has arranged for me to study with Karl Heinrich Barth next year, and to play several concerts for the Berlin Philharmonic."

"That's wonderful, Arthur! What will you play?"

"Perhaps Mozart, Chopin, Schumann, or a Saint-Saëns concerto."

"Maybe I can come hear you," Bronislaw says. "Do you miss living in Lódź?"

"Not really. Too much smoke from all the smokestacks and fires. Berlin is nicer. But I miss my family. What about you?"

"I'm tired and taking a break from concerts for a while."

"When will you go back?" Arthur asks.

"Not sure."

"I don't think I'll ever want to stop playing concerts, Bronislaw. I don't know what I'd do without my music. Music's not just a hobby for me— music *is* me!"[1]

During his two years away from concert halls, and with the valuable time to rest and study, Bronislaw grows more mature and much healthier, and plans to extend his break from concert life. But in 1902, his situation changes abruptly. He is forced to give up his study of music and step back into the world's crowded concert halls.

CHAPTER 13

The Life-Changing Death

A judgment of Huberman is quickly rendered. He is simply a phe-nomenon, an apparition before whom criticism ceases. . . . Huber-man was never that which is known as a "child prodigy." At the age of six years, he was already a miraculous man who, far from being reduced to normal stature, kept himself at an illustrious height.

Theodor Leschetizky, December 25, 1898[1]

In 1902, in her home in Częstochowa, Alexandra walks into the room where her husband lies in bed.

"Are you feeling any better, Jacob?" she asks.

"No!" he says. "I am in great pain. How can I get better with all the noise in this house?"

"Boys," Alexandra calls into the parlor, "please be quiet. Papa is ill.

"I am sorry you're sick, Jacob. I'll make you something to eat. That might help." She walks toward the kitchen.

Some time ago, Alexandra began to notice signs of her husband's illness. His knees often buckled and caused him to fall. He complained about pain in his arms and legs. Sometimes he seemed disorientated or unable to speak. The doctor told Alexandra that, most likely, Jacob had suffered a stroke, damaging his central nervous system.

"Paralysis," the doctor diagnosed. "His condition will probably worsen, and soon Jacob may not be able to move at all."[2]

Alexandra accepts the prognosis without visible reaction. The doctor remains by her side for a few moments, ready to assist her if she needs to be comforted. But she does not.

"Call me if you need me, Alexandra," the doctor says. "As for Jacob, I'm sorry I can't do any more for him."

Alexandra stays by her husband's side, caring for him in his sickness, listening to him complain about the noise and his pain, trying to fulfill his constant demands. Jacob seems to grow weaker in strength and meaner in temperament with each passing day. Alexandra does her wifely caretaking, and she patiently waits.

That winter, Alexandra awakes one morning and discovers that Jacob has died in his sleep. She gulps a deep breath of air, audibly exhaling it hard and long.

"It's over," she whispers aloud.

She feels no sadness. Instead, she experiences a welcome sense of deep, satisfying relief. With a neighbor's help, she bathes and dresses Jacob's body and arranges to hold a small funeral in Częstochowa.

As Alexandra prepares her husband's corpse for burial, she reflects on their tumultuous marriage.

"Jacob," she says aloud. "I have put up with your anger, your explosive temper, your violence and abuse to me and my children, and your many job losses. You have broken my heart with your cruel comments, your selfishness, and withheld affection. You have been a miserable husband and father. The children have grown up terrified of you, shuddering whenever you walked into the room."

Alexandra looks at the dead body of the man she has feared and tolerated for so many years.

"Jacob," she tells him as if he is alive, "you have pushed my firstborn son so hard that he has become a nervous, fearful, and resentful young man. You have selfishly thrust your own failed dreams onto his frail shoulders. You have made my son's life miserable, almost unbearable."

She grits her teeth, her nostrils flaring as she recalls her husband's past abuse.

"You will *not* be missed, Jacob—not by me, not by Bronislaw, not by anybody."

Bronislaw travels home to Częstochowa and helps Alexandra bury Jacob. Few family members, friends, or neighbors attend the burial service. Bronislaw spends time with his mother, helping her put Jacob's things in order.

He worries about his mother, who seems filled with fear and anxiety. At length, he listens to her talk about her old dreams and fantasies about the future.

"With Jacob gone, I am free to marry a duke," she tells him. "When I find one, I will live in a beautiful palace."

Knowing his mother's mind is unstable, Bronislaw changes the subject.

"Mama," he asks, "where did Papa keep his papers and money?"

"I don't know. I never saw any of his money," she says. "He kept all those things hidden from me."

"My concerts have earned a small fortune," he tells her. "We need that money to feed the family, and it will also allow me to continue my schooling."

That afternoon, Bronislaw visits his father's bank. He discovers that Jacob has saved little of his son's hard-earned money, and the money he *has* deposited is listed under his own name, not Bronislaw's.

"Jacob stipulates in his will that this money is to support Alexandra and your two brothers," the barrister tells him. "The money is not yours, Bronislaw. It belongs to your family."

"He put all the money I earned in *his* name? None of it is in *my* name?"

"That's correct," the lawyer says. "Your mother is named as the money's manager."

"If that's the case," Bronislaw says, "then I am flat broke."

CHAPTER 14

The High Price of Purpose

The true mission of the violin is to imitate the accents of the human voice, a noble mission that has earned for the violin the glory of being called the king of instruments.

Charles-Auguste de Beriot[1]

In 1903, in one of the world's finest hotels, Bronislaw Huberman wakes early. He stretches his arms and legs, and opens his eyes. Nothing looks familiar.

"Where am I?" he mumbles. "Vienna? Berlin? Brussels? New York?"

He cannot remember. With his constant travels and back-to-back concerts, he often forgets where he is.

"Oh, well," he says aloud. "I guess it doesn't really matter. I do the same thing in every city—play my violin. Who cares where in the world I am?"

His eyes dart instinctively to the side of his bed where he keeps his Gibson Stradivarius encased in its custom-made box.

"Safe," he mumbles. "Must keep it close. It is my voice."

Bronislaw has grown to depend upon his violin. He and the Strad have become inseparable.

Since his father's death, Bronislaw travels alone. He appreciates the newfound solitude and freedom, as well as the respite from his father's criticism. He now controls his own concert schedule, declining some invitations but accepting most.

With each performance, Bronislaw's reputation grows. At only twenty-one years of age, he has risen to international fame, becoming one of the world's greatest and most celebrated violinists. Bronislaw has also become totally absorbed in his art. Music has become his life's central focus, the reason for his existence. Few things in life divert his attention.

With an extensive travel schedule, hours of grueling practice, and little time to rest, life leaves no room for anything else—not women, not marriage, not children, and certainly not pleasure.

Fame pushes Bronislaw into the company of society's affluent—the moneyed, celebrated, and crowned. Lavishing him with accolades and gifts, the world's wealthy and influential beg his presence at their glamorous events, dropping his name generously to their well-to-do friends. He sleeps at the most expensive hotels, eats at the world's finest restaurants, and keeps company with the rich and royal.

As the sole means of support of his family, he supplies both their necessities and their increasing demands for luxuries. He wonders if he should limit their money, put them on a tighter budget. But, in the end, he finds that giving them money is easier than listening to them whine and complain about not having enough.

He keeps a frantic schedule, paying a staggering personal price for his relentless work. His physical appearance announces his feverish, joyless lifestyle to the world. His complexion deathly pale, his face reveals his loneliness, sadness, and worries. He rarely smiles. His eyes often stare unfocused into the distance for long periods of time, and stay bloodshot and strained. His shoulders slump from exhaustion, hours of practice, and little sleep.

As his success grows to more tremendous heights, Bronislaw becomes more private, more inwardly inclined, introspective, and more protective of his personal space. At times, he suffers severe sadness and depression.

Nonetheless, the violinist struggles to guard his main priority, mission, and purpose in life—his music. He lives and breathes and personally sacrifices to play the violin, to further excel in his art. *L'art pour l'art.*

Theodor Herzl continues his hard work encouraging others toward his Zionist goal.

"I see increasing anti-Semitism in czarist Russia," he tells his delegates. "More and more Jews—up to forty thousand of them—are leaving Eastern Europe and settling as pioneers in Palestine. They are reviving the Hebrew language and publishing Hebrew literature and newspapers."

But Herzl does not live long enough to realize his dream for a Jewish state in Palestine. On July 3, 1904, the forty-four-year-old Theodor Herzl dies.[2]

CHAPTER 15

The Beautiful Actress

*His left hand lifted the violin and pressed it tightly to his shoulder
and chin, while his right hand lifted the bow, and there emerged
a tone sweeter, more powerful, more sublime than I had ever heard.*

Elsa Galafrés[1]

In Vienna, in 1909, the beautiful and renowned actress and singer Elsa
Galafrés, and her hostess, Mrs. Keller, wife of the director of concerts,
enter the hall, find their box seat close to the stage, and wait eagerly to hear
the violinist Bronislaw Huberman.

"I have heard from many people about the gifted Mr. Huberman," Elsa
says. "I am grateful to you, Mrs. Keller, for inviting me to attend tonight's
concert."

"You are most welcome, Elsa. I chose this box so you can better hear
him. This young man—our dear friend Broni, is quite famous. You've no
idea the number of beautiful women, like yourself, who are . . . ah . . .
after him. A single man of his status is quite the catch."

"Well, Mrs. Keller, if he is anything like his reputation, I just might,
myself, be 'after him.'"

Elsa smiles. She feels unusually restless tonight, finding it difficult to
sit still and wait for the handsome Mr. Huberman.

"I am happy to be the one to introduce you to him," Mrs. Keller says.
"Broni's concerts in Europe, and around the world, are sold out long before
the concert season begins. Only the most influential people in society can
acquire tickets."

"I'm glad, Mrs. Keller, that you are one of the *influential* women in this city," Elsa says, wondering if Mrs. Keller will recognize her subtle mockery.

Mrs. Keller reaches over, winks, and squeezes Elsa's hand.

"Yes, Elsa. And I am delighted to know you, such a beautiful actress. I have arranged a private dinner after the concert for you, me, and Broni."

"That will be lovely," Elsa says, patting in place the waves in her light brown hair.

Bronislaw Huberman slept little the night before. He spends most of the day practicing in his hotel room, trying hard to keep from yawning. He stretches his back to straighten his stooped shoulders. Glancing in the mirror, the young man sighs when he sees his heavy eyelids and pasty-faced reflection.

"I'm not excited about this performance," he says aloud. "I feel tired, and I wish I could go back to bed. But I can't. The show must go on."

That evening, before a large audience, he shuffles onto the stage without acknowledging the listeners. As the orchestra begins Bronislaw lifts the violin and presses it under his chin. With his right hand, he lifts the bow and joins the orchestra playing Brahms's Violin Concerto.

Elsa leans forward in her seat to take a better look at the violinist on the platform. Her hand flies to her mouth.

"Can this poor man with sagging shoulders and such an ashen face be the great Huberman?" she mumbles. "Is this a nightmare? He is far too young to look like . . . like . . . this! Oh . . . he's pitiful!"

Mrs. Keller leans over and whispers into Elsa's ear: "Dear, I can tell that you are . . . uh . . . disappointed at Mr. Huberman's appearance."

Before Elsa can answer, Bronislaw pulls the bow across the strings of the Stradivarius. Elsa's mouth drops open.

Oh my . . .

Elsa is spellbound as she listens to him play, for the moment her thoughts distracted from his surprising appearance.

"Mrs. Keller! His music is magic!" she whispers.

A deafening applause follows the final note. Elsa notices a weak forced smile on Bronislaw's lips as he bows stiffly to his audience, ignoring all calls for encores, and quickly leaves the platform.

"Well, Elsa," Mrs. Keller asks, "what do you have to say now?"

"He is certainly *not* what I expected in appearance, but he's quite the musician!"

Mrs. Keller takes Elsa's arm: "Let's go," she says. "I have many people to speak to before we meet Broni for dinner at the Hotel Imperial! And, if he arrives before us, we must not keep him waiting."

When they arrive at the Hotel Imperial, Mrs. Keller guides Elsa to the table where Bronislaw sits. He does not acknowledge their presence as he talks with a waiter and sips champagne. Mrs. Keller is embarrassed when she sees the half-empty bottle and the leftover scraps on his dinner plate.

"Broni, dear!" she says loudly, smiling and trying to hide her reaction. "Your playing tonight was divine!"

Huberman glances in her direction, but does not stand to greet her. She feels her face blush.

"Ah . . . Broni . . . let me introduce you to my good friend, the wonderful actress Elsa Galafrés," Mrs. Keller says. "Perhaps you have seen her perform?"

Bronislaw looks up, giving Elsa a quick glance.

"No, I haven't. And excuse me if I don't get up," he says to Elsa. "I'm terribly tired. I've spent some awful nights on the train, and endured all kinds of noises in the hotel. I suffer from rankling insomnia. I wish this season were at an end."

Reaching for the champagne bottle in front of him, he fills his glass to the brim and drinks it with a long, loud gulp.

"I am no particular friend to alcohol," he says, "but it helps me over the initial fatigue."

Elsa is repulsed at Mr. Huberman's behavior. She notices looks from the other diners, as if they recognize her from the theater.

When the waiter brings Huberman's dessert, Elsa watches him fill his mouth full, completely ignoring her and Mrs. Keller, who are both still standing beside the table. In his rush to eat, his elbow knocks over a water glass. As it crashes to the floor, the noise startles him, and he jumps. He gives Elsa a startled look.

"Don't bother to clean it up," he tells her. "The waiter will do it."

"Broken glass brings good luck!" Elsa says, smiling and attempting to save him from embarrassment.

"Luck?" he says, rolling his eyes to the ceiling.

Mrs. Keller motions for Elsa to sit down. Then she pulls out a chair and joins her while Huberman continues to eat. Elsa feels ill at ease, not knowing what to say during the long, uncomfortable silence.

After a few moments, Elsa tries to make small talk, but Huberman seems uninterested. When the waiter appears to take Mrs. Keller's and Elsa's menu orders, they both order "just coffee."

"Mr. Huberman," Elsa says, "we both know artists whose work and art are sublime. Yet, as human beings, they are small, petty, and filled with vanities and weaknesses that make a very poor comparison with their art."

Huberman stops eating, wrinkles his nose, and looks closely at Elsa for the first time.

"Perhaps, Miss . . . ah . . . Galafrés, is it? Perhaps you put too much weight on external, perceivable things," he says. "Life can be so complicated that the complications prevent one from living."

He wipes his lips on the linen napkin and tosses it on his empty plate.

"I think—" Elsa starts to say, but he interrupts her.

"I must go now! My train leaves at seven in the morning."

He rises from his chair, nods to Mrs. Keller, and leaves.

Mrs. Keller's face turns crimson. Elsa reaches across the table and takes her hand.

"Thank you, Mrs. Keller, for the lovely evening. I wanted to thank Mr. Huberman, too, but I didn't get the chance."

Mrs. Keller blinks her eyes rapidly, and says nothing.

B ronislaw does not sleep well that night. He wakes up later than usual, dresses quickly, and rushes to West Station to catch the train.

Before he boards, he hears someone call his name. Turning around, he sees Elsa.

"Ah . . . Ellie . . . no . . . I mean, Elsa . . . ah . . . Galafrés . . . isn't it?" Huberman says. "What a surprise to see you. If I had known you were to be here, I would have come a few minutes earlier. Now I must board my train."

Ignoring him, Elsa hands him a bunch of violets she grabbed from the hotel lobby vase. "I so enjoy Parma violets. I hope you do, too," she says. "How did you sleep last night?"

"Hardly an hour. And I have many more months until the end of the concert season. It just goes on and on."

"Well, please take care of yourself, Mr. Huberman. You must take some time away from work and try to enjoy life a little."

"*Enjoy* life?" he says as he boards the train.

CHAPTER 16

The Dresden Sanatorium

Huberman had met the singer Elsa Galafrés . . . but it was a chance meeting at the Weisser Hirsch sanatorium in Dresden that led to their romance. The sanatorium promoted healthy living, with cold showers, brisk walks, and food that consisted mainly of salads and fruit. Perhaps, if the food had been better, Elsa and Huberman would have spent less time together?

Patrick Harris[1]

Several weeks later, Elsa Galafrés checks into the Weisser Hirsch sanatorium in Dresden, Germany, resting from a busy theater season. As she laughs and lunches with friends on the warm summer day, she is surprised to see Bronislaw Huberman approaching her table.

"Do I interrupt?" he says. "I learned only today that you were here."

She smiles. "If I had known you were to be here, I would have waited before beginning my lunch," she says. "Now my friends and I have finished. But, please, Mr. Huberman, sit down and join us."

The couple sits at the table, talking long after the others leave. He is so warm, attentive, and talkative, Elsa can hardly believe he is the same man she met only weeks before.

After a while, he stops talking. "I've been far too egotistical," he says. "I have talked only of myself. Please, Elsa, tell me about you."

Elsa speaks freely about her life, career, family, and about European politics in general. When she finally stops, Bronislaw takes her hand and looks deep into her eyes.

"You, too, are lonely, Elsa. I can hear it in your voice," he says. "You, too, are searching."

She pauses, wondering how he could so accurately sense her innermost feelings.

"Yes," she says. "I am."

Becoming lovers, Elsa and Bronislaw leave the Weisser Hirsch sanatorium. At his invitation, she moves into his rented two-story villa on the outskirts of Vienna, and they fill their hours with passionate lovemaking and long walks in flowered parks, and attend theaters and concerts around the world. Elsa thrills in the excitement of new romance, dreaming and hinting, early in the relationship, about becoming Mrs. Bronislaw Huberman.

"We should become engaged, Broni," she says. "People are asking me when we plan to announce our engagement."

"I am not the marrying type, Elsa," he says.

When Elsa tells her mother about her romance and growing relationship with Huberman, her mother stares at her with wide eyes.

"I love him, Mother," Elsa says. "And . . . we . . . we are . . . living together . . . in his villa in Vienna."

"Elsa!" her mother cries. "It cannot be! You must *not* associate with this . . . this Huberman—he is a Jew from Poland! If your father was still alive, he would most definitely forbid it!"

"But I told you, Mother, I love him! And nothing else matters! I will not give him up!"

"Don't be stupid, Elsa!" her mother shouts. "Your attachment to him will damage your career. Please, Elsa, think about what you are doing—to yourself and to me!"

When Elsa returns home, she tells Bronislaw about her mother's reaction to the news of their affair.

"If your mother is concerned about us doing something stupid—like getting married—she has nothing to worry about, Elsa," he says. "I do not want the obligation of marriage, not now and not ever."

CHAPTER 17

The Complication

As a tree can be shaken to its roots by a thunderstorm, so the knowledge brought to my consciousness the scandal! But only for a flash, then a feeling of inexpressible joy.

Elsa Galafrés[1]

When Elsa walks into the main room of their Viennese villa, in the summer of 1910, she finds Bronislaw at his desk making final arrangements for his upcoming concert tour in London.

"Broni," she says, smiling, "I have some wonderful news."

"Can we talk later, Elsa?" he asks. "I must finish this. We are to leave for London in a few days, and I have deadlines to meet before we go."

"We must talk *now*, Broni, not later. My news cannot wait."

"What is it, Elsa?"

"Broni, I am to become a mother."

Huberman jerks up his head, drops his jaw, and glares at Elsa. For the next few seconds, he doesn't speak.

"What?" he finally shouts. "What did you just say?"

"Darling, I am pregnant. You are to become a father!"

Bronislaw closes his mouth and frowns, his eyes still glued on Elsa's.

"Well, Elsa," he says, taking a deep breath and exhaling it slowly, "I guess we must marry immediately. The bigger you become, the harder it will be to hide your secret. Otherwise, there will be a scandal, and it will damage my career. We can marry in a synagogue in London between my two scheduled concerts."

"A synagogue and not a church?" she asks.

E lsa's mother cries when her daughter reveals her pregnancy and upcoming marriage to Huberman.

"Elsa, what have you done? Your baby will have Jewish blood! You know how Vienna and Europe hate the Jews. You have made a big mistake, Elsa, and we will all suffer because of it."

D uring the summer of 1910, Elsa and Bronislaw arrive in London, marrying on July 19 between concert performances, by the clerk of the district court in a quick civil service ceremony. Elsa insists on a honeymoon at the North Sea resort in Cromer. When they arrive at the honeymoon suite, she pins the official marriage license on the wall above their bed.

"Elsa," Bronislaw whispers to his new bride in the middle of the night, "I am unable to sleep. Your every movement wakens me. Will you please move into the adjoining bedroom?"

Elsa obeys, slipping into the next room's bed, burying her face into a pillow and crying.

After the final concert performance in London, Elsa and Bronislaw go home to Vienna to prepare for the upcoming autumn–winter concert season, and to get ready for the birth.

"When will the baby be born?" Bronislaw asks. "I hope the delivery doesn't interrupt my winter concert schedule."

"You and your music always come first, don't they?" she shouts, angered by his seeming indifference to the birth of their child. "Do you care anything about me and our unborn child? You love only yourself, and this . . . this . . ."

She grabs the Stradivarius from its case, her hand firmly gripping its fingerboard. Holding the violin high above her head, as if threatening to throw it, she screams: "This . . . this is the thing you most adore! Not me! Not our child!"

"Elsa, no! Not my Strad!" Bronislaw shouts.

Elsa sees the horrified look on her husband's face. Feeling the sharp blade of truth stab deep into her heart, she pauses, lowers the violin in resignation, and places it back into its case.

"It's true," she whispers, wiping her eyes with her hand.

Elsa's contractions start at home in early December. After thirty-six hours of hard labor, she gives birth to a healthy son. During the delivery, Bronislaw seems emotionally detached, showing little interest in Elsa or the child. When a nurse places the newborn in his arms, he holds his son stiffly. But, as Elsa watches her husband's face, the baby cuddled and cooing in his arms, his appearance begins to change. The hard, serious expression softens into a smile.

"Look at those beautiful eyes," he says.

He tilts his head forward, kissing the child's tiny hands and feet, seeming to be suddenly smitten with the brand-new life.

"This is *my* son! My *son*! My own flesh and blood! We will name him 'Johannes,' after Johannes Brahms."

Bronislaw holds his son for a long time, staring into the child's eyes as if hypnotized by his beauty. He gently hands the baby to Elsa, takes his violin and bow, and plays the Concerto penned long ago by the child's namesake. He seems to delight in sharing his music with his new son.

Bronislaw adores his son, but with a new baby in the home, he finds little quiet time to work. The infant's cries interrupt his daytime work as well as his nighttime sleep. With his perfectionist traits, he feels more frustrated each day, facing deadlines he cannot meet in the midst of the commotion. Within days of his son's birth, Bronislaw jumps into a chaotic

Christmas concert season, and Elsa returns to the stage. Both must travel, often working away from home for long periods of time. Elsa's mother, Oma, moves into the villa to care for the baby.

When together at home, Bronislaw and Elsa argue constantly. One day, she waves a newspaper in his face, screaming at him: "Who is she?"

"What are you talking about, Elsa?"

"The St. Petersburg aristocrat! I demand to know who she is!"

Bronislaw takes the newspaper, scanning the article that lists his name. It reports he will soon divorce his actress wife to marry a St. Petersburg aristocrat.

"This is nonsense, Elsa!" he says, laughing.

"Who is she?" Elsa demands. "Why would a newspaper print a story that isn't true?"

Bronislaw shakes his head, throws his hands into the air, and leaves the room.

As arguments between them grow more bitter, Bronislaw stops inviting Elsa to accompany him on his frequent concert tours. He finds welcome relief when he travels alone to faraway places for extended periods of time.

Elsa sits quietly in the parlor, holding the now three-year-old toddler in her lap, pondering her life with Bronislaw, who is on tour in Russia. She recalls the quick marriage ceremony and disastrous honeymoon. Life has become humdrum, the passion of their love fading. She misses the relationship they once shared and wonders if she will ever experience it again.

Feeling unusually bored and lonely one evening, Elsa asks her mother to care for Johannes. Dressing in a long elegant gown, she wears her most exquisite gems and wraps herself in furs. Going alone to a concert in Vienna, she knows she risks causing a scandal. But she doesn't care. At the end of the concert, she stands and applauds the handsome Hungarian conductor Ernő Dohnányi. And for the first time in a long time, she feels something deep within her stir.

CHAPTER 18

The Parting

*When he appeared on the conductor's stand, the applause poured
over him in great waves of sound. Then the hall darkened. He
waited until the excited murmurs died down. There was a little
pause, an undercurrent of something, which had nothing to do with
the performance. But, in Vienna, what love affair, or hint of one,
can remain uncovered?*

Elsa Galafrés, speaking of Ernő Dohnányi[1]

From the conductor's platform, Ernő Dohnányi scans the audience and
recognizes the actress Elsa Galafrés. Her off-the-shoulder gown, showing
her china-white shoulders, and the low neckline, revealing ample cleavage,
arouse his attention. He wonders why her husband is not with her.

The thirty-five-year-old conductor is also an accomplished composer
and pianist. His credentials are impressive, studies at the Royal National
Hungarian Academy of Music in Budapest, successful published composi-
tions, a prestigious teaching position at the Hochschule in Berlin, endorsed
by Joseph Joachim. Dohnányi often uses the German form of his name—
Ernst von Dohnányi, the "von" suggesting an ancient ancestor's assumed
nobility.[2]

Dohnányi keeps a demanding concert schedule, most often traveling
alone. His wife of ten years, pianist Elisabeth Kunwald, stays home, caring
for their two young children, Hans and Greta.

After the concert, Ernő Dohnányi arranges to meet Elsa. He invites
her for a drink in a nearby café.

"Where is Mr. Huberman tonight?" he asks her as they sip coffee.

Elsa smiles flirtatiously, looking into his eyes.

"Russia," she says, lifting an eyebrow.

"How convenient," he whispers.

"Yes, isn't it?" Elsa responds.

Elsa welcomes and encourages Ernő Dohnányi's advances, arranging to spend every available moment with her new lover. Their relationship deepens. Dohnányi asks Elsa to divorce Bronislaw and to marry him.

"We have so much to gain by being together and so little to lose," he tells her, promising Elsa he will divorce his wife and officially adopt Johannes.

Elsa and Ernő telephone their lawyers, setting the wheels of divorce into motion.

When Elsa tells Bronislaw she has filed for divorce, he says little.

"I admit that life with me hasn't been easy, Elsa," he tells her. "I am hypersensitive and uptight because I suffer from chronic insomnia. I admit I haven't been a perfect husband. But a divorce, Elsa? Johannes needs both his mother and father. What will become of him?"

"Ernő has agreed to adopt Johannes," she says. "You can visit him anytime you wish."

"No, Elsa. Because of Johannes, I will not agree to the divorce."

When Elsa learns that Elisabeth will not grant Ernő a divorce either, she and Ernő find a home together in Vienna. They invite Elsa's mother, Oma, to live with them, to care for Johannes. They wait impatiently for their respective spouses to grant divorces so they can marry. In the meantime, Elsa gives birth to Ernő's child, Matthew.

With the work of caring for young children and a home, Elsa's mother becomes tired and sick. One night, she dies suddenly from a stroke. Elsa has Oma's body cremated, and hosts a simple memorial service in a Viennese chapel. After the service, Elsa notices an arrangement of Parma violets at the foot of Oma's casket. The accompanying note, handwritten by Bronislaw, expresses his deepest condolences.

Bronislaw stays busy performing back-to-back concerts around the world. He yearns to be with Johannes, greatly missing the child who touched, with such warmth, his overburdened heart.

To ease his pain, Bronislaw buries himself in his music, trying hard to find some deeper meaning in his fame, success, and wealth. He decides to grant the divorce, but his heart is torn when he learns that Ernő will adopt Johannes. Shortly after his divorce, he hears that Elisabeth has also granted Ernő his freedom, allowing Elsa and Ernő to marry. Without his wife and son in his life, Bronislaw works hard, traveling the world and perfecting his art. Playing the Stradivarius becomes, even more than before, the sole love and purpose of his life.

After the loss of his family, the insomnia worsens, leaving Huberman tired all the time, unable to find rest day or night. When he travels, he books an entire floor of hotel rooms, in an effort to create a hall of silence so that he might sleep.

CHAPTER 19

The Golden Age of Security

The Great Powers of Europe stumbled or sleepwalked into the war of 1914. . . . German, Russian, Austria-Hungarian, British, and French politicians were apparently shocked by it, awoken as if from some peaceful reverie.

Paul Ham, *The Eve of War* (1913)[1]

Performing sold-out concerts in society's finest halls, dressing in expensive suits and calf-leather shoes, and dining in fabulous restaurants with the rich and royal, Bronislaw Huberman travels the world in 1913, staying busy and trying to put aside his sadness, loneliness, and anger over losing his wife and son to Ernő Dohnányi.

He reaches out for all the world's riches, finding them immediately within his grasp. He lives the "good life," receiving more invitations than he can possibly accept, earning more money than he can possibly spend. He enjoys lavish luxuries and glowing accolades, the stuff most musicians can only dream of.

He thinks about his father, Jacob, now gone for almost a dozen years.

"How Papa would have reveled in the lifestyle and fame I now know," he mumbles. "Papa so desperately yearned to leave the peasant's life, becoming rich and famous, and caring so little the cost to me, his son."

Living and working in 1913, the affluent and prosperous golden age, soon takes a toll on the thirty-one-year-old violinist. Bronislaw suffers constant exhaustion as well as severe depression. He talks with every doctor in Europe, finding no medication or medical advice to help him sleep.

He looks out the train window as he travels to another concert in another city, watching the countryside and cities pass by, pondering the present circumstances of Europe, rich, healthy, and stable.

"It is a good time to live in Europe," he whispers.

Huberman feels hopeful about the continent's future, with Kaiser Wilhelm II, King George V, and Czar Nicholas II so at peace with one another that they attend family weddings and other social occasions together. Although some conflicts exist among the individual countries, Europe seems politically and diplomatically sound.

Not only does the future promise peace, but Huberman is also aware of Europe's new industrial boom—global trade thriving, middle-class people now able to buy more luxuries, and whole families traveling by express steamers and deluxe sleeper-car trains. Each day he hears of another new invention. Telephone and tram lines thread through Berlin's busy boulevards, making communication, travel, and shopping easy for consumers. Industry works hard to keep up with the growing demands for practical, work-saving products.

Huberman sees advances, and new interest, in intellectual pursuits and the arts. Cafés spring up on every street corner, drawing society's sophisticated thinkers to meet, drink, and express a constant flow of new ideas. Europeans are eagerly relishing music and art, rushing en masse to Paris to attend the recent gala opening of Igor Stravinsky's *The Rite of Spring*, an avant-garde ballet and orchestral concert. Huberman is witnessing groups of artists aggressively giving birth to a popular form of art—German Expressionism. Europeans, seemingly filled with a new enthusiastic optimism, believe the peaceful, prosperous future will always be ripe with fresh opportunities and new inventions as they relax and recreate in 1913's golden age of security.

But in spite of Europe's present fortune and harmony, Huberman feels an unsettling stir in the pit of his stomach, like the harbinger of an approaching disaster. He senses a strong political fault building beneath the surface of prosperity, a tremor of deepening anti-Semitism and violence, threatening Europe's peace. As hard as he tries, he cannot shake this sense of impending doom, fearing a seismic event of enormous magnitude ready to erupt, its epicenter the heart of Europe.

Part 2

WAR!

All the bridges between our today and our yesterday and our yesteryears have been burnt. The golden age of security [is] gone.

Stefan Zweig, Austrian novelist[1]

CHAPTER 20

Earthquake!

I see how people are set against one another, and in silence, unknowingly, foolishly, obediently, innocently slay one another.
Erich Maria Remarque, *All Quiet on the Western Front* (1929)[1]

On a sunny morning, June 28, 1914, as they head to Sarajevo, Archduke Franz Ferdinand, heir to the Austro-Hungarian crown, extends his hand to his wife, the Archduchess Sophie, helping her into the 1911 Gräf & Stift Bois de Boulogne phaeton automobile.

"Let's leave the top down," Sophie suggests. "It's such a beautiful day. I want to enjoy the sunshine."

"Yes, Sophie," he says as they settle into their seats. "I am happy you are able to join me on this trip. In your present condition, I wasn't sure you could."

Sophie places her hand on her swollen belly.

"I am fine, dear," she says. "The morning sickness has gone, and I feel much better. Anyway, I wouldn't want to miss the anniversary remembrance of the First Battle of Kosovo."

"Yes, we must celebrate this five-hundred-and-twenty-fifth-year anniversary," he says. "I also plan to inspect Bosnia and Herzegovina's imperial armed forces while on this trip."

Ferdinand notices a large crowd gathered ahead of their car. The archduke keeps a serious expression when their car glides alongside them, ignoring the people and staring straight ahead. Sophie smiles, nodding as they pass the people who wave their hands in wild adoration.

Suddenly, to his left, Ferdinand sees a man run up to the car and throw something toward them. The small hard object hits the side of the carriage and rolls away, falling down the back of the car. Ferdinand grabs his wife to protect her. The crude device hits the ground and explodes, rocking the car.

"Sophie!" Ferdinand shouts.

The guards, running alongside the car, tackle the would-be assassin, a Serbian nationalist, Nedeljko Čabrinović. An officer jumps into the car, pushing the couple to the floorboard.

"Stay down!" he shouts. "That was a bomb thrown at you!"

Ferdinand raises his head slightly and looks around him. Crowds of screaming people run in all directions. An officer bleeds, and some bystanders lie on the ground groaning in pain.

"We are unhurt!" Ferdinand shouts. "Move ahead to a safe place away from people!"

Guards push the people away from the car and tend to the injured. The driver brings the carriage to a calm clearing and some parkland.

"Sophie," Ferdinand says, helping her from the floor and into her seat, "are you hurt? Is the child safe?"

"I'm fine, dear," Sophie tells him. "Just shaken. The baby is unhurt."

"Take us home!" Ferdinand orders the driver. "And do it quickly!"

"We are both safe," Sophie says. "Let us continue our journey, and attend the reception at the town hall. We must not disappoint the people."

"But we are not safe, Sophie. That was a close call."

A guard walks to the car. "Sir, the man who threw the bomb is in our custody. You are safe now."

"See, dear. We are no longer in danger," Sophie says. "I have so looked forward to this event."

"We will go to the town hall as planned," Ferdinand tells the driver. "Go quickly!"

Sophie adjusts her long, elegant dress and straightens her hat and veil. She glances to her husband's face, noticing his distinguished handlebar mustache and medal-adorned uniform.

"Ferdinand," she says, smiling and trying to lighten the gloomy mood, "even at fifty years old, you are still so handsome and dignified."

When the couple and their entourage arrive at the Sarajevo Town Hall, the driver parks the car beside the impressive marble columns at the building's front entrance. Surrounded by city leaders, the archduke and his wife are escorted up the stairs and led into the festive hall.

The mayor greets them, welcoming them on behalf of the city.

"Your Highness," the mayor says, smiling wide and showing teeth, "we want to welcome you to—"

"What is the good of your speeches?" Ferdinand shouts. "I come to Sarajevo on a visit, and I get bombs thrown at me!"

"I am sorry, Your Highness," the mayor says. "I am terribly—"

"It is outrageous!" Ferdinand shouts.

Before the official ceremonies end, the Austrian commander General Potiorek pleads with the archduke: "Your Highness, the city is seething with rebellion. You are not safe here. May I urge you to leave quickly, and to take the shortest route out of town."

"Yes," Ferdinand agrees. "Have the car brought around. We are most eager to leave Sarajevo. I, too, feel the tension."

The driver receives directions from General Potiorek, and with a bodyguard riding on the car's running board, the couple heads out of the city.

"I will be relieved when we are home," Ferdinand tells Sophie.

The driver slows down to negotiate the V-shaped roadway at the bridge, making a sharp turn to cross over the River Nilgacka.

A sickly, twenty-year-old man, Gavrilo Princip, stands beside the bridge spanning the River Nilgacka, waiting for the archduke's car to pass by. A member of the secret Black Hand Society—a nationalist movement favoring a Bosnia-Herzegovina and Serbia union—Princip is one of three assassins sent to Sarajevo by Dragutin Dimitrijević, chief of the Intelligence

Department in the Serbian army. Their assignment? To murder the archduke.

Princip puts his hand in his pocket, feeling for the phial of cyanide, the loaded revolver, and the grenades. Dimitrijević has instructed him to swallow the cyanide immediately after he assassinates the archduke.

Princip coughs, wiping a drop of blood from his mouth. Suffering from tuberculosis, he knows he won't live long. He is grateful the cyanide will end his growing pain, and he feels patriotic in serving his country before he dies.

When the assassin sees the Gräf & Stift Bois de Boulogne slow down to cross the bridge, he lunges toward the car, aims the gun, and fires a shot. The bullet lodges in Sophie's abdomen. He watches her grab her belly and fall forward. Princip points his automatic pistol at the archduke, and pulls the trigger.

Ferdinand hears the first gunshot. He looks down at his wife with horror as she lies limp and bleeding on the floorboard. The second shot enters the archduke's heart. He grabs his chest, gasping to breathe, his chin resting on his torso. Before he dies, he whispers softly: "Sophie."

His job done, Gavrilo Princip reaches into his pocket for the poison-filled phial. It is not there. He points the gun to his temple, but before he can fire, strong hands seize him, throwing him to the ground and beating him until his world goes black.[2,3]

In his hotel room, preparing for an evening concert, Bronislaw hears of Ferdinand's assassination.

"The earthquake erupts," he says aloud. "Just like I predicted. Surely, this will bring war!"

Over the next few days, he watches European tensions flare. Fragile social bridges, built among royal families and countries, collapse. He knows the golden age of security has shattered.

Within weeks, he learns Austria-Hungary's emperor, Franz Joseph, has declared war on Serbia, and that Russia, Belgium, France, Great Britain, and Serbia are lining up against Austria-Hungary and Germany. To his expected horror, the Great War begins.

CHAPTER 21

The Arrest

You will be home before the leaves have fallen from the trees!

Kaiser Wilhelm assures his troops as they leave for the front,
August 1914[1]

Princess Cecilie, wife of Crown Prince Wilhelm, the oldest son of Kaiser Wilhelm II of Germany, is one of Huberman's most loyal fans. The strikingly beautiful princess attends most of his concerts in Germany and elsewhere. Like other Germans, she appreciates his music's "unforgettable moments of exaltation and ecstasy."

"His music takes me into a different world when I hear it," she tells her friends.

"I so admire his solemn dedication to the arts. How I and Germany adore Mr. Huberman!"

Princess Cecilie arranges for tickets to Huberman's concert in Berlin during the first week of August 1914. Her husband, preparing to take charge of the Fifth Army, cannot join her. She and her affluent friends sit in a box seat, whisper among themselves, and wait anxiously for the concert to begin.

"The audience seems terribly tense tonight," Cecilie tells her guests. "No doubt people are nervous, apprehensive about the events happening here in Europe."

"Yes," a guest responds. "It is a frightening time. With Germany declaring war on Russia, France, and Belgium, Europeans are afraid."

"I heard just this morning," another guest says, "that Austria-Hungary is beginning to fight with Serbia and Russia, and that Australia, Canada, and New Zealand are teaming up with Britain preparing to fight against *us*."[2]

"These are difficult and frightening times," Cecilie says. "But my husband assures me this war will end quickly."

The lights dim. Cecilie watches Huberman walk onto the stage, and is somewhat surprised by his strange movements. He hardly acknowledges the audience's applause, and seems intensely nervous. In agonizing motions, the violinist takes a piece of rosin from his back pocket, drawing it across the hairs of his bow. Turning each peg, he tunes his violin, again using rosin on the bow. Drawing the Stradivarius to his chin, he lifts the bow and prepares to play.

But before he plays the first note, Cecilie hears a disturbance at the back of the hall. Looking back, she sees a group of uniformed German officers storming down the aisle. They jump to the platform, surround the violinist, and grab his arms, sending the Strad and bow crashing to the floor.

B ronislaw feels strong hands grip him roughly and lead him off the stage. The audience members gasp and begin talking among themselves.

"What do you want?" Huberman asks the men. "Where are you taking me and why?"

"You are under arrest, Bronislaw Huberman," an officer shouts. "You are a Pole, a citizen of Russia, and therefore you are now an enemy of the state of Germany!"

"An enemy of Germany!" Huberman cries. "What are you talking about? I have been playing concerts in Germany my entire life!"

"Not anymore!" the German says, pushing Bronislaw toward another officer. "Take this enemy to the prison! Lock him up," he orders.

The audience members jump from their seats, noisily dropping purses, top hats, and canes, scurrying toward exit doors.

An officer forces Huberman into the back of a car. Speeding away, the car arrives at the Berlin jail, and Huberman is locked into a small dark cell.

"Please," he asks a nearby guard, "will you have someone retrieve my violin and bow? I dropped both on the stage."

"No! Mr. Huberman, you should worry less about your violin and more about your life!" the guard spits. "Germany is at war, and you are now our enemy!"

Princess Cecilie is horrified by the arrest. She moves quickly down the stairs toward the stage, gently picking up the Stradivarius and bow.

Writing a brief note, the princess summons a messenger from the palace. "Take this message directly to my husband," she tells him. "It is urgent." The messenger bows and rushes out the door.

Bronislaw sits quietly in his jail cell, his face livid with anger and embarrassment. A long noisy night passes in the prison as he lies on a thin, dirty mattress. His eyes wide open, he worries about his violin and his life, and in that order.

"An enemy of Germany?" he tells the morning guard. "I love this country and its people. They are my biggest supporters."

The guard ignores him, announcing: "Huberman, you have a visitor."

Bronislaw stands when Princess Cecilie approaches his cell. He looks into the eyes of the tall, slender princess, still dressed in her elegant floor-length flowing gown.

"Princess Cecilie," he says, bowing his head toward her.

"My dear Mr. Huberman," the princess says, putting her small ivory hand through the bars to take his hand. "Please accept my personal apology for this . . . this embarrassing, humiliating incident."

Cecilie hands a note to the guard.

"My husband orders Mr. Huberman released from this cell at once!" she demands.

The guard reads the note and fumbles with the keys, rushing to unlock the iron-barred door.

"Mr. Huberman," Cecilie says, handing him the Stradivarius, "as far as I can tell, the violin hasn't been damaged. I have asked an aide to retrieve the case from your dressing room in the concert hall."

Huberman takes the violin, clasping it to his chest.

"Thank you, Princess Cecilie. I am in your eternal debt," he says.

"It is my pleasure," she tells him. "We Germans need your music now more than ever before. Mr. Huberman, stay safe until this terrible conflict ends. And please come back to us someday."

"I will certainly try," he says. "Will you please thank your husband for me?"

"Certainly, Mr. Huberman. I have arranged safe transit papers for you, and my car will escort you safely out of Germany," she says. "Again, on behalf of myself, my husband, and our country, please accept our heartfelt apology."

The violinist steps swiftly into the waiting car, holding the violin and bow tight in his trembling arms.

"Surely," he mumbles to himself, "art has found a new purpose today. It has rescued me from my captors, prison, and punishment! Perhaps it has even saved my very life!"

CHAPTER 22

The Scientist

My pacifism is an instinctive feeling, a feeling that possesses me because the murder of men is abhorrent. My attitude is not derived from intellectual theory, but is based on my deepest antipathy to every kind of cruelty and hatred.

Albert Einstein[1]

In the winter of 1914, the German-born scientist Professor Albert Einstein sits in his office at the University of Berlin, smoking his pipe and taking a break from his heavy workload. He looks out the window, contemplating the three great passions in his life: science, world peace, and music.

A decent, amateur violinist, he possesses a deep appreciation for good music. Einstein often tells his friends: "Had I not been a scientist, I would have been a musician."

He smiles when he remembers what a friend once told him about his musical ability.

"Albert, there are many musicians with much better technique, but none, I believe, who ever played with more sincerity or deeper feeling than you do."[2]

To that statement, Einstein responded: "Life without playing music is inconceivable for me. I live my daydreams in music. I see my life in terms of music . . . I get most joy in life out of music."[3]

Although he has a passion for the music of Mozart and Bach, Einstein cares little for Richard Wagner's music, even though all of Germany worships Wagner. He considers it indescribably offensive.

Einstein was thirty-five years old when he moved to Berlin, four months before the war began, serving as the director of the Kaiser Wilhelm Physical Institute and professor at the University of Berlin. He renounced his German citizenship at age seventeen, choosing to become a Swiss citizen instead. But in light of his new teaching position in Berlin, he has returned to his country's roots, renewing his German citizenship. He won international acclaim back in 1905 as a result of his famous equation of special relativity: $E=mc^2$. By now, Einstein is the most famous Jew in the world.

A confirmed pacifist, Einstein detests violence and war. He urges Europe's side-by-side neighbors to reconcile, to strive for peace and unity, a cause that makes him an unpopular Jew in an anti-Semitic Germany. At one of his recent lectures, a student openly threatened to "cut that Jew's throat." Germany does not listen to Einstein's pleas for peace. His dream of European cooperation and tranquility seems far away, and not likely to become a reality anytime soon.[4]

CHAPTER 23

The World at War

The lamps are going out all over Europe; we shall not see them lit again in our lifetime.

Sir Edward Grey, British Foreign Secretary[1]

Bronislaw follows news of the war closely. He notices how the war begins with enthusiasm, all sides hoping for a quick victory. But as months drag on, the costly battle and trench warfare bog down, resulting in pain and bloodshed, promising no end in sight.[2]

At the war's beginning, Britain, France, Serbia, and Imperial Russia battle Germany, Austria-Hungary, Ottoman Turkey, and Bulgaria. But soon the hostilities spread, and the whole world wages war. European armies build massive fortifications, string barbed-wire barriers, and dig trenches from the North Sea to the Swiss border. Thousands of soldiers die in brutal fighting along the Western and Eastern Fronts. Combat takes place in the sea, and, for the first time in history, in the air.[3]

Bronislaw detests the barbarism he witnesses all around him. He worries about the safety of Elsa and Johannes living in Hungary.

In New York, Arturo Toscanini, conductor of the Metropolitan Opera, misses his Italian home and worries about the war raging in Europe.

"It is time for me to return home to Italy," he tells his friends and colleagues in the spring of 1915. "I plan to leave New York on May first, and have booked a suite on the passenger ocean liner *Lusitania* to Liverpool. It is rumored to be the most modern, comfortable, and fastest ship on the North Atlantic run."

Toscanini is one of the world's most celebrated conductors, garnering international acclaim for his detail of phrasing, dynamic intensity, classical conception of form, and for his phenomenal memory. But now he is experiencing some awkward issues with the Met's financial management. He also feels overwhelmed by the relentless workload, as well as disappointed that his recent performance of *Carmen* did not go as well as expected.

But the main reason Toscanini wants to leave New York is a personal one. A connoisseur of beautiful women, the conductor has enjoyed a passionate and secret love affair with the famous singer Geraldine Farrar.

He met the dark-haired, doe-eyed diva when he first arrived at the Met. He saw how her international audiences loved her, often comparing Farrar to singers Maria Malibran, Jenny Lind, and Adelina Patti. He enjoys watching her perform, especially when she wears costumes of "two small groups of jewels, inconspicuous but essentially located."[4]

Toscanini endeared himself to Geraldine when she lost her voice in the middle of performing *Faust*. He knelt by her side, nursing, adoring, caressing, and encouraging her until she fully recovered. Until recently, Miss Farrar seemed happy in her role as his mistress, but lately she has been wanting more.

"I'm tired of waiting for you to divorce your wife and marry me," she tells him. After seven years of Toscanini's promises of marriage, she finally gives him the ultimatum—a wedding or a publicly exposed affaire de coeur.

Toscanini, a Catholic, has no interest in divorcing his wife of eighteen years, Carla De Martini, or remarrying. He sneaks out of the city a week early, abruptly canceling his reserved May 1 passage on the *Lusitania* and taking instead a slow, nondescript Italian liner home.

The long voyage across the Atlantic proves uneventful. Toscanini enjoys a reunion in Italy with his wife and children, thousands of miles away from the badgering Farrar.

On May 1, 1915, two thousand passengers and crew board the luxurious *Lusitania*, setting sail for Liverpool, England, on its 101st roundtrip voyage across the Atlantic. The vessel's captain denies the rumor that the ship carries 173 tons of war munitions for Britain. He purposely ignores Germany's warnings about the titanic consequences for passenger ships secretly transporting ammunition for British guns.

The voyage is smooth, and people are happy as they wine, dine, and dance across the Atlantic. But on May 7, a German submarine off the south coast of Ireland spots the ship. Receiving orders to destroy it, the submarine fires a single torpedo at the thirty-two-thousand-ton *Lusitania*, tearing into the hull on its starboard side and causing a huge explosion. A second explosion rips through the massive ship, sinking it in eighteen minutes, taking thousands of lives down with it to the bottom of the icy Celtic Sea. More than 1,100 people drown, freeze, and perish, including 128 Americans.

Citizens of the United States are outraged by the German attack on a passenger liner, turning public opinion against Germany and putting pressure on President Woodrow Wilson to enter the war.[5]

When Arturo Toscanini learns the tragic fate of the *Lusitania*, the passenger liner he had originally planned to take from New York to Liverpool, he shudders with horror and relief, silently thanking Geraldine Farrar for indirectly saving his life.

CHAPTER 24

Discouragement and Depression

A nation like Germany, after having forced the issue, will only give in after it is beaten to the ground. This will take a very long time. No one living knows how long.

Lord Horatio Kitchener, Britain's war secretary, August 1914[1]

By November 1916, the war is in full swing. One of the largest and bloodiest battles of the war, the Somme Offensive, has just ended near the Somme River in France. More than 620,000 Allied and 500,000 German soldiers die, making this one of the deadliest battles in history.[2]

On the same day, Bronislaw learns that eighty-six-year-old Franz Joseph has died. The emperor has reigned for sixty-six years. His wife, Elisabeth, preceded him in death, assassinated in Geneva, in 1898, by an Italian anarchist.

Bronislaw takes the Stradivarius from its case and examines the instrument, the exquisite gift given to him two decades before by Emperor Joseph and his wife.

He runs his fingers along the instrument's smooth varnish, recalling the emperor's continued kindness to him for many years, how he so faithfully stayed in contact with Bronislaw, encouraging him and promoting his performances.

"Rest in peace, dear generous friends," he whispers, holding the Strad to his heart.

For the past few weeks, Bronislaw has felt unusually tired, depressed, and alone. As with most inhabitants of Europe, he stays abreast of the war happenings, following the bloody battles, worrying about the safety of loved ones, and hearing of the violent deaths of family, friends, and neighbors. He, too, is war-weary, wondering when and how it will all end.

But Huberman suffers something deeper in his soul than the depression brought on by war and loss. He is experiencing the deep darkness of heart, the gnawing fathomless fear that his whole life is falling apart. He broods about his career, and how the war has interrupted his concert schedule. He misses his son, Johannes, who is turning six next month. He frets about the roles he has allowed others to play in his life—his father, Jacob; his ex-wife, Elsa; and his thieving rival, Ernő Dohnányi.

He places his violin and bow back into its case, deciding not to practice today, and maybe not tomorrow, or the next day either.

The violinist is famous, successful, and wealthy, having no unfulfilled needs or desires, insulated from life's inevitable hardships, safe and secure. But fame and money cannot grant him the life-enabling gift of sleep, or soothe his troubled soul, or gift him with the deep loving friendships he craves, or keep him from hating Dohnányi or missing his little boy. The load of life, with its worries, frustrations, and complications, hits Huberman with full force for the first time in his thirty-four years, knocking him off his feet. The invisible force overpowers and conquers him, rendering him unable to practice, bathe, dress, eat, or sleep. He spends the days staring out the window, thinking, pondering, and resenting his tormentors. The long nights pass in anxious, sleepless agony.

Gripped in the jaws of a debilitating depression in the early months of 1917, Huberman makes the decision to get away, to find rest and relief. With his last vestiges of physical and emotional strength, and in need of healing, Huberman reserves a suite at a Viennese health clinic.

CHAPTER 25

The German Nurse

How far that little candle throws its beams!
William Shakespeare, *The Merchant of Venice*[1]

Ida Ibbeken walks into Huberman's darkened room at the clinic, turns on a soft light, and reads his medical chart. Six feet tall, her slim body dressed in a stiffly starched uniform, a white shoulder-length nurse's veil covering her carefully combed brown hair, she makes a competent-looking and somewhat intriguing figure.

"Mr. Bronislaw Huberman," she says, and smiles. "My name is Ida Ibbeken. I am your nurse."

"Miss Ibbeken," he says, lifting his hand to shake hers. "I promise to be a good patient, causing you little trouble. I just need to rest and recover."

"Recover from what, Mr. Huberman?"

The stately German nurse sits in an iron chair, her back straight, her head held high on her long neck.

"Many things, Miss Ibbeken."

"Well, sir, you will find healing here. I will personally make sure of that."

Nurse Ibbeken writes something on the chart, rises, and pours a glass of water.

"I am an admirer of your music, Mr. Huberman," she says, handing him the glass.

"You've heard of me, Miss Ibbeken?"

"Certainly. I have attended several of your concerts."

"I hope you enjoyed them. I play few concerts now with the war raging across Europe. Trying to further the cause of art and music is impossible when people are war-weary, and have little money and food. Art must always take a backseat to sheer survival."

"I understand, Mr. Huberman. But this is only true if you consider art as self-serving, art for art's sake alone, or as the French say, *l'art pour l'art.*"

"How else are we to consider art, Miss Ibbeken?"

"Well, sir, I believe *true* art serves larger purposes than just its own desire for excellence."

"Your belief is quite revolutionary, Miss Ibbeken, and completely contrary to what most of us believe about art and music."

Ida smiles as she leaves the room.

The next morning, Nurse Ibbeken delivers Bronislaw's breakfast, opens the thick curtains, and tucks a linen napkin under his chin.

"I hope you are hungry, Mr. Huberman."

"Not so much," he says. "But I will try to eat."

While he nibbles at eggs and toast, Ibbeken sits beside his bed.

"I've always thought the life of a famous musician exciting and glamorous," she says. "Surely, many musicians yearn for the position and popularity you have attained."

"Exciting? Glamorous?" he asks. "It's hardly that, Miss Ibbeken. It involves much more work than most imagine. In fact, it's quite routine, ordinary, and thoroughly exhausting."

"What do you mean, Mr. Huberman?"

"I must spend hours studying and practicing. Before I can perform a work, the music must seep into my subconsciousness, and mature. It must be part of me before I can truly play it."

"This is obvious from the way you play your music," Ida says.

"Not only must I practice and learn the music, but I must pack, travel, and learn the geography of railways, the customs of different nations, and the details of promotion. And I spend many sleepless nights in noisy hotels. Perhaps this is why I am exhausted."

"I understand, sir. I had no idea of the work involved."

"Few people do. My work also aggravates my stomach, causing me to suffer greatly at times. I grew up with a strict father, and I learned as a boy to suppress my anger, keeping my mouth shut when I wanted to scream."

"Restrained passion can cause internal pain, an upset stomach. I will help you find healing."

"I should like nothing better, Miss Ibbeken."

"I'll begin your treatment with a head rub," she says.

"Thank you, Miss Ibbeken." He grins, his eyes lighting up. "I am in great need of a head rub."

CHAPTER 26

The Birth of a Friendship

A friend is one that knows you as you are, understands where you have been, accepts what you have become, and still, gently allows you to grow.

Anonymous

Bronislaw spends weeks at the clinic resting, reading, walking, dining, and enjoying the care of Nurse Ibbeken. He knows that he, a thirty-four-year-old Polish Jew, has little in common with the twenty-two-year-old German Protestant nurse except for a mutual love of music. He finds healing in Ida's company, looking forward to her company and her head rubs. Tensions drain from his body as she massages his temples, relaxing his body and easing his troubled soul.

Bronislaw and Ida eat most of their meals together, often discussing world politics, music, and art. One evening, Bronislaw plays his violin for her. She closes her eyes and relaxes her head on the sofa's back, seeming to relish the music.

"I feel honored that you would play just for me, Mr. Huberman."

A nurse enters the room, holding a small, folding vest-pocket Kodak camera.

"I heard the music from down the hall," she says. "May I take your photograph, Mr. Huberman?"

"Of course," he says, motioning Ida to join him at his side.

Huberman tells Ida about performing, as a boy, for Johannes Brahms at Vienna's Musikverein Hall, and about receiving the Stradivarius from

Emperor Franz Joseph. He places the violin in her hands and watches her hold it gently, reverently.

Huberman spends hours each day with Ida, feeling unusually comfortable and natural in her presence, experiencing an ease he has never known with a woman. He finds himself wanting to share his innermost thoughts with her. After enduring four years of marriage to the self-centered Elsa Galafrés, he welcomes Ida's plain looks, disinterest in clothes and jewelry, and her modest simplicity. Nurse Ibbeken seems content with life, and grateful to be entrusted with the care of his health.

Bronislaw also enjoys Ida's quick wit, and is challenged by her knowledge of people, world events, and the arts. He loves the way she laughs at his attempts to be humorous. After spending several weeks with her, he begins to care a little more each day for Ida.

"I appreciate you, Ida," he tells her, taking her hand between his. "You possess rare gifts of patience, humility, and warm sensitivity. I know few people with your strength of character, affection, and compassion. You are a refreshing individual, and a tremendous help to me."

Ida smiles, lowering her eyes and blushing.

Ida also enjoys Bronislaw's company, treasuring her time with him and sensing a deep mutual closeness developing. She finds him easy to talk with, seeming to be genuinely interested in her opinions. She looks forward to their long walks and daily meals together, and their discussions about music and art. When he plays the violin for her, she listens with joy and great admiration. She works hard to care for him with sweet compassion, desiring nothing more than to provide healing for the body and soul of the overworked violinist.

But as much as she desires his healing, she wants him to stay there with her, and dreads the day when he must leave the clinic.

"I love him," she finally admits aloud. "But he is wealthy and famous, constantly surrounded by beautiful women. I'm plain, a 'nobody' in his sophisticated circles. Could Mr. Huberman possibly be interested in me?"

With his health restored, Bronislaw makes plans to go home. Ida has been a bright light in his life, caring for him with tenderness, helping him recover, and becoming his friend. He is ready to leave the clinic, but he is *not* ready to leave Ida.

On the day of his departure, Bronislaw takes Ida's hand in his, looks into her eyes, and says softly: "Ida, I must say good-bye. Thank you for taking such good care of me, and for becoming my friend. I will miss you."

"And I will miss you, too, Mr. Huberman," Ida says. "I pray you will stay well, and continue bringing joy to the world through your music."

A nurse holding a photograph runs to Bronislaw. "I had the photograph developed for you," she says, handing him a small square picture, and rushing back inside.

Bronislaw and Ida look at the photograph, taken weeks before, he holding his violin, Ida sitting close beside him, and both smile. He tucks it into his coat pocket.

Huberman feels the urge to wrap his arms around Ida, hold her tightly, and ask her to come with him. But he restrains himself, keeping secret his deep feelings for her.

Suddenly he feels awkward, hardly knowing what to do or say next.

"Ah . . . we must stay in contact, Ida. Maybe we can see each other again at one of my concerts . . . or somewhere."

"Yes, Broni," she says, her expression professional. "I will look forward to it . . . ah . . . at a concert . . . or somewhere . . . one day."

Bronislaw pauses for a moment before releasing her hand.

"Ida, I . . . I . . . ah . . . would you . . . ?" He stops abruptly midsentence. Pressing his lips together, he smiles, releases her hand, turns, and walks toward a waiting car. The driver opens the back door for him, and then places his suitcase in the trunk. He bends to sit down, but then hesitates, looking back a last time at the nurse standing by the clinic's door.

I cannot leave without her. I could search a lifetime, and never find another woman I love like Ida. But . . .

He climbs into the backseat, and the car pulls away.

I da feels tears well in her eyes as she watches the car drive away.

I will never see him again.

She retreats to her room and, for a long afternoon, ponders the loving relationship she has known with the great violinist, Bronislaw Huberman.

CHAPTER 27

The Missing Months

Love is that condition in which the happiness of another person is essential to your own.

Robert A. Heinlein, *Stranger in a Strange Land* (1961)[1]

Bronislaw thinks about Ida during his drive home, yearning to have the driver turn around and go back to the clinic, back to Ida. He struggles with the decision. He loves her, but he has already tried marriage, and for him it didn't work. Elsa had convinced him, during the four years of their painful marriage, that he was not suited to be a husband. And he didn't want to break another heart—especially not Ida's heart—and risk another divorce.

As he travels through the cities and countryside, he ponders the war that still consumes Europe. He has known a brief respite at the clinic, an intermission from the bloody devastation. But now he is going home, returning to the thick of war, his brief sabbatical at an end.

Daily, he reads the papers, so weary of war, and yearning to see the conflict end. But the war goes on; strong and constant it continues. In March, he hears news of revolution in Petrograd, and the abdication of Russia's czar Nicholas II. Enduring mutinies, low morale, starvation, and the desertion of soldiers, the three-hundred-year Romanov dynasty collapses. On April 6, 1917, he reads that President Wilson has declared war on Germany, bringing the United States into the battle.

During long days of waiting for the war to end, and for his concerts to resume, he practices intensely and learns new repertoire. But every time he plays the Strad, he wishes Ida could be with him, listening to the piece and offering her loving encouragements. Every meal he eats alone, he dreams of Ida sitting beside him, sharing the food and keeping him company. He misses Ida, her kind ways, her spontaneous laughter, her sweet words, the way she blushes when he compliments her. He also misses the head massages, those gentle hands that chase away his headaches, the way her tender touch drains the anxiety from his soul.

Many times during spring and summer, he picks up the telephone to call her. But he never completes the call.

Ida has cared for many patients at the clinic since Bronislaw left. She often wonders how he is, what he's doing, where he's traveling. Not hearing from him for months, she comes to believe her love for him was one-sided and not mutual.

In the summer of 1917, Bronislaw wonders if the war will ever end. The fighting is still intensely strong, slowing little. German planes bomb London, causing the city to suffer its greatest number of civilian casualties of the war. The British retaliate with deadly bombing raids against Germany. At the end of June, the first American troops land in France, launching the next deadly phase of this brutal war. On July 2, Greece joins the effort, declaring war on the Central Powers.[2] The world is in chaos.

By fall, Bronislaw feels unusually discouraged. He slips on his coat, deciding to take a walk. In the pocket, he finds the photograph made at the clinic with Ida. Staring at the picture of Ida, for the first time he finally admits he is desperately lonely, that he loves and misses Ida, and that he no longer wants to live without her.

Holding the photograph, he telephones Ida at the clinic. Expressing his heartfelt desire to see her, Bronislaw invites her to visit him. Ida accepts his invitation and travels to his home, and at Bronislaw's heart-felt insistence, she remains there with him as his companion, secretary, and friend.

Part 3

THE GREAT
WAR ENDS

*From the first gunshot fired in anger in 1914 until the
11th hour of the 11th day on the 11th month in 1918,
The Great War took its toll on human life. Of the 65
million men who fought in World War 1: eight million
men were killed in battle; two million died of illness
and disease; 21.2 million were wounded; 7.8 million
were taken prisoner or went missing in action; 6.8
million civilians were killed.*

James Paterson,
from "The Human Cost of War"[1,2]

CHAPTER 28

The Eleventh Hour of the Eleventh Day of the Eleventh Month

Peace came, not the peace they expected, in the shape of a white dove with an olive branch, but like a withering blast from some destroying angel, which swept away names once dear, and things once sacred. . . . The Imperial House is no more; its Emperor and Empress, its Court, and its insignia have vanished like shadows.

An unnamed reporter, Vienna, 1919[1]

On the afternoon of November 11, 1918, in the living room of their home, Ida sits on the sofa holding Bronislaw's head in her lap, gently massaging his temples. She glances at her wristwatch.

"It's eleven o'clock—the eleventh hour of the eleventh day of the eleventh month. The war is finally over. I am so glad."

"Yes, I, too, am glad. It was such a foolish war. But I sense it won't be the last war in Europe during our lifetimes, Ida."

"Oh, Broni, I pray it was truly the war to end all wars. I can't imagine another one. Europeans will be mourning their wounded, lost, and dead for a long, long time."

Most Europeans are still scrubbing blood off the streets of their war-torn countryside when, on a snowy February morning in 1919, Bronislaw and Ida step into a Viennese hotel. The Great War has ended, leaving Europe's populace with steep inflation, widespread poverty, a scarred landscape, and unfathomable human suffering. Bronislaw is glad to be receiving concert invitations again in parts of Europe.

"Your concert is in a few hours, Broni," Ida tells him. She reaches out and gently strokes his face with the back of her hand. "You need to rest after the long drive."

"Ida, I need to practice."

The thirty-seven-year-old violinist glances out the window at the lightly falling snow, picks up his Stradivarius, and begins to practice. Ida empties his suitcase, hanging up his suits and shirts and stacking his toiletries neatly on the bathroom sink.

After a while, Bronislaw stops, stretches his neck and arms, and again looks out the window. A group of people stand idly on the street beneath him. Like most Europeans after the war, they look bruised and battered, impoverished, hungry, and weary.

The violinist turns away and continues to play, trying to ignore the beaten-down people who now live on the streets and have no warm place to go. But something catches his eye. He looks closer, and sees a young mother, clad in dirty rags, holding a baby. He lowers his bow and watches the woman.

Where is her husband? Was he a soldier, now buried in a mass unmarked grave along the Western Front? Is she a widow without money, without home, and with a child to rear alone?

His sympathy for the mother and child catches him by surprise. Peering out the window, he spots a soldier still wearing a battle-worn uniform, his right arm missing.

A one-armed man. Where did he fight? What work can he do with only one arm?

He closes his eyes, picks up the bow, and starts to play again.

"I need to practice, not peer out the window!" he admonishes himself aloud.

But he cannot keep his eyes closed, his mind refusing to focus on the music. Something draws his eyes down again to the wretched, suffering people below.

He sees young children gathered on the street, thin, dirty, their faces showing despair, hopelessness.

He stops playing for a moment and watches the children. They stand barefoot in the snow, wearing tattered clothes that give no warmth or protection from Vienna's freezing February weather. They look at each other with hollow eyes, as if already mourning the memories of a childhood lost, never to be recovered. One small boy, wearing a faded brown coat, stands out. Huberman looks more closely at the boy's misshaped spine and bowed legs.

"Rickets," he whispers.

He focuses on the child's face.

"Ida," he asks, "please open the window."

"Broni, it is freezing outside. You'll get a chill. . . ."

"Please, Ida, open it."

She shakes her head in frustration, walks to the large window, opening it an inch or two.

"Open it wider," he says.

She obeys, pushing the window up as high as it will go.

"But just for a little while, Broni, then we will close it."

Concentrating on the boy, Huberman plays. The sweet violin music floats from the open window to the ears of the small disabled boy. The child's face lights up with the look of pure joy as he seems to drink in the sounds of the soul-soothing music. The boy jumps up and down, responding with loud excited cries and spontaneous applause.

The violinist continues to play, watching others emerge from the shadows to join the boy. Little by little, the crowd grows. Huberman smiles as he watches the people's reactions to his music, as if they are oblivious to hunger, cold temperatures, and falling snow. Their heads tilt upward as they wave their arms with elation, visibly expressing their delight.

B ronislaw Huberman sighs as he plays, remembering prewar Vienna, the impressive capital of the once-powerful Austro-Hungarian Empire that could boast of fifteen nations and more than fifty million inhabitants. He recalls those forever-gone days when Vienna's women walked along beautifully paved streets, carrying lace parasols, stopping occasionally to admire statues of heroes mounted on stallions atop ornate buildings. He knows the Empire is no more.

He closes his eyes and reflects back to lavishly decorated concert halls, packed to capacity with music-loving people, women dressed in sequined gowns and white elbow-length gloves, men wearing black top hats and tails. How they applauded when the famous violinist walked onto the finest concert stages of Vienna, the city he has known since his early childhood, the hub of art and culture, palaces and paintings, universities, museums, parks, and miles of manicured landscapes. The rich, powerful, talented, and famous flocked to the city from all parts of the world in those grand long-lost days.

His heart begins to hurt for the war-torn city, its politics in chaos, its empire stripped, its anti-Semitism heightened, its once-affluent finery turned to filth, and its people shocked and depressed. Now shabbily dressed women search through discarded piles of garbage on street corners looking for an evening meal. Famine, social unrest, high infant mortality rates, and the dreaded tuberculosis—dubbed the "Viennese malady"—plague the suffering city.[2]

Huberman opens his eyes and looks for the peasant boy in the crowd below. But the boy in the brown coat is gone. Unexpected tears form in the violinist's eyes as he searches for the child, and plays for the war-wounded people who stand below him.

As he watches the people react to the music, he notices, perhaps for the first time, how the music of a single violin seems to strengthen and encourage the suffering listeners.

"The music is feeding their hungry hearts," he whispers to himself.

Huberman plays the final notes, scanning the crowd once more in search of the boy. But he cannot find him. The violinist lowers his bow, walks to the bed, and sits on its edge.

Ida jumps up, closes the window, and picks up a blanket, spreading it snugly around Bronislaw's shoulders.

"You seem unusually downcast, Broni," she says, standing close beside him.

"I was just thinking about the war," he replies, leaning his head against her arm, "and how deeply it has hurt these people."[3]

CHAPTER 29

The Boy in the Brown Jacket

We need to decide that we will not go to war, whatever reason is conjured up by the politicians or the media, because war . . . is always indiscriminate, a war against innocents, a war against children.

Howard Zinn[1]

Bronislaw Huberman stretches his body across the bed, his hand instinctively reaching for the Stradivarius. Without awareness, his fingers run lightly along the instrument's fine Cremona wood. He has been playing this 206-year-old violin for more than two decades. Since his youth, he and his cherished Strad have produced sweet sounds unlike any violin he has ever heard. It is his very voice, an essential part of him. He pulls the Stradivarius close.

He tries to relax, to ready his body and mind for the evening's concert, but something inside his spirit draws him back to the window. As he looks outside, he sees groups of shivering people still standing on the street below, their eyes staring up to his closed window. They seem to be in no hurry to leave, or to find warmth and shelter. They continue to wait, as if hoping and hungering for more music. He opens the window wide. A sudden blast of cold air hits his face, and an uncomfortable wet chill saturates the room. He positions the beloved violin under his chin and plays for them.

L ater that evening, Bronislaw's performance is received with an over-whelming response. Performing encore after encore for the audience, Huberman honors their endless requests for more music, and performs late into the night.

"Let us go quickly," he usually tells Ida after he plays the last note and takes a final bow. She always helps him escape the admiring crowds who wish to engage in what he calls meaningless chatter.

But tonight is different. Bronislaw stays in the hall, allowing his audience to surround him, engage him in conversation, and touch him—as if one touch might bring them a shred of hope and happiness. Huberman smiles at the admirers who greet him, an expression his audience rarely sees.

T hat night, Bronislaw finally drifts off to sleep in the dark, early morning hours. He dreams he plays for the crowds who gaze up to his window, their empty eyes silently begging for music. The sunken faces and thin, diseased bodies haunt his dreams as the people cry for music instead of bread.

When he spots the small brown-jacketed boy, partially hidden in the crowd of starving peasants, he lays down his violin, racing from his room down into the street. People reach out to touch him, grab him, wrapping bony hands around his arms and legs, preventing him from reaching the boy. Gently pushing the peasants away, he claws his way to the child, who lies facedown in the wet street. He kneels, picking up the small limp body and turning the child's head up toward him. He looks into the dead child's face. It looks just like his son, Johannes.

"Johannes! Johannes!" he screams, awakening from sleep and startling himself.

From the adjoining room, Ida rushes to his bedside, rubbing her eyes as if trying to wake up.

"Broni? What's wrong? Why are you screaming?"

She sits on his bed, enveloping him in her arms until his violent trembling ends.

"I saw a boy—a dead boy—out on the street, and he looked just like my son, Johannes!"

"You've had a bad dream, Broni," she whispers, rubbing his back. "Try to go back to sleep."

CHAPTER 30

The Theft

There was a war, a great war, and now it is over. Men fought to kill, to maim, to destroy. Some return home, others remain behind forever on the fields of their greatest sacrifice. The rewards of the dead are the lasting honors of martyrs for humanity; the reward of the living is the peaceful conscience of one who plays the game of life and plays it square.

Lieutenant Lewis Plush, a twenty-six-year-old
soldier of the American Expeditionary Force[1]

Later that morning, Ida massages Bronislaw's head and neck until he is calm.

"Broni, let's dress and go downstairs for breakfast. Food will help you feel better."

Before they leave, Bronislaw reminds Ida to hide the Stradivarius under the bed.

"We want no hotel staff touching it if they clean the room before we return," he says.

For the next half hour, Ida and Bronislaw sit quietly in the hotel's café, eating a light breakfast.

"I'm glad to see you eat, Broni. I was worried about you."

"I am much better now," he says, and purposely changes the subject. "I miss the old days of Vienna, Ida."

"So do I, Broni."

fter breakfast, the couple returns to their room. Unlocking the door, Bronislaw steps inside as Ida follows.

"They have not yet cleaned our room," he says. "Maybe I can sleep a few hours before we leave the city. I am awfully tired."

"Good idea, Broni. While you rest, I will pack our suitcases and keep the cleaning staff out of the room.

He smiles at Ida and walks to the unmade bed.

"No! No! No!" he suddenly screams.

On the floor beside the bed, the violin case is flung open, and the Stradivarius is gone.

I da runs to Bronislaw, dropping to her knees beside him, horrified to see the empty case. She cries, places her arms around him, trying to comfort him. But he is inconsolable.

"How dare someone steal my violin!" he shouts, jumping to his feet, heading to the door.

"Broni," Ida begs as she rises to follow him. "Please calm down. We will find it."

Running down the stairs and outside into the street, they find a police officer standing on the corner. He listens to their story and escorts them to police headquarters. Ida files a theft report and then joins Bronislaw, sitting beside him on a cold metal bench inside the station. Bronislaw's head is lowered, his face buried in his hands.

"Go back to your hotel," an officer tells them. "We'll let you know if . . . I mean . . . *when* we find the violin."

While they wait in their room to hear some news, Ida again tries to reassure him.

"Broni," she says softly, motioning him to put his head in her lap. "Please do not worry so. It'll upset your stomach."

Ida begins massaging his head and neck, whispering to him, trying to soothe his growing anxiety.

"I will never see that violin again. I have kept it safe all these years, and now . . ."

Ida pulls a plain white handkerchief from the sleeve of her blouse, tenderly wiping Bronislaw's face and tucking the handkerchief into his hand.

"The police will find it," she says.

Hours drag by as Ida and Bronislaw wait. One minute, Ida convinces him to sit down, put his head in her lap, and allow her to massage it. The next minute, he's on his feet, pacing the floor, shouting with anger, and staring out the window.

Ida feels helpless to comfort him.

Late that afternoon, a police officer knocks on Bronislaw's hotel room door.

The door swings open, and he smiles at the tall, plain-faced woman who greets him.

"I'm lookin' for Mr. Huberman," he says. "I've got his—"

Ida's face lights up. She snatches the Stradivarius from the officer's hand, turning toward Bronislaw.

"They found it, Broni!" she shouts.

From the open door, the officer sees the violinist take the Strad, embracing it like a starving man given a loaf of bread.

"Please come in," Ida tells him.

"Did you catch that good-for-nothing thief?" Bronislaw shouts, his right hand forming a fist.

"Yes, sir," the officer says. "We got 'im! Caught him red-handed in the alley, tryin' to sell it to somebody on the street. He's in jail now."

Looking more closely at the violin, the officer asks: "How much is that worth anyway?"

"It is worth a lot to me," Bronislaw says.

"It don't look damaged," the officer says.

Bronislaw pulls several folded bills from his pocket, placing the money in the man's hand.

"Tell me, sir," Bronislaw says. "Do you have a son?"

"Yes, Mr. Huberman. I'm father to four small boys."

Bronislaw reaches deep into his pocket, pulling out four more large bills and placing them in the officer's hand.

"Take good care of them," he tells the officer.

B ronislaw says little as Ida drives their car across the war-ravaged countryside, returning home to Vienna. He feels relieved to have recovered his violin.

"Are you feeling ill, Broni?" she asks, putting her free hand up to his forehead.

"No, Ida. Just thinking."

"You are remembering those people who stood below our window at the hotel, aren't you, Broni, the ones who listened to your music?"

"Yes, Ida, and I am remembering that dead child in my dream," he says. "The boy in the brown coat who wore the face of my son."

CHAPTER 31

The Treaty

There are no humane methods of warfare, there is no such thing as civilized warfare; all warfare is inhuman, all warfare is barbaric; the first blast of the bugles of war ever sounds for the time being the funeral knell of human progress. . . . What lover of humanity can view with anything but horror the prospect of this ruthless destruction of human life?

James Connolly, 1868–1916[1]

In the summer of 1919, almost five months after the Stradivarius was stolen in Vienna, Bronislaw and Ida read the morning papers and eat breakfast in the dining room of a plush hotel in Zurich.

"The war is now officially over," Bronislaw tells her, his eyes glued to the newspaper. "It says here the Germans will sign a treaty today in Versailles."

"The war may be over," Ida says, "but Europeans are still struggling with the devastation. Especially my fellow Germans."

"It will take a long time for people to heal, Ida. They are hungry, homeless, and dying from disease."

"Yes, and European politics are in chaos," she says. "I can't even imagine what will happen to my family and friends."

On June 28, 1919, several French soldiers wearing worn uniforms climb atop chairs and tables, peeking through windows into the Hall of Mirrors at the Versailles Palace near Paris. The great hall, with its 578 mirrors and seventeen large windows, is breathtakingly beautiful. Large, extravagant glass chandeliers cast sparkling colors and light throughout the palace hall.

The war came to a halt on November 11, and today the Allies are forcing the Germans to sign the devastating Treaty of Versailles, an official document outlining Germany's punishment for starting the war, downsizing their military to prevent future combat, and billing them heavily for the war's damages.

"I understand why they chose this hall for the signin'," a soldier observes, grinning and elbowing his buddy.

"'Cause it's a gorgeous place that the German bombs didn't destroy?"

"No, 'cause with all the mirrors, the Allies can watch every move these devious Germans make. If they stumble, sneer, or even insult the Allies, it'll be reflected thousands of times for everybody to see!"

"Yeah! Further humiliation!" The soldier laughs.

The soldiers, as well as hundreds of important guests, watch and listen to the three invited world leaders as they make presentations: David Lloyd George of Britain, Georges Clémenceau of France, and the American president Woodrow Wilson.

The soldiers hear hundreds of angry men outside shouting: "Hang the Kaiser! Make Germany pay! They started the war! Make 'em pay for the damages!"

Inside, a group of old soldiers talk among themselves.

"This'll bring ol' Germany to her knees," one says. "They've lost land and soldiers, and most of their tanks, airplanes, and subs."

"Most of their battleships, too!" another says, and smirks. "No way for Germany to protect herself now, much less start another war! They're sunk."

"There's no way they can pay for all the damage they caused. Their money's no good now anyway. Takes 'em two years' salary just to buy a loaf of bread!"

"Serves 'em right. The Allies won't let 'em join the new League of Nations neither. They'll never survive the bloody mess they've made. Never."

"Do you boys realize it's been five years to the day since old Ferdinand

and Sophie were gunned down?" one of the soldiers asks. "We've put up with five long years of bloody conflict. The Germans are gettin' just what they deserve 'cause they brought it on themselves."

"From what I hear," says another, "it sounds like this treaty'll make 'em suffer real good!"[2]

Forty-six days after the Allies force Germany to sign the treaty, a thirty-year-old Austrian drifter, Adolf Hitler, attends a beer hall meeting of the German Workers' Party in Munich, Bavaria's capital. Failing as an artist in Vienna before the war, Hitler found some success as an enlisted soldier in the German army, receiving the Iron Cross First Class, the Iron Cross Second Class, and a certificate for bravery. Since Germany's defeat, Hitler has served with the remnant of the German army, helping to process the release of French and Russian prisoners of war. Seven months earlier, army intelligence assigned the anti-Bolshevik to investigate the German Workers' Party, a small anti-Semitic group meeting in beer halls and seeking to support working Germans.

At his first meeting, on September 12, 1919, Hitler jumps from his seat, interrupting the speaker and rudely denouncing the leader's opinion.

"Your idea is ruinous!" Hitler shouts. "Bavarian independence from Germany will divide and weaken Germany! Your idea is only fit for a traitor!"

The young man's crude boldness impresses the attending party leaders, and they invite him to come again.

He eagerly accepts. Soon Hitler becomes a regular speaker at the party's growing gatherings, harshly denouncing German Jews, as well as Berlin's Social Democratic government leaders.

"They are Marxists!" Hitler screams. The people listen to him, enthusiastically applauding their agreement. He affirms with praise the party's chosen symbol—the swastika, a three-thousand-year-old symbol representing life, sun, power, strength, and good luck.[3]

With an innate confidence and passion in his orations, Hitler speaks to party members about the Aryans—European invaders who were ancestors of the ancient Greeks.

"A superior people," he tells them, "right and natural in their superiority, conquerors of inferior people. To this day, the halfhearted and the lukewarm remain the curse of Germany." Hitler's words inflame German hearts, urging them to regain their national pride and their German empire.[4]

"The Jews are a tuberculosis of the people!" he screams to his audiences, bringing him roaring applause and cheers. "Germany's ultimate goal must be the removal of the Jews altogether!"[5]

Empowered by the support of his growing audience, Hitler joins the German Workers' Party. The party accepts his leadership, and with the hate-fueled Austrian as their frequent star speaker, it becomes the National Socialist German Workers' Party, or "Nazis" for short. The racist, fanatical group of Nazis quickly expands to more than six thousand members.[6]

The newly designed red-and-white flag, stamped with the fearsome black swastika, comes to symbolize Nazi violence, murder, death, and extreme hatred for Jews.[7]

CHAPTER 32

The Rabble-Rouser and the New German Party

We have faith that one day heaven will bring the Germans back into a Reich over which there shall be no Soviet star, no Jewish star of David, but above that Reich there shall be the symbol of German labor—the swastika!

Adolf Hitler, 1923[1]

Over the following months, Bronislaw hears more and more about the rising popularity of Adolf Hitler.

"This man is gaining power quickly in Germany," he tells Ida. "He's a compelling speaker, and Germans seem to be listening to him, and worse, supporting him."

"I hear he promotes violence and anti-Semitism," Ida says.

"He is a rabble-rouser! Hitler and this new party are dangerous," he says. "With Germany's government so unstable since the war, any violent, anti-Semitic lunatic can stir up a mob and take leadership. I fear he is cultivating a whole new level of hatred and harassment for European Jews."

"Maybe more European Jews will turn to Zionism," Ida says. "Perhaps they do need a nation just for themselves, a place they can live together in harmony and safety."

"Ida, Palestine is an uncultured, hot, dangerous desert. Why would anyone want to leave Europe and live *there*?"

Without answering his question, Ida stares into Bronislaw's eyes with a look of frustration. "Broni, why do you so adamantly oppose Zionism?"

"Because I strongly disagree with Herzl and the World Zionist Organization when they encourage Jews to settle in Palestine. The Jews will lose far too much if they leave Europe."

"Perhaps they might gain more than they will lose," she says.

Bronislaw raises his voice slightly. "Ida, the Jews have assimilated deeply into European culture. They live and work as professionals in medicine, music, business, science, and industry—hardworking citizens who contribute greatly to European culture. Just consider how many Jewish musicians are employed by the Berlin Philharmonic Orchestra, as well as other first-class orchestras in Europe? Nothing in Palestine could entice them to leave Europe, give up good careers, uproot their families, and move to a barren desert that offers few, if any, opportunities for education, art, music, or culture. They should not leave their homes and jobs in Europe. They belong here!"

"I understand, Broni, but if the Jews are despised here, treated with gross injustice, and their lives threatened constantly, how can you blame them for wanting to get away from it?"

Bronislaw takes a deep breath, in obvious exasperation. "If they leave, Ida, they will pay a high price. It will be a tragedy if Jewish people sever their deep ties with Europe."

Ida looks down, pressing her lips together tightly and saying nothing.

Bronislaw softens his voice and smiles. "I don't want to argue with you, Ida, but you'll never convince me that Zionism is a good idea. I am wholeheartedly against it."

He places his hand on her face, stroking it tenderly. "I admire your compassion for the hurting in society, Ida, and I, too, feel sorry for the Jewish people and what they must endure."

Ida's eyes dart up and meet his. She leans forward, moving her face close to his.

"*Your* people, Broni. The Jewish people are *your* people. They are safe

Bronislaw with the haircut popular among Polish boys of the time.

A young Bronislaw Huberman with his father, Jacob.
Courtesy of Joan Huberman Payne

Bronislaw Huberman in an early publicity photo.
Courtesy of Amnon Weinstein

The German composer and pianist,
Johannes Brahms.

The card that Brahms scribbled for the young Huberman
after hearing the boy play his concerto.

An 1896 silhouette depicting the fourteen-year-old Bronislaw playing the Brahms Violin Concerto at Vienna's Musikverein Hall on January 29, 1896. The composer and other musicians of the time are clearly recognizable, including Anton Bruckner, Hans Richter, Johann Strauss, and Karl Goldmark.

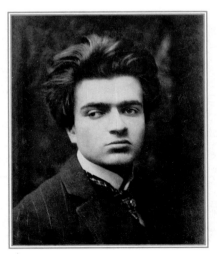

The young Huberman at the height of his teenaged fame.
Courtesy of Amnon Weinstein

Bronislaw Huberman in one of many early publicity photos.

Bronislaw Huberman and Elsa Huberman-Galafrés at their summer home, "Rekawinkel," in Austria. *Courtesy of Joan Huberman Payne*

Bronislaw with his wife, Elsa Galafrés, and their son, Johannes, in good times.
Courtesy of Joan Huberman Payne

A portrait of Elsa and Johannes, 1911.
Courtesy of Joan Huberman Payne

Ida Ibbeken when she was a nurse in the clinic where she met Bronislaw.
Photo circa WWI era.

Huberman having a rare moment of relaxation in Palestine, 1931.

Huberman and his friend Albert Einstein at the physicist's home
in Princeton, New Jersey, in April 1936.
Courtesy of the Murray S. Katz Photo Archives of the IPO

The young Wilhelm Furtwängler,
conductor of the Berlin Philharmonic.
Library of Congress, Prints & Photographs Division

Ida Ibbeken and Huberman on a fundraising concert tour.

nowhere on this planet. And do not forget that your Jewish blood also runs through the veins of your son."

L ong into the dark early-morning hours, Bronislaw lies awake in bed, pondering Ida's words.

"I know I am Jewish. I don't need Ida to remind me of that fact," he whispers. "But I consider myself first a violinist, second a Pole—then a European, and lastly, a Jew."

Bronislaw knows that because he is a wealthy, prominent violinist, protected by fame and money, he has been insulated from the violent abuse most European Jews suffer.

Sometime before dawn, Bronislaw succumbs to sleep. But it is a restless, fidgety sleep filled with nightmares.

CHAPTER 33

The Decision

The year, 1918, has gone: a year momentous as the termination of the most cruel war in the annals of the human race; a year which developed a most fatal infectious disease causing the death of hundreds of thousands of human beings. Medical science, for four and one-half years, devoted itself to putting men on the firing line and keeping them there. Now it must turn with its whole might to combating the greatest enemy of all—infectious disease.

A reporter for the *Journal of the American Medical Association*[1]

The world seems a strange and different place to Bronislaw, Ida, and the planet's suffering populace after the Great War finally ends. Families bury loved ones and mourn, struggle to bind up deep national wounds with new leaders and governments, work hard to clear rubble cluttering their countryside, and strive to get back on their feet, build new homes and businesses, and heal from the widespread anguish of death, destruction, and war.

Not only did four and a half years of heavy combat kill legions of people, but during the past two years, the deadly "Spanish flu" claimed more casualties worldwide than perished in the Great War. The world has lost millions upon millions of its citizens, more than enough to forever alter the course of world history.

A s 1919 turns into 1920, the memory of the boy in the brown coat continues to haunt Bronislaw, upsetting his stomach and aborting all attempts to sleep. He feels restless. Disturbed. Resentful. He yearns for something that seems missing in his life, but has yet to discover what his soul so craves. By the end of the old year, the violinist is eating little, rarely smiling, and seldom speaking. It is as if he carries the weight of the whole weary, war-ravaged world on his shoulders. Bronislaw spends most of his time at home in Vienna, staring out the window into winter's thick shroud of fog.

During the early days of the new year, however, the fog begins to lift. Only slightly at first, but just enough to allow a bit of sunshine to peek through the darkness, penetrating the gloom and bringing some semblance of hope to Vienna's overcast winter sky and to Bronislaw's comfortless soul. For the first time in many months, the corners of the violinist's lips slant slightly upward, and he invites Ida to join him for afternoon tea.

"Ida," he says as he sips hot tea. "Now that the war is over, I want to see Johannes. It has been far too long since I have seen my son."

Ida smiles, closes her eyes, and nods.

"Johannes is growing up in the home of German and Hungarian Protestants," he says, wrinkling his forehead, knitting his brows. "I want him to know his Jewish roots."

"He is now old enough to travel with us, Broni."

"Yes, Ida. At nine years old, he will appreciate learning about his Jewish heritage, as well as spending more time with me. I want to take him to Poland, introduce him to my family, show him where I grew up."

"To Częstochowa?"

"Yes, and also to Tomashov, the part of Poland where my grandfather Chaim Eliezer lived and worked, and where my father, Jacob, was born."

"Tomashov? I did not know this, Broni."

"Yes. My grandfather was born there in the early 1800s. He married and had four sons—the third son, born in 1857, was my father. Grandfather found work in Tomashov on a large farm owned by a German Gentile named Huberman."

"This is where you received your name?"

"Yes. Huberman made my grandfather his general foreman, and was so pleased with his work that he gave him his family name."

"Did your grandfather's family practice Judaism?"

Bronislaw nods. "My grandfather taught his sons Yiddish, and they observed faithfully the ancient rituals in their home. My father, however, failed to share Chaim's Jewish ways with our family."[2]

"I wish I had met your father, Broni."

"Consider yourself fortunate, Ida, that you did not. Papa yearned to become a professional violinist, but his father's lack of money quickly quashed his ambitions. So Papa pushed his dream onto me."

Bronislaw pauses, remembering the pain of a childhood long ago.

"My family suffered under Papa's harsh control, especially my mother and me. He made me quit school as a mere boy. I have always resented him for that. Years before he died, he became an angry, frustrated, brutal man whose abrupt outbursts of unbridled rage cost him his jobs and intimidated everyone around him, including me."[3]

Ida says nothing as she gazes downward and wipes her eyes with a handkerchief.

"I am determined, Ida, to be a better father to Johannes than my father was to me."

Late that night, Huberman lies in bed, reflecting on his memories of his father. Over his lifetime, he has allowed anger and resentment toward his father to nearly eat him alive. Now, for the first time in his thirty-seven years, he is able to slip his own feet into his father's shoes.

The thoughts of Jacob flood his mind and hurt his heart as he envisions this man suffering from deep, unfulfilled dreams, no job, little money, and a family to feed and shelter. The knot of resentment that has long been lodged in Bronislaw's throat, at times almost choking him, begins to move. For the first time ever, he feels unexpected compassion for his father.

"Papa was a poor, hungry peasant. Was he like the cold, miserable people who stood beneath the window of my hotel in Vienna?" he whispers, as if asking out loud will give him a greater understanding of the tragedy of his father's life.

As Bronislaw ponders his father's poverty, as well as a suffering, war-scarred populace, he begins to reflect on his own life, his father's, and those of the other people in the world. He compares his own extraordinary circumstances to theirs.

"I am comfortably ensconced between clean, linen sheets," he whispers. "In my kitchen pantry is bacon, eggs, bread, butter, and jam for my breakfast in a few hours. My closet is filled to overflowing with fashionable clothes, starched white shirts, comfortable shoes, socks, and freshly laundered underwear. Gold and silver tie pins rest near my vast assortment of silk ties. I have a skill and a career I love, one that brings wealth, as well as worldwide praise and adoration from the rich and royal. Surely, I have so much more than Papa, and most Europeans today. I am a rich man in so many ways."

Bronislaw pauses, taking a moment to ponder more deeply.

"Papa was a merciless disciplinarian and a harsh teacher, and I hated him for it. Nothing can change that. But would I have any of these comforts, or this career, had he not forced his ambitions onto me? Had he not made me practice the violin until my fingertips bled?"

As tears drop from his eyes, Bronislaw feels the lifetime's resentment slowly begin to drain. The bitter poison, so long harbored in his heart, seems to pour out from some place deep within him.

Bronislaw sits up in bed and wipes away his tears. He swallows hard, and discovers that the choking knot in his throat, which he has lived with much of his life, has been dislodged; it has disappeared. In the darkness of his bedroom, he whispers: "Oh, Papa, I forgive you."

By morning light, Bronislaw has forgiven his father, and has made an important, life-changing decision. When Ida awakes, he tells her his plans.

"Ida, all night I have pondered the suffering of people, including that of my own father. I realize now that I know so little about world politics and the human situation, about what causes people to bear arms against their neighbors and cause such devastation, death, and the mauling of beautiful cities. I have had so little formal education. I feel as if I know nothing about the ways of man and the world. I have decided to cancel all my upcoming concerts and become a full-time university student. Perhaps in Paris."

Ida's mouth drops open, and her eyebrows fly up on her forehead. But after a few seconds, she smiles. "I admire you for making this decision, Broni. Shall I help you cancel your concerts?"

Bronislaw and Ida take a train to Paris. During the next two years, Bronislaw refuses to give concerts, immersing himself instead in deep studies of social and political sciences at the Sorbonne University. He meets many influential people who, like him, are sick of war and weary of watching people suffer.

Inwardly projecting the impact of another European war, and already predicting its approach in the political undercurrents he feels brewing, Bronislaw Huberman ponders deeply the importance of peace, aggressively planning the public stand he must take to help ensure it. He decides to use his art and music, his worldwide popularity and fame, to propose and promote his politics of world peace. He joins the small but powerful Pan-Europa movement, presently gaining strength and numbers in Europe. The organization promotes a vision of a politically, economically, and militarily united Europe. Its founder, Coudenhove-Kalergi, the son of an Austrian diplomat, launched this great political movement years before, sensing a future war that would totally collapse Europe.[4]

"Europe needs to unite its individual countries, rule as one democratic government, and prevent the coming war," Bronislaw tells Ida, explaining the Pan-Europa concept.

"This new political system is ideal for Europe, staunchly anti-Communist from its inception. It has four basic principles: liberalism, Christianity, social responsibility, and pro-Europeanism. At the same time, Ida, it welcomes and acknowledges the contributions of Judaism and Islam."[5]

Within the Pan-Europa group of supporters, he meets and forms friendships with France's prime minister Aristide Briand, the Austrian neurologist Sigmund Freud, the pacifist scientist Albert Einstein, and others of world influence.

By the end of 1922, the Pan-Europa cause has turned Bronislaw's head, giving him a vision that points his life and work in a new direction. A feverish passion has taken root in his heart. He emerges from the Sorbonne with a new group of powerful friends, and a strong, fresh desire to work with them in promoting international harmony and world peace.

CHAPTER 34

A Fanatic's Promises

I scanned the revolutionary events of history and put the question to myself against which racial element in Germany can I unleash my propaganda of hate with the greatest prospects of success? I had to find the right kind of victim, and especially one against whom the struggle would make sense, materially speaking. I can assure you that I examined every possible and thinkable solution to this problem, and, weighing every imaginable factor, I came to the conclusion that a campaign against the Jews would be as popular as it would be successful.

Adolf Hitler[1]

Germany's humiliating war defeat, and forced signing of the Treaty of Versailles, enrages Adolf Hitler. The treaty's harsh and punishing terms add even more fuel to the fire of his mounting anger. Postwar hyperinflation is devastating Germany's middle class, and they blame the German government. Hitler and his Nazis seize every opportunity to create political chaos, promoting their hate-driven agenda and becoming wildly popular with the masses of suffering people.

Attracting wide attention when he speaks to large, frequent rallies, Hitler has the look of a mad fanatic as he captivates the audience as if by hypnotic spell. The nature and sound of Hitler's speech seems to mesmerize the throngs, his vocal cords, damaged by a gas attack in the war, giving his voice its strange yet captivating quality.[2]

B ronislaw Huberman's deep intuition senses a dangerous stirring in the hearts of Germans as they hang on to Hitler's harsh words, offering him more and more political power over their lives.

"We are racing down the road toward another bloody world war," Bronislaw tells Ida. "I can feel it."

Chills run down his back when Huberman hears Hitler's promises to the German people, vowing that his first and foremost task, when he comes into real power, will be the total annihilation of the Jews.[3]

Hearing Hitler's pledges to the German people compels Bronislaw to involve himself personally in politics, to take a strong public stand for peace, and to try his best to stop this madman.

I n the winter of 1923, Adolf Hitler sits in a Munich jail, imprisoned for political crimes, and begins writing the first volume of his book, *Mein Kampf* (My Struggle). His friend and avid supporter Frau Winifred Wagner, daughter-in-law of the great German composer Richard Wagner, supplies the stationery Hitler writes on. In his book, Hitler carefully outlines his political ideology and his plans for Germany.[4]

CHAPTER 35

Sojourn in the States

All roads may not lead to Rome, but all roads do lead to a United States of Europe—the road of reason, the road of material prosperity, and the roads of ethics, of religion, of pacifism, of Christian love for our neighbor, and of the instinct of self-preservation.

Bronislaw Huberman[1]

During the mid-1920s, Bronislaw and Ida travel to the United States, his fourth extended sojourn there, and spend an entire winter. In light of his new political commitment, Bronislaw's time in the States proves unusually fertile.

"I have never seen such generous people as here in the United States," he tells Ida. "Universities, research institutions, museums, libraries, conservatories, symphony orchestras with grand concert halls—these are all a direct result of the public-spirited private citizens here."

"I have never seen so many people wearing silk stockings and fur collars, and riding around in their own personal automobiles," Ida says, her eyes wide.

"Yes, Ida, it's true. But it's not just the wealth and generosity of Americans. There is a strong standard of contented well-being among them. It is remarkable, and so unlike Europe. Just imagine how a United States of Europe, built on this same principle, would transform the conflicted and competing European societies, offer greater educational and cultural opportunities, and bring people together for the benefit and blessing of the entire nation.

"It's my dream, Ida. I plan to make use of my celebrity to take a strong stand for this cause."

"Broni, it's a noble dream. But, you have always believed in *l'art pour l'art*. Won't using your music for political purposes contradict that belief?"

Bronislaw looks into Ida's eyes in quiet puzzlement, saying nothing.

That afternoon, Bronislaw and Ida board a train with a deluxe sleeping car, traveling overnight to another state. With a schedule of upcoming concerts, Huberman practices the violin almost nonstop during the trip.

A black porter serves them tea, and takes a moment to listen to Bronislaw practice. When Bronislaw stops playing, the porter engages him in conversation.

"I own a Vic'rola myself," the porter says. "And I've collect'd a' least a hundred Vic'rola recordin's—Kreisler, Elman, ol' Heifetz, and eve' some of yors, too, Mr. Hubr-man. I cert'ly enjoy yor' playin'!"

"Thank you," Huberman says, tipping the friendly porter. "I appreciate your compliments, but I feel recorded music leaves much to be desired. How much more beautiful the violin and other instruments sound in person in a concert hall."

"I ain't disagreein' 'ith ya, sir. But I feels rit'ly for-tunat' ta be listenin' ta ya playin' right in m' own livin' room. It's a cert'n lux'ry my daddy didn' have."

Bronislaw and the black man continue the conversation, covering a wide range of subjects related to classical music. Bronislaw is amazed that a low-paid porter can speak so intelligently about the subject, revealing such knowledge of the musical world.

When the porter leaves, Huberman sits speechless for a moment, and then tells Ida: "In Europe, we would never meet a railway porter of low wages and status who could talk with me so appreciatively about the quality of my playing as reproduced on Victrola records!"

"You should give him a ticket to one of your concerts," Ida suggests.

"He probably can't afford the admission cost, and perhaps has never heard music in a concert hall."

Huberman smiles, encasing the Strad and leaving the room to search for the porter. When he finds him, he hands the man a ticket to one of his performances in the series scheduled in the city where the porter lives.

"Oh, t'ank ya, Mr. Hubr-man," the porter says. "But I ar'dy have season tick'its for ya' whole concert ser'res!"

"Ida," Brownislaw says when he returns, "the porter has already bought season tickets to the entire series!"

Ida laughs out loud. "I am so impressed with this country," she says.

Bronislaw nods and smiles. "It impresses me, too, Ida. I hope to see Europe follow this pattern. Do you think it will ever happen?"

"Perhaps, Broni, perhaps."

"Oh, Ida, I sense it is this same American spirit that produces this clearly discernible physical resilience in the American people. Nowhere else can you hear the grass of progress grow the way that you can here!"[2]

CHAPTER 36

The Movement

Universal prosperity, a general content, and a certain pride in belonging to a great, united nation, take the place of our irritating class-distinctions, of the mutual hatred between bourgeoisie and proletariat, and of our national animosities.

Bronislaw Huberman, speaking of the United States[1]

Over the next few years, Bronislaw Huberman becomes even more deeply involved in his struggle for a United States of Europe, working actively with the Pan-Europa movement's members, giving concerts and speeches, writing books and pamphlets, and traveling throughout the world to promote world peace. Through the miles and years, Ida travels by his side.

"I am convinced," he tells everyone who will listen, "that the abolition of frontiers is crucial to avoid further wars. America can serve as a model for us in Europe. Those who help us do not do so only altruistically . . . but they protect themselves and their dear ones from the destruction of property, from poverty, from collective murder, and from their own ruin."

But in spite of his hard work, years of labor, and hopes for the future, Huberman watches the rise of fascism in Europe deal a hard death blow to the Pan-Europa movement, thus destroying his dream.

Albert Einstein, Huberman's friend and colleague in the Pan-Europa movement, has also been deeply affected by the tragedy and bloodshed of the Great War. Like Huberman, he worries about current and future political turmoil.

"This war has deepened my beliefs about pacifism," he tells his wife, Elsa. "The killing of human beings is even more abhorrent to me now. I believe educated people in all countries should use their influence to bring about a peace treaty that will not carry the seeds of future wars," he says. "War must be abolished at all costs."

Einstein and Huberman are in complete agreement about the horror and tragedy of global conflict, and both are working hard to promote the idea of a peaceful and united Europe.[2]

Both men sense that another war is looming as they watch Germans suffer, the poor becoming poorer, the middle class dissolving, and the populace following the fanatical new leader, Hitler, for some hope.

While they agree on many issues, Huberman and Einstein disagree about Zionism.

"European Jews must assimilate even deeper into European society," Huberman argues.

"Bronislaw," the scientist says, "I feel strongly that there should be a developing Jewish colony in Palestine. I will be relieved when there is a tiny speck, a place on this earth where the members of our tribe are not considered aliens."

"Albert, we know that Jews have been returning to Palestine for almost a hundred years, trying to create a political, national, and spiritual resurrection there in the midst of a half-million Arabs," Huberman says. "So, yes, a small group now lives there, but I cannot imagine masses of the world's Jews moving to Palestine."[3]

"You are wrong, Bronislaw. This upswing of persecution against Jews will push more European Jews to take up the cause of Zionism, and they will go to Palestine," Einstein says. "But the dream of Zionism will have a hard path for a long time to come because of the local population. Already there is Arab resistance to Jewish immigration. Of course, you know the League of Nations has made Britain responsible for Palestine, but the British mandate is not able to properly protect the Jewish population. There are reports of more and more looting, violence, and murder by Arab residents who revolt against the numbers of Jewish immigrants moving to Palestine. It's going to be a long road. But it's vital that Israel one day emerge as a state for the Jews."

"I have been invited to perform in Palestine," Huberman says. "It will be my first trip there. I look forward to seeing the situation firsthand."

"I think you will be greatly impressed, Bronislaw, by the community that is growing there. You may even return to Europe with a changed perspective, perhaps as an ardent Zionist."

Bronislaw laughs. "Change my opinion about Zionism? I don't think so, Albert."

CHAPTER 37

Of Conductors and Crashes

The most important thing for a performing artist [is] to build up a community of love for the music with the audience, to create one fellow feeling among so many people who have come from so many different places and feelings. I have lived with that ideal all my life as a performer.

Wilhelm Furtwängler[1]

In Vienna, in 1927, Morris Grunschlag combs his son's hair, smiles, and pats the thirteen-year-old's back.

"David, Mr. Bronislaw Huberman is one of the most famous violinists in the world. Please, son, be on your best behavior. When I introduce you to him, shake his hand and bow with respect like I've taught you to do."

"Yes, Papa," David says, taking a deep breath, sticking out his chest, and standing up taller.

After introductions, handshakes, and bows, Morris Grunschlag thanks Huberman for taking the time to hear his son play.

"We are a music-loving family, Mr. Huberman. I have two daughters, Rosi and Toni, who play the piano. They, too, are quite accomplished."

"Yes, I understand," Bronislaw says.

"David has been studying with Adolf Bak. He believes my son is a child prodigy."

"Yes, I know about child prodigies," Huberman says. "David, please begin."

The boy places the violin under his chin and begins to play the instrument with the skill of someone much older.

"That was well done, David," Huberman tells him. "Will you please wait outside while I talk with your father?

"Mr. Grunschlag, your son is already an excellent violinist and I am impressed with his playing."

"Thank you, sir," Grunschlag says.

"If you will allow me to take over his musical education I would like to send him to the Hochschule für Musik in Berlin to study with Willie Hess and Arnold Schoenberg, and perhaps with Alban Berg and Franz Schreker."

"Most certainly, Mr. Huberman. They are great musicians and teachers. How wonderful if my son can study with them, and with you!"

"Then, we have an agreement, Mr. Grunschlag?"

"Yes," he says. "But may I ask, sir, the cost of living in Berlin, and studying with you and the masters?"

"You need not worry, Mr. Grunschlag. I will take care of every detail, including David's accommodations, living expenses, and tuition payments."

Grunschlag's mouth drops open. For a moment he is speechless. He grabs the violinist's hand, shaking it vigorously. "I don't know how to thank you, Mr. Huberman. This is my dream come true for David!"

Bronislaw keeps his promise to Mr. Grunschlag. After several years of study at the Hochschule für Musik in Berlin, Bronislaw takes David, now sixteen years old, to Vienna. In spite of his busy concert schedule, Huberman personally supervises the young man's musical education.[2]

In 1929, Wilhelm Furtwängler, the Berlin-born, world-famous conductor of the Berlin Philharmonic Orchestra, discusses with his Jewish secretary, Berta Geissmar, the upcoming 1930 Bayreuth Wagner Festival.

"I am glad Toscanini has agreed to conduct the 1930 Bayreuth opening season. He will give great prestige to the festival."

"Very good! Especially since we will be broadcasting on European radio stations for the first time," Berta says. "Hopefully in the next few years, Germany's politics will become more stable. But for now, I see Hitler and his brand of anti-Semitism becoming much stronger, and I worry about myself and our Jewish orchestra members."

"I try to stay out of politics, Berta, but I believe Hitler poses no real threat to our Jewish players," Furtwängler says. "This hissing street peddler will never get anywhere in Germany! He and his Nazis are a passing phase. Anyway, Hitler, as you know, is an enthusiastic supporter of music. Who knows, he may actually end up helping the orchestra."

"I think you might see Hitler in a different light, Wilhelm, if you were Jewish."

"Perhaps, Berta. But I am sure the German authorities will look the other way before they apply anti-Jewish racial laws to the orchestra. The German people will never allow our homeland's rich cultural and musical heritage to be threatened."

"I hope you are right, Wilhelm."

"We certainly cannot afford to lose our Jewish musicians, Berta. But I see no threat of that. To that point, I have decided to invite my Jewish friend Bronislaw Huberman to perform with the orchestra for the 1934 opening season."

That same year, Bronislaw Huberman walks up to the platform in a Vienna concert hall and, without introduction or pleasantries, begins his address to the large Jewish audience who has invited him to speak about the Pan-Europa movement.

"Somebody made an allusion to my professed political ideas on Pan-Europa, a United States of Europe," he begins.

He hears a slight stirring in the audience, but ignores it and continues.

"An ardent Jewish politician in Poland recently asked me: 'Mr. Huberman, where does the Jew come in regarding Pan-Europa?' I told him: 'In many respects, he would be one of the beneficiaries.' He asked me: 'Why a "beneficiary"'? 'Because one of the most dangerous elements of anti-Semitism is envy, jealousy,' I told him. 'When there is bread for both anti-Semite and Jew, the anti-Semites will lose much of their resentment against Jews, even in Germany.'"

An old Jewish man in the crowd stands and asks: "What about Zionism, Mr. Huberman. What part will it play in Pan-Europa?"

"A good question, sir," Huberman says. "I am of the opinion that there is nothing more European than the Jews. The whole structure of what we call our Western civilization is built on two main columns: the Greeks and the Jews. No matter how great the share of the other nations were in the upbuilding of European civilization, they had to build upon the basis laid down by those two peoples."

Huberman catches Ida's eye in the crowd. She is smiling, as if encouraging him.

"We got our sense of beauty, of philosophy from the Greeks," he continues, "and our conception of the one and only God from the Jews. Now the Greeks have vanished, but the Jews still exist, and they are going on with their mission within the Western European civilization."

Another man in the audience stands. "Yes, that is all true, but please, Mr. Huberman, answer the gentleman's question."

"As I said before, and as I hardly need say to anybody, Jew or Gentile, we got our monotheism from the Jews. It is only a step from the idea of the Almighty, the one and unique and ever-present God, to that other idea of the one humanity of brethren."

The audience again stirs, and Huberman hears some people whisper among themselves.

"Therefore," he continues, "it is not a mere chance, it is just, I daresay, a mathematical consequence that the nation which developed the conception of the one God has become a leader in social development, leading in the struggle for social justice among humanity. Where there is only one God, there can be only one humanity; where there is the conception of one humanity, in the long run, social injustice cannot be tolerated. The Jews have been mostly responsible for the transformation of the industrial and financial structure of Europe."

"You, then, Mr. Huberman, are not a proponent of Zionism, of Jewry establishing its own colony and state in Palestine?" another asks.

"Sir, I have asked myself, when the problem of Zionism presented itself to me, whether such a thing would hamper or help the fulfilling of this mission of the Jews in the world."

"And what is your answer, Mr. Huberman?" a woman asks.

"This mission can be fulfilled only if Jews are allowed to assimilate into the world's cultures while remaining loyal Jews—in Poland as Polish Jews, in Germany as German Jews, in America as American Jews, and so on."

"Some of us here are Zionists, Mr. Huberman," several people shout in unison.

"I have a great reserve toward Zionism," Huberman says. "Jews need to stay and assimilate even more deeply within European society."

"But we are unwanted in European culture, Mr. Huberman!" someone says.

Huberman responds: "I don't conceal the fact that, while I am a loyal Jew, whenever the moment of displaying this loyalty arises, I also feel very Polish, and at the same time, very European. I was always a European nationalist. This feeling was so strong, so imperative, that I could not help embarking actively in what is called the Pan-European movement, a political movement aiming at the formation of the United States of Europe."[3]

On October 30, 1929, the morning papers in Europe carry the news of the previous day's Black Tuesday stock-market crash in the United States.

"Stock prices have collapsed on Wall Street," Bronislaw tells Ida. "I wonder what this will mean for Germany and Europe?"

"I think we can expect global economic collapse," she says, frowning. "Could Germany be hurting financially any more than she already is?"

~·~

G ermany suffers from the 1929 Depression, with staggeringly high inflation and unemployment. Hitler takes full advantage of the crisis.

"All these misfortunes that have befallen Germany are because of the Jews!" Hitler shouts to the listening multitudes. "It was Jewish conspiracy that caused us to lose the war! The Treaty of Versailles, another Jewish conspiracy, was designed to bring Germany to her knees. The Jews tried to destroy the Fatherland with the hyperinflation of 1923."

The suffering German masses hang on to his every word.

"The Jew hates the white race," Hitler says, "and wants to lower its cultural level so that they can dominate . . . was there any form of filth or crime . . . without at least one Jew involved in it? If you cut . . . into such a sore, you will find, like a maggot in a rotting body, a JEW!"[4]

The Jews become the scapegoat of Hitler, who blames them for all Germany's problems. The German people, desperate for a new direction, begin to believe, blindly, in his anti-Semitic diatribes. For the first time since the war, the people sense a tiny sparkle of hope in Hitler.

Part 4

THE BEGINNING OF TRANSFORMATION

I was never so touched as I was by these audiences . . . people of every part of society came. Here were people with such a passion for music, and they were so idealistic about their culture.

Bronislaw Huberman,
1929, on his first trip to Palestine

CHAPTER 38

The Trip to Palestine

I am making a vow never to say another antagonistic word about Zionism. To do so now, after this rich experience, would be like Dolchstoss in den Rucken—*a knife in the back.*

Bronislaw Huberman, 1929, on his first trip to Palestine

In the summer of 1929, upset by disputes over religious issues and sacred sites, the Arabs of Palestine riot against the Jews in Safed, Hebron, Jerusalem, and Motza. Before the rioting ends, more than one hundred Jews are dead, many hundreds more injured. Similar incidents had taken place in 1920 and 1921.

The British administration respond as they have done before—with seeming indifference to the escalating violence and rising threats to Jewish settlers.[1]

Tensions between Palestinian Jews and Arabs continue to brew and erupt. Some people feel that Jews and Arabs cannot coexist. The British want to sharply curtail future Jewish immigration.[2]

In the spring before the riots, Bronislaw and Ida make their first visit to Palestine. Huberman has agreed to give four concerts in Tel Aviv and Jerusalem. They are delighted by Tel Aviv, and overwhelmed by the shimmering beauty of Jerusalem, fifty-six kilometers away.

"Ida," Bronislaw exclaims, "I feel an unexpected feeling of . . . of . . . *mysticism* here, as if it emanates from the soil. Do you feel it, too?"

"Yes, Broni, I do."

The concerts sell out immediately. Huberman receives a tremendous reception by the people in Palestine. He watches them crowd into concert halls, claim their seats, and wait enthusiastically for the music to begin.

Something within the violinist comes alive as he mingles with the people, hearing them express their excited hopes and dreams about establishing a state of their own.

"Even the people's ordinary everyday activities seem elevated to some higher spiritual place," Bronislaw tells Ida. "The people are truly glad to be building this country, each one seemingly conscious of the link between the historic past, a very complex present, and an unknown future. I must admit, Ida, I am surprised by it all!"

"I'm surprised by your reaction, Broni," Ida says. "Are you beginning to lean in the direction of Zionism? And, if so, does Zionism not conflict with your Pan-Europa beliefs?"

"Conflict? Not at all, Ida. Zionism and Pan-Europa are not in conflict. The Jews have given the world monotheism, and in my opinion, it's just a step away from the idea of one humanity of brethren."

Ida smiles.

"And, Ida, in answer to your first question, I am still an internationalist, more European than Jewish, and rather anti-Zionist."

After performing four sold-out concerts, Bronislaw marvels about the unusually high attendance and extremely appreciative, responsive audiences.

"How many people have attended my concerts here, Ida?" he asks when the tour ends.

"In all, more than eight thousand people," Ida tells him. "And many of these were not well-to-do people, but laborers with low incomes."

"That high attendance is astonishing, Ida, for a country of only two hundred and eighty thousand Jews! If these concerts were given in New York, and the same proportion of the Jewish population came, then every symphony concert would be attended by three hundred thousand people!"

"The Jewish people here certainly love music intensely, Broni, the workers as well as the most educated."

"Yes, Ida. They seem to *feel* the music deeply, not just as beautiful harmony and tone, but as something much deeper, something *spiritual*."

"So, you are feeling differently now about Palestine?" Ida says.

"Ida, I am so impressed by the monuments of idealism, of the creative energy of the people here, that I am making a vow never to say another antagonistic word about Zionism."

CHAPTER 39

The Rehearsal

The most important political force in Bavaria at the present time is the National Socialist German Workers Party. . . . Adolf Hitler . . . is the dominating force in the movement . . . his ability to influence a large audience is uncanny.

Truman Smith, an American spy based in Germany[1]

Until 1929, the Nazi Party was small, had little funds, and seemed destined for political obscurity. The Wall Street stock-market crash in October, however, seemed to help save the Nazis. America loaned Germany money that year, allowing some economic growth in the country. But after the stock-market crash, America called back the money they loaned, leaving Germany effectively bankrupt.

By 1930, with high unemployment, poverty, and nationwide starvation, the German people take new interest in Hitler's hopeful ideas. He appears to them a savior of sorts, and they take his propaganda promises to heart.[2]

The English-born Winifred Wagner, the young daughter-in-law of the late Richard Wagner, sits in the audience of musical directors and other guests, eager to see the great Arturo Toscanini prepare the orchestra and cast for the opening of the Bayreuth Festival's 1930 summer season.

Sitting beside her is Siegfried, her husband, thirty years her senior, and in poor health.[3]

Siegfried Wagner has been the director of the festival since his aged mother, Cosima, the widow of Richard Wagner, passed the job to him in 1906. Siegfried pays his performers far below the going rate, considering the prestige and privilege of an invitation to participate at Bayreuth a big enough incentive.

Wilhelm Furtwängler, the co–musical director of the Bayreuth Festival, welcomes Arturo Toscanini to the platform. Winifred senses that the audience is thrillingly aware that they are witness to an historic moment as they see, side by side, the two greatest conductors in the world.

Winifred watches Toscanini take his baton from its black case and give the downbeat. But soon after the musicians start to play, the Italian conductor abruptly stops the rehearsal.

"No! No! NO! This is not Wagner!" he shouts in Italian. "I must hear a clearer line!"

Frau Wagner's mouth drops open, astonished by Toscanini's sudden outburst and criticism of the orchestra's skills.

"He should be grateful to be here!" she whispers to Siegfried. "After all, he is a non-German, and we are allowing him to conduct on the hallowed soil of Bayreuth! How dare he criticize our musicians!"

Toscanini resumes the rehearsal, but, as before, he stops the musicians abruptly with an outburst of temper.

"No! No! No!" he screams, his face becoming red. "Not like that! Like this!" He taps his baton hard and impatiently on the podium to beat out the rhythm for the players.

"Siegfried," Winifred whispers, "look at the musicians' faces. They betray their feelings about this arrogant conductor."

She smiles: "He shouts 'no, no, no' so much, perhaps we should call him 'Toscan-*no-no*.'"

The third time Toscanini halts the orchestra, he appears unusually perturbed.

"I do not like the way the second violins play that passage," he shouts.

Winifred's eyes widen when the silver-haired conductor strikes the stand so forcefully with his baton that it breaks in half. Her hand flies to her mouth when he throws the baton's pieces over his shoulder and begins stomping his foot, visibly enraged at the musicians' seemingly inferior performance.

"What terrible and unacceptable behavior," Winifred whispers to her husband.[4]

Winifred Wagner is relieved when the long, painful rehearsal is completed, and Toscanini finally seems satisfied that the orchestra is ready to perform Wagner his way.

The attendees at the Bayreuth opera performances that summer are impressive, and include members of the Wagner family as well as the many devoted Wagnerites, who are fortunate enough to get the highly coveted, very expensive tickets.

Despite Winifred's horror at Toscanini's iron-willed demands of her orchestra, his performances of *Parsifal* and *Tannhäuser* receive spectacular reviews.

As the season ends, Winifred approaches Toscanini and says, "We look forward to your conducting the 1933 Bayreuth Festival."

The conductor bows slightly, cocking his head to one side, and politely takes his leave.

By September 1930, Bronislaw Huberman as well as other European Jews are alarmed when they hear that Germany's unemployment rate has risen to more than three million, and that many more Germans are starving and filing for bankruptcy.

Bronislaw isn't surprised when the parliamentary coalition that governs Germany falls apart, and new elections boost Adolf Hitler's National Socialist Party to Germany's second largest political party.

"Hitler's call for radical change, his seemingly sincere devotion to Germany, his appeal to enforce stricter morality laws and stamp out corruption in its cities, makes him look better and better to a hurting populace," Bronislaw tells Ida.[5]

"The people are certainly being deceived," Ida says.

CHAPTER 40

The Second Trip to Palestine

Surely, there is nothing more European than the Jews. But I am becoming less ambivalent about Zionism, as I come to better understand and appreciate the idea of reestablishing a Jewish nation here in Palestine.

Bronislaw Huberman, 1931

When the Jewish people in Palestine invite Bronislaw to return in 1931 to play four more concerts, he jumps at the opportunity. Tickets to his performances are immediately purchased by thousands of music enthusiasts.

While in Palestine, Bronislaw and Ida enjoy dinners in the homes of immigrant Jews, most of whom have already lived in Palestine for a generation. After the meal, they spend long evenings in conversation, discussing politics, anti-Semistism in Germany, the cohabitation of Jews and Arabs in Palestine, and the Jewish people's passion for music in the Holy Land.

In every home they visit, Bronislaw witnesses this deep love of music and the yearning for more of the cultural heritage that European artists have brought and shared with them.

"We miss the European culture of our youth and younger years," they tell him. "Here in Palestine, we are far from the center of that culture."

Over dinner in a Jewish home after a concert one evening, Bronislaw asks his host about the local orchestra he played with that evening.

"As you experienced yourself, Mr. Huberman, the orchestra we have here is not very good," the host tells him. "The musicians aren't properly trained. But it's what we have."

"The people here love music so much," Bronislaw tells him. "How wonderful it would be if you had a first-class orchestra of your own, made up entirely of Jewish musicians."

"Yes," the man says, his eyes lighting up. "Yes. That is exactly what we so desperately need. But can you imagine first-class musicians leaving their positions in European orchestras to come to Palestine and settle in this barren land? I can hardly imagine a scenario in which they would be willing to do this."

Long into the night, Bronislaw, Ida, and their host family talk about that possibility, and the joys and the prestige, a top-quality orchestra would bring to Palestine.

But by the end of the evening, Bronislaw agrees with his host about the obstacles to such a far-fetched dream. "Palestine is a world away from the culture of European art and music," Bronislaw admits. "And this country offers so little to European musicians and their families compared to what they now have. It does seem impossible that one could create a premier orchestra here."

In May 1931, in Italy's Bologna Municipal Theater, Arturo Toscanini stands on the podium, about to begin the sold-out opening night of the opera. In the audience sits a host of high-ranking Fascist officials, including Count Ciano, the undersecretary of the Ministry of the Interior, and father-in-law of Premier Mussolini's daughter.

Toscanini has agreed to perform the first Italian edition of *Tristan und Isolde*, gratis, in honor of his friend composer/conductor Giuseppe Martucci.

Ordered by Mussolini to play the Fascist anthem, "Giovinezza," Toscanini has refused. Turning to his audience that night, he announces pointedly that he will lead the orchestra in the traditional Italian anthem.

The next evening, as Toscanini approaches the opera house to conduct the second concert, he is met by a group of Fascist thugs who beat him black and blue and splitting his lip. Toscanini's driver intervenes, pushing him into the car and speeding away to a local hospital.

After being treated for his injuries, Toscanini immediately returns to the concert hall, where the conductor is again told to play the Fascist anthem. As Toscanini once again refuses and plays the traditional Italian anthem, the Fascist watchdogs in the grand tier boxes noisily stomp out of the hall.

To punish Toscanini, Mussolini confiscates his passport and visa and orders him kept under strict police surveillance.[1]

Toscanini writes Mussolini, complaining vociferously, but receives no response. The international press eagerly covers the story, the *Chicago Tribune* reporting:

"Toscanini's steadfast independence long has made him a thorn in the side of Fascism. His concepts are veritable rites of art, in which nothing incongruous is permissible. Consequently, he has steadfastly refused to play national or political anthems during his concerts."[2]

The international outcry on Toscanini's behalf forces Mussolini to back down, returning the conductor's passport and visa. Toscanini immediately leaves the country, vowing never again to conduct in Fascist Italy.[3]

CHAPTER 41

The Deal

A tireless, tenacious agitator with the gift of paralyzing opponents by a guileful combination of venom, slander and insinuation, [Joseph] Goebbels knew how to mobilize the fears of the unemployed masses as the Great Depression hit Germany, playing on the national psyche with "ice-cold calculation."

Nazi Party member[1]

By 1927, Nazi Party leader Joseph Goebbels had become the most feared demagogue in Berlin. Often referred to as the "Marat of Red Berlin," Goebbels spread terror throughout Germany, so impressing the powers that be in the party that in 1929, they appointed him Reich propaganda leader of the National Socialist German Workers' Party (NSDAP). Goebbels and Hitler developed a close bond when Goebbels helped him in the election campaign of 1932.[2]

Berlin-born Wilhelm Furtwängler, who became director of the Berlin Philharmonic Orchestra in 1922, has made the Philharmonic one of the most prestigious orchestras in the world.

Since twelve years of age, Furtwängler has loved Beethoven, memorizing most of the master's works and playing them on the family piano. He wanted to be a conductor as early as he could remember. By the age of ten, he had already written six piano sonatas, trios, and quartets. Performing and conducting helped support his family after his father's death. Working hard over a lifetime to achieve his musical dreams, he has become one of the most celebrated conductors in the world.

In 1930, Furtwängler took on added responsibilities and garnered more prestige when he became the music director of the Bayreuth Festival. He has reached the peak of his extraordinary career.

He glows with pride when he thinks about the annual festival, the spectacular event established by Richard Wagner, and known to all of Europe as the "crown of German culture."[3]

Opposed to the Weimar Republic, Furtwängler is at first drawn to the Nazis' power and promises. The Berlin Philharmonic was hurting financially, and he hoped the Nazis' oft-expressed dedication to the nation's arts would translate into their support.

"My greatest desire is beautiful music," he claims. "I have no interest in politics, and politics have no place in art."

But when he learns that the Nazis have made no financial commitment to supporting the Berlin Philharmonic and that they intend to rid Germany of all its Jewish musicians, he is shocked.

Furtwängler has a number of Jewish musicians in the orchestra, and is friendly with many of them. Deeply concerned about his orchestra, he arranges a meeting with the Reich minister of propaganda, Joseph Goebbels.

Furtwängler tries to explain how art must bring artists together, not separate them.

"I only recognize one line of separation: between good and bad art," he tells Goebbels. "At present, the division is drawn between Jew and non-Jew, while the separation between good and bad music is neglected."

He asks Goebbels to allow his Jewish musicians to keep their positions in the orchestra. In defense of this request, he reminds him that the German violinist and teacher Joseph Joachim, as well as the great German composer Felix Mendelssohn, were both Jews, and, like many Jews, had been an important part of Germany's musical history.

"I believe," Furtwängler says, "that ridding the Fatherland of its superb Jewish musicians would not be in the best interests of Germany's cultural life, because artists anywhere are much too rare for any country to be able to dispense with their work without loss to culture. The quality of our music and orchestra depends on all our musicians, including our Jewish members. We cannot afford to lose any of them."[4]

Furtwängler then lets Goebbels know he has been offered important conducting posts in other countries, but he prefers staying in Berlin, in order to preserve the highest qualities of German musical art.

"I am trying to decide whether or not to stay in Germany," Furtwängler says. He does not want to leave his post or his beloved fatherland.

But, if he is to make this decision, he wants Goebbels's promise not to fire his Jewish musicians, and to promise the financial support required for the orchestra to continue at the highest level.

I am glad you are still here in Germany," Goebbels says. "Germany's other renowned conductors—Bruno Walter, Otto Klemperer, and Erich Kleiber—have all turned cowardly and have left. You have no competition here in Germany now."

He smiles thinly: "You will always be our *Das Wunder Furtwängler*, the Miracle Furtwängler!"

Goebbels stands up, walks to the corner of his office, and pours himself a drink. He stares for a long time at the conductor sitting uncomfortably in his office. After taking several sips of his drink, he says finally: "If you stay with us, Maestro Furtwängler, conducting the Berlin Philharmonic, I will personally guarantee you financial support for the orchestra."

"That will certainly help us," Furtwängler says.

"I can make you that promise," Goebbels states.

"But," Furtwängler tells him, "I must also receive your promise to keep my Jewish musicians. They are an essential part of the Philharmonic. We need them to bring the high quality of music and *good* art to the Fatherland."

"Maestro, it is true that art must be good," Goebbels responds. "But beyond that, it must also be responsible, professional, popular, and aggressive."[5]

Goebbels finishes his drink, placing the empty glass down hard on the table.

"I just believe that fighting against real artists is not in the interest of the cultural life in Germany," Furtwängler says.

Goebbels responds quickly: "In the center of our musical life must be the cultivation of *good* German music."

"Yes, I agree," the conductor says. "But just because a musician is German does not mean he produces *great* German music."

Goebbels pauses for a long moment and glares into Furtwängler's eyes. "If there are bad Germanic artists," he shouts, purposely emphasizing each word, "it is only because they are already infected with Jewish blood!"

Furtwängler furrows his brows as if trying to understand what Goebbels is saying. "Sir, I simply *must* be allowed to keep my Jewish musicians."

"Maestro," Goebbels says, "every *true* artist must perform in Germany without consideration of his race."

"Yes," Furtwängler says, and nods. "Then you will protect my Jewish musicians?"

"Yes!" Goebbels shouts, his eyes rolling to the ceiling. "I will show leniency toward *certain* key Jewish players in the orchestra, in return for your commitment to stay in Germany as the Philharmonic's conductor."

Still standing, Goebbels meets the conductor's eyes. "Is this satisfactory, Furtwängler? Will you now agree to stay?"

"I will give it my deepest thought and consideration," he answers.

Goebbels frowns. "Herr Furtwängler," he says firmly, "there will be consequences if you decide to leave."

"Consequences, Herr Goebbels?"

"If you desert us, we will forever bar your return to the Fatherland."

"Yes, I would expect that," Furtwängler responds. He takes a deep breath and looks Goebbels directly in the eye: "But that does not affect my decision, sir."

"Well, Herr Furtwängler, perhaps this will. I would regret if anything might happen to your personal secretary, Berta Geissmar. She is Jewish, yes? And, Herr Furtwängler, I know your dear *mutter* lives in Germany. Even though she is not Jewish, I would hate for your mother to be imprisoned."[6]

Wilhelm Furtwängler freezes, his head lowered, staring hard at the floor.

"You would do that?" he whispers slowly.

"Yes! I would, and I will!" Goebbels shouts back at him suddenly, his blistering words hanging in the air.

The two men are silent for a long moment.

"And if I commit to stay in Germany and continue conducting the orchestra," Furtwängler finally asks, "you will vow to keep my mother and secretary safe and unharmed?"

Goebbels looks at him opaquely. "Of course I will."

"And will you honor these commitments you've made regarding the orchestra's Jewish musicians? None of them will be fired."

"I will. And, Maestro Furtwängler," he adds, "I hope you will not only stay and conduct for us, but will also join and support the Nazi Party."

Furtwängler's face goes blank, and for a long time he doesn't speak.

"If you cannot do this," Goebbels tells him, "then we will make you a *Staatsrat*—a state councilor, for life."

"By doing so, Herr Goebbels, you know you are effectively silencing me outside of Germany," Furtwängler says, his face turning red with anger.

"I should think the consequences of refusing to stay and support the party would have greater and more disturbing consequences for you," Goebbels says, closing the meeting and dismissing the maestro.

"Such a coward!" Goebbels says out loud as Furtwängler leaves his office. Goebbels calls an aide.

"Generate news stories and press releases that tell the public the famous Wilhelm Furtwängler is staying in Germany," Goebbels orders his aide. "And add that Furtwängler is eagerly remaining at his post and aggressively supporting the Nazi Party."

Wilhelm Furtwängler leaves Goebbels's office in a daze. He overheard Goebbels's insult as he left the office. *Coward. Coward. Coward.*

For hours, he wanders the almost empty streets, thinking about his conversation with Goebbels and feeling trapped in Berlin.

A dull rain blows through the woods of the Tiergarten across from the Berlin Philharmonic Hall. He pulls his collar closer to his neck, wiping water from his face and drawing close to the stage door to escape the rain. A night guard recognizes him, opens the door, and lets him inside.

Wandering the dark, eerie halls of his theater, he feels alone, sad. He hears no sounds in the building, except his own footsteps. Inside the theater, he finds a seat in a remote corner. As he becomes aware of the pregnant silence, he closes his eyes, envisions the faces of those who have begged him to take a stand against Hitler, to protest the new party and their anti-Semitic actions, and to leave Germany. But he has waited too long to make the decision, and now it's too late.

"*Das Wunder Furtwängler*, they call me," he says aloud. "But today I have earned a new title: *traitor*. I will stay in Germany. I don't have the courage to fight against such a powerful enemy. But I swear, I will never pledge my allegiance to Goebbels, or to the Nazi Party! Never!"

For several hours, he remains in his seat, contemplating the severe consequences of his decision to stay in Germany. He vows never to admit to a living soul his most private thoughts that night as he sits alone in the dark theater.

"I should have already left Germany," he whispers. "And I should have taken my mother and Berta with me. But I have made a deal with the Devil. Goebbels is right, I *am* a coward."

CHAPTER 42

The Madman Comes to Power

Once the hatred and the battle against the Jews has been really stirred up, their resistance will necessarily crumble in the shortest possible time. They are totally defenseless, and no one will stand up to protect them.

Adolf Hitler[1]

The events of 1933 bring nightmares to the Jews living in Germany. On January 30, Adolf Hitler is named chancellor of Germany by President Paul von Hindenburg, who naively believes he can control and limit Hitler's power and brutality.[2]

The new chancellor steps arrogantly to the podium on January 31, standing straight and tall, promising the German people a powerful, unified one-party state devoid of disruptive politics.

"More than fourteen years have passed since that unhappy day when the German people, blinded by promises made by those at home and abroad, forgot the highest values of our past, of the Reich, of its honor and its freedom, and thereby lost everything. Since those days of treason, the Almighty has withdrawn his blessing from our nation. Discord and hatred have moved in. . . ." he shouts to a large, cheering audience.

In his inaugural speech, he tells of Germany's heartbreaking disunity and her loss of freedom. He pledges to the people: "The National Government will therefore regard it, as its first and supreme task, to restore to the German people unity of mind and will. It will preserve and defend the foundations on which the strength of our nation rests. It will take under its firm protection Christianity as the basis of our morality, and the family as the nucleus of our nation and our state. Standing above estates and classes, it will bring back to our people the consciousness of its racial and political unity, and the obligations arising therefrom."[3]

Hitler appoints Joseph Goebbels as Reich minister for public enlightenment and propaganda, giving him total control of the media—radio, press, publishing, cinema, and the other arts.[4]

In the spring, Hitler demonstrates his absolute power and savage cruelty. With the simple signing of his name, Hitler's bills become law in Germany within twenty-four hours.[5]

Hitler also opens the first concentration camp in Dachau to house political prisoners, as well as those people he considers *unfit* to live in the new Fatherland.[6]

With Goebbels's help, the new chancellor suspends the freedoms of the press, speech, and assembly. Anyone opposing Hitler's laws is confronted by his special security forces—the Gestapo, the storm troopers (SA), and the Schutzstaffel (SS)—facing arrest and/or execution. By summer, all non-Nazi parties, organizations, and labor unions no longer exist. Goebbels and the Nazi Party fire almost all the Jewish musicians in Germany's orchestras, leaving only a handful of them in the Berlin Philharmonic.

Hitler and his Nazis promote their ideology of the pure Aryan race—the German master race—and put into practice laws that harshly and unfairly affect Jews, Roma (Gypsies), and the disabled. Hitler knows that Jews in Germany number only 525,000—less than one percent of her population, but he convinces the German people that the Jews are to blame for Germany's severe economic depression and humiliating defeat in the world war.[7]

Hitler calls for a boycott of all Jewish shops and businesses, outlawing books and music written by Jews and others unapproved by the state. That year, more than thirty-seven thousand Jews emigrate from Germany to other parts of the world.[8]

In March 1933, Arturo Toscanini is outraged by the increasing anti-Semitism and Jewish persecution in Germany. He makes a decision, one he knows will have serious political and public consequences. He contacts Wilhelm Furtwängler and abruptly cancels his contract to conduct the 1933 Bayreuth Festival.

"I am an avowed anti-Fascist," Toscanini tells Furtwängler. "And I must refuse to conduct in Germany following the Nazi Party's assumption of power!"

He announces his decision publicly so that newspapers around the world will report his protest of Nazi policies in Germany.

With the unexpected news of Toscanini's cancellation—just a few months before the festival, Furtwängler drops his head into his hands, sick to his stomach, shocked that the Italian conductor has refused to honor this most prestigious of all performance engagements in Europe.

Furtwängler paces the floor nervously, wondering how he will replace Toscanini at such short notice. He dreads having to approach Winifred Wagner with the terrible news.

He takes a deep breath, trying not to panic, and visits Winifred that afternoon, telling her of Toscanini's decision and hoping she has the influence to make him change his mind.

"How dare he!" she shouts, throwing her arms in the air. "He refuses to conduct, and cancels at this late date? Right before rehearsals begin?"

"This is not acceptable!" she cries. "He dares to cancel on the fiftieth anniversary of the Bayreuth Festival, the series that commemorates my father-in-law's death? His cancellation demeans Richard's memory and work! This . . . this arrogant Italian should be honored to be invited to conduct at Bayreuth!"

"Perhaps, Frau Wagner, you can talk to him, and persuade him to change his mind. Otherwise, I will need to find another conductor to replace him."

"There is no conductor alive who can fill his shoes and replace him, Herr Furtwängler!"

Wilhelm Furtwängler looks at the floor, trying not to appear angry or embarrassed by the naked affront to him, a truly great maestro by anyone's standard.

"Will you talk with him?" he asks.

"I will do better than speak to him myself!" Wagner says. "I will ask *Unser Seliger Adolf*—our blessed Adolf—to convince Toscanini to come."

CHAPTER 43

The Primacy of Richard Wagner

Wagner remains the only composer imaginable who could have simultaneously supplied the Führer with an incandescent aesthetic experience, an anti-Semitic virulence, and a Weltanschauung *that so perfectly meshed, matched, and stimulated his own. Wagner's extra-musical credo attracted Hitler as much as his music.*

From *Music in Exile: Émigré Composers of the 1930s*[1]

On April 3, 1933, during a visit from the hysterical Frau Wagner, Adolf Hitler tells his secretary to write a letter to Arturo Toscanini.

"Address the letter to the 'Honored Maestro,'" Hitler says. "Tell him I am a friend of the house of Wahnfried,[2] and have always had the satisfaction of seeing a high artistic mission in the Bayreuth Festivals. Explain to him how much joy it will bring me to be able to thank him *personally* for his cooperation and participation in Wagner's work—something like that. Sign it 'with sincere respect' and 'sincerely yours.'"

After his secretary leaves, Hitler puts his arm tenderly around Frau Wagner's shoulders. "Winnie," he says, "at the age of twelve, I saw the first opera of my life, *Lohengrin*. In one instant, I was addicted. My youthful enthusiasm for the Bayreuth master, Wagner, knows no bounds."[3]

"Thank you, my Führer," she says, smiling, her eyes looking intimately into his. "I knew you could change his mind."

"Yes, my letter to Toscanini will take care of our little problem," he says, and pats her back tenderly. "Now, my dear Winnie, don't worry anymore about it. After Toscanini reads my letter, he will agree to come and conduct at Bayreuth. I personally guarantee it."

A t the end of May, after nearly two irritating months of waiting to hear from Toscanini, Hitler finally receives a reply to his letter of April 3. The Führer again meets with Frau Wagner.

"I have just received the maestro's answer," he says, his face red with fury and indignation. "He waits almost two months to tell me that he *still* refuses to come to Bayreuth!"

"Why?" Frau Wagner cries.

"He says it is for the 'sake of his tranquility and mine'!" Hitler spits, tearing up the letter and tossing it to the floor.[4]

Frau Wagner sits stunned, quietly murmuring and wiping her eyes with a lace handkerchief. The Führer takes her hand in his, stroking it gently.

"I am sorry, Winnie," he says, "but as you can see, Toscanini refuses to come, even after receiving *my* personal letter. I suggest we engage another conductor . . . perhaps Richard Strauss, to conduct *Parsifal*—not only this year, but next year also."

Mrs. Wagner looks to the ceiling and sighs. "To my knowledge, my Führer, Strauss has conducted *Parsifal* only four times in his whole career, and he hasn't conducted anything at Bayreuth since 1894. I don't think he is a good choice. But I will contact him if you wish."[5]

T o punish Toscanini for his abrupt withdrawal from Bayreuth on the fiftieth anniversary of Wagner's death, Hitler takes immediate revenge.

"Start a smear campaign against Toscanini," he orders Joseph Goebbels. "Call him a . . . a 'Friend of Vicious World Jewry.' Tell our storm troopers to ransack Germany's record shops, and to seize and destroy all of Toscanini's recordings."[6]

In April of 1933, just three months after Hitler's coming to power, the sixty-nine-year-old Richard Strauss was the most famous composer in Germany and a favorite of Hitler's. Just months earlier, propaganda minister Joseph Goebbels had named Strauss president of the Reichsmusikkammer, the State Music Bureau. He later claimed he did not realize his job was not only to promote good German music but was, in reality, to utterly Aryanize it by blacklisting Jewish composers.

Like conductor Wilhelm Furtwängler, whose relationship with the Nazis became a quagmire, Strauss would later claim to be unpolitical—just an artist dedicated to maintaining the quality of German music and in writing his own works. He was at times known to be anti-Semitic and wrote at least one letter in support of Hitler's policies. But he also had many Jewish friends and collaborated with Jewish writers. When the name of Stefan Zweig, his Jewish libretist, was left off the program of their opera *The Silent Woman*, he insisted that it be included or he would stop the production. Throughout the Nazi reign he walked a delicate line, trying to both maintain his favor with Goebbels and Hitler while protecting his legacy and his ability to operate as an independent artist. Ultimately, Richard Strauss was not viewed as a collaborator, but rather as an egotistical opportunist whose first priority was always himself.

So, in April of 1933, just months after Hitler came to power, he was exceedingly pleased to receive Frau Wagner's most prestigious invitation to conduct the Bayreuth festival that summer.

Strauss began reading Wagner's opera scores when he was a teenager and had placed him high in his personal pantheon. Strauss considered him a god, and his theater at Bayreuth, holy ground. He once commented publicly that Richard Wagner was "the only composer besides Mozart who could be taken seriously."[7]

Hitler attends the 1933 Bayreuth opening reception at Wagner's villa, Wahnfried. With his wife, soprano, Pauline de Ahna, on his arm, Strauss approaches Hitler. The Führer makes a showy display of welcome, even adulation, to the famous soprano. Strauss thanks Hitler for his appointment as president of the State Music Bureau and suggests that the new government subsidize Bayreuth by levying a one percent royalty on every Wagner performance in Germany. Hitler refuses.

"We have no legal precedent to do so," he tells Strauss.[8]

When Ida hears the news that Arturo Toscanini has broken his contract to conduct the Bayreuth season, she runs to tell Bronislaw.

"Yes, I already know. Good for him!" he says. "It doesn't surprise me. Arturo is steadfastly against fascism."

"Yes! And his refusal is a slap in Hitler's face!" Ida says.

"I admire Arturo for doing this, Ida. I would do the same thing."

"I doubt you'll ever be given the opportunity, Broni."

"I know," he replies, laughing. "I can't imagine Furtwängler inviting me, a Polish Jew, to perform with the Berlin orchestra!"

"I read that Richard Strauss is taking Toscanini's place," Ida says.

"Nobody on this planet can fill Arturo's shoes!" he replies.

CHAPTER 44

Creation of the Kulturbund Deutscher Juden

The Kulturbund *and its theatre would "cultivate the artistic and scholarly interests of the Jewish population and provide work for unemployed artists and scholars." Theatre performances, concerts, lectures, and exhibitions would be "attended fundamentally by Jews."... The* Kulturbund *thus became the locus for Jewish-born actors, musicians, scenic artists, stage technicians, lecturers, and theatre-goers to congregate.*

Rebecca Rovit[1]

At the Bayreuth Concert Hall in the summer of 1933, Richard Strauss displays his finest skills as he conducts *Parsifal*. When, from the stage, he looks at the audience, he sees Adolf Hitler and Joseph Goebbels, as well as every influential leader in Germany. At the opera's end, he bows toward them, feeling highly satisfied with his performance.

He feels quite proud of himself until the next morning, when he reads a newspaper's review of *Parsifal* that criticizes Strauss for hurrying the opera, completing it in four hours and eight minutes, and comparing it unfavorably to Toscanini's four-hour-forty-eight-minute version at Bayreuth in 1930.

"I'm not surprised reporters compare me to Toscanini," he tells his wife, Pauline. "But it hurts just the same."

"I know, Richard," Pauline says. "And I'm sorry."

Later, he reads a newspaper review that makes him feel even worse, calling his performance of *Parsifal* second rate and unworthy of the orchestra.

He crumples the newspapers, tossing them into the trash.

"I may not be the 'great' Arturo Toscanini," he tells Pauline, "but my performance was certainly *not* 'second rate'!"

"Your performance was first rate, Richard!" Pauline tells him. "They have invited you to perform at Bayreuth next year, too," she reminds him. "Are you still planning to do this for them?"

"Why, of course, Pauline!" he snaps. "I would never turn down an invitation to Bayreuth!"[2]

In Berlin, by 1933, more than eight thousand Jewish musicians, actors, and other artists have either left on their own or have been fired from their positions with German orchestras, opera companies, and theater groups. Almost all the Jewish musicians have lost their positions in the Berlin Philharmonic in spite of Wilhelm Furtwängler's pleas to Goebbels to protect and keep them.

With all the unemployed Jewish artists in Germany, Kurt Baumann, a young Jewish production assistant in Berlin, comes up with a unique, job-saving idea.

"Since we no longer hold positions in Germany's public sphere, let us create a new artistic organization, one just for Jewish artists—the Kulturbund Deutscher Juden, the Culture League of German Jews," he proposes.[3]

"Are we allowed to do this?" someone asks. "How will it work, and will the Nazi government permit this new organization?"

"My idea to found a Jewish cultural circle is based on very simple numbers. At the present time, five hundred and forty thousand Jews live in Germany—a hundred and seventy-five thousand live in Berlin alone; many other big cities have, percentage-wise, similar numbers," Baumann explains. "I figure that a city of a hundred and seventy-five thousand inhabitants can have their own theater, opera, symphony orchestra, museum, lectures, and even a *Hochschule*, an institute of higher education, and this with the population of a midsized city.[4]

"I fear the Zionists will not support the organization," someone says. "If they do, they will want all the activities in Yiddish or Hebrew."

"And I think the majority of German Jews will not respond to an all-Jewish cultural circle," another says. "They will say, 'We are not going voluntarily into the *ghetto*!'"

"I will work on a proposal, and contact Dr. Kurt Singer. I worked with him for two years when he was director of the Städtischen Oper, the Berlin State Opera. Dr. Singer is Jewish, and has the clout and abilities to make this happen."

Kurt Singer has also been dismissed from his many roles in Germany's musical life. A medical doctor as well as an accomplished musician, the flamboyant Dr. Singer served as an army doctor during the Great War. Germany awarded him an Iron Cross for his extraordinary service. Singer meets with Kurt Baumann and likes his idea of the Kulturbund Deutscher Juden.

"I, too, have envisioned a similar organization," he tells Baumann.

"We believe you are the perfect choice to champion the Kulturbund."

"I accept the challenge!" Singer says as the two men shake hands.

Hans Hinkel, the dark-haired, sharp-nosed, Nazi-appointed head of the Preußischen Theaterausschuß, the Prussian Theater Commission, agrees to meet with Kurt Singer. Hinkle, an SS officer, listens silently to Singer's idea.

Hinkel immediately understands the benefits for the party in allowing the creation of the Kulturbund. It will help show the world that Germany's Jews are not being mistreated and it will cut down on social unrest. Hinkel also foresees that this organization could facilitate the end of the Jews' involvement in Aryan German culture.

"Yes, I see several good reasons for us to support the Kulturbund," Hinkel says, his expression serious and unfriendly.

"Then we can negotiate the operating terms for the creation of the Kulturbund?" Singer asks.

Hinkel, an SS officer who has no intention of negotiating anything with a Jew, says, "Yes, but there are several stipulations. The Kulturbund can only be staffed and financed by Jews."

Hinkel believes this will further isolate Jewish activities from the German population, allowing the German government to fund only the accepted Aryan musical institutions, and it will give them the means, by issuing membership cards, to keep track of the Jews who join the Kulturbund.

"I think we can agree on that," Singer says. "It will be by Jews for Jews."

"Another stipulation," Hinkel says. "Only the Jewish press is allowed to report on Kulturbund events. Not the German press. And the organization must submit all programs to me for my personal approval before the performances."

In this way, Hinkel knows he can control their repertoire, determining if it is appropriate for a Jewish organization and will promote Jewish culture.

"Two more stipulations," SS officer Hans Hinkel adds. "Jewish members can attend only two cultural events per month. And each member must present an identification badge proving Jewish descent before being allowed into the hall."

"I see no problem with these stipulations," Singer says. "We will very much appreciate the government's approval and support."

After Singer leaves his office, Hinkel takes a deep breath and smiles. "Hitler will be glad I am doing my job well and removing the Jews from Germany's cultural undertakings," he says aloud. "The Kulturbund will help us do that."

In May 1933, Hermann Göring, Hitler's new prime minister, agrees to meet with Hans Hinkel and Kurt Singer to talk about the creation of the new Kulturbund.

"We give our approval of the Kulturbund," Göring tells Singer. He then issues a severe warning: "If all of you Jews do everything right . . . then everything will go well. If all of you Jews behave badly, then there'll be trouble, you know that."

"Yes," Singer says. "We understand."

During the Kulturbund's creation, Göring closely watches Kurt Singer, making sure he meets all the government's stipulations, keeps the group's repertoire "Jewish," and includes and involves only the homogeneous Jewish community.

For the next several years, Göring, Hinkel, and the party allow the Kulturbund to exist, and even flourish, among the Jews in Germany. It grows from 12,500 members in October 1933 to more than 20,000 by winter.[5]

In January 1933, Albert Einstein and his wife, Elsa, travel for the third time to America. When they arrive in Pasadena, California, they receive an unexpected and frightening wave of angry, violent protests, criticizing Einstein's past actions promoting pacifism.

By mid-March, the Einsteins decide to return to Europe. On the way home, aboard the ship *Belgenland,* they hear through regular telegrams of alarming new and increased anti-Semitic brutality in Germany.

"I just learned that death threats are awaiting me," he tells Elsa. "The Nazis have confiscated our house and frozen our bank account."

Tears form in Elsa's eyes. "I think we must avoid Germany, Albert. Our lives may depend on it."

"I agree, Elsa. We will make our home elsewhere. Perhaps Belgium or England."

The Einsteins decide not to go back to Germany. Albert cables his resignation to the Berlin Academy, where he has taught since 1914. He vows never again to step on German ground.

Soon Einstein and Elsa decide to make their new home in the United States. He accepts a post in Princeton, New Jersey, at the Institute for Advanced Study, a research center for theoretical research and intellectual inquiry.[6]

From Princeton, Einstein continues to promote his long-held philosophy of pacifism, and his interest in Zionism continues unabated as he watches Palestine's Jewish immigrant population steadily grow.[7]

CHAPTER 45

Hitler's Propaganda Minister

Dr. Goebbels was gifted with the two things without which the situation in Berlin could not have been mastered: verbal facility and intellect. . . . For Dr. Goebbels, who had not found much in the way of a political organization when he started, had won Berlin in the truest sense of the word.

Adolf Hitler[1]

One early morning in 1933, Joseph Goebbels sits on the edge of his bed cursing his weak, misshapen foot, a result of childhood polio. Born into a strict Catholic working-class family, the black-haired, puny-framed man still feels bitter that his deformed foot kept him from serving his fatherland in the Great War. He knows he has never measured up to the expectations of his family or his country. As a journalist in Germany, he tried his hand at writing, yearning to become a published author. But publishers rejected all of his books.

To compensate for his physical and intellectual failures, his self-hatred and inferiority complex, he was drawn to the excesses, anti-Semitism, and rigidity of the Nazi Party. It fueled his deep-rooted psychological issues, and Goebbels became a near-perfect Nazi officer. Since becoming Hitler's Reich minister for public enlightenment and propaganda, he alone has total control of Germany's communications—media, radio, press, publishing, cinema, and all the arts.

Goebbels has spent a long night pondering new ways to make Germany's Jews suffer, and to promote the Führer myth, portraying Hitler as a deity figure, a messiah-redeemer, the ultimate savior of the Fatherland. It is his job. He rises from bed and dresses.

Goebbels dreams about molding Germany's youth, including his stepson and baby daughter, to one day hold positions that will empower them to continue building the German Reich, promising its endurance for millennia to come. Goebbels knows the Führer wants strong, educated future leadership, and the weaknesses of all Germany's children hammered away.

When Hitler's youth grow up, the whole world will tremble!

Goebbels thinks back to his wedding several years before. He had married the divorced Magda Quandt, who had a young son, Harald, from her failed first marriage. At the wedding, Harald, clad in his new Hitler Youth uniform, stood beside Goebbels's best man, Adolf Hitler. As the newlyweds walked down the aisle, the guests celebrated their marriage with the *Hitlergruß*, the Nazi salute.

Goebbels's daughter, Helga, a lovely baby with sparkling blue eyes, has become a favorite of Hitler's. The Führer often holds her on his lap during late-night meetings with her father.

Goebbels glances at the black band on the left arm of his uniform, runs his fingers slowly across the swastika emblazoned on it, and remembers Hitler's words to him about Germany's children.

"I want a brutal, domineering, fearless, cruel youth," the Führer told him. "Youth must be all that. It must bear pain. There must be nothing weak and gentle about it. The free, splendid beast of prey must once again flash from its eyes. That is how I will eradicate thousands of years of human domestication. That is how I will create the New Order."[2]

"Germany has been transformed into a great house of the Lord," Goebbels says aloud. "The Führer as our mediator stands before the throne of God. Surely, with my help, Hitler will one day rule the world!"[3]

Goebbels considers his new importance and whispers to himself, "I will help the Führer accomplish this, and one day we will deport all the 'undesirables' from Germany, exterminating them, and ridding the Fatherland of its 'parasites' once and for all!

"And we, the Nazis, shall go down in history as the greatest statesmen of all times."

He takes a deep breath and frowns, envisioning the tender innocent faces of Harald and Helga, and wonders what might happen to them if, by some unforeseen chance, Germany's Nazi Party fails.

How will my children think of us then? Will they see us as the greatest statesmen? Or as the greatest criminals?[4]

CHAPTER 46

The Invitation

In the last few years, [Bronislaw Huberman] has exchanged his bow for the pen of the political agitator, and has not alone endeavored at all costs to place himself among front line fighters for the Pan-European idea, but, besides being an active propagandist for the aims and interests of international Jewry, [he] openly attacked German artists and artistic life, and regarded himself as the mouthpiece of those large groups and cliques which despise the words "nation," "nationalism," "folk," "loyalty."

Pro-Nazi newspaper in Vienna, *Wiener Neueste Nachrichten*[1]

Even though Goebbels has fired most of the Jewish musicians throughout Germany, Furtwängler still believes the propaganda minister's promise to show leniency toward his orchestra's *key* Jewish players, and guest Jewish soloists. Furtwängler invites Bronislaw Huberman—as a *special-skills* Jew, to be the soloist for the Berlin Philharmonic's 1934 opening season. He posts the letter to Huberman and waits, expecting an immediate and positive response.

In his summer home in Italy, on July 10, 1933, Bronislaw practices his violin while Ida sits at her desk busily writing letters for him to sign. When the day's mail is delivered, Ida interrupts his practice to give him Wilhelm Furtwängler's letter.

Huberman reads it slowly, his face gradually flushing red with anger.

"I can't believe that Furtwängler is defending himself, declaring that he is standing up for German culture by conducting this music, and hopes I will support this idea!" he fumes.

"Furtwängler expects *me* to play with the Philharmonic?" he continues. "Me, a Jew—when both the German Nazis and the German *non*-Nazis are doing such terrible things to the Jews and to Jewish musicians!"

He stands still for a long time, gripping the letter in his fist and staring icily across the room.

"We certainly will not lend our art and fame to these kinds of policies!"

"Broni," Ida asks, "shall I write him, telling him you decline his invitation? Like Toscanini did?"

"Of course!" he shouts. "Tell him *no!*"

"Shall I say no so forcefully?"

"No, Ida. Address him as 'friend,' and tell him I admire his fearlessness, determination, tenacity, and sense of responsibility for rescuing the concert stage from destruction by those racial 'purifiers,' but that I cannot accept *his* government's declarations as sufficient for my return to German concert life."

Huberman stops and thinks for a moment.

"Tell him that the gap between Germany and the cultural world is getting bigger every day, and that I will refuse to play in Germany until Germany stops discriminating against Jews!"

A few days later, Furtwängler receives Huberman's refusal to perform with the orchestra. He bites his lip as he reads.

"First Toscanini, and now Huberman!" he tells Berta. "I can't believe Bronislaw would turn down my offer to open the Berlin season? Is he mad? It's the most prestigious concert engagement in Europe. He knows that."

Berta types as Furtwängler dictates a hasty reply to Huberman.

"Tell Huberman I regret that he has refused my invitation, but that I understand his reasons, although I feel they are not justified, and that his attitude and explanation are incorrect.

"Write to him that the foreign press exaggerates these things, and that during the legal revolution currently going on in Germany, an artist has to accept the inevitable course of events as reality, whether he approves of it or not.

"Tell him that he . . . no . . . *one* must accept the inevitable course of events, and build anew upon them, and that I regret he refuses to support me in my efforts to keep the pure sphere of art free from politics.

"End the letter in this way, Berta: 'I fear that the Germany of today will not be in a position to repeat its offer through me, to you. I know you can, of course, do as well without Germany, as it can do without you. Whether this attitude is in the best interest of art remains another question.'"

When Huberman reads Furtwängler's reply, he balls his hand into a fist and shouts, startling Ida: "Wilhelm Furtwängler is one of those German *non*-Nazis who helps make Nazism possible! I am a Pole, a Jew, a free artist, and a Pan-European, and by each of these identities, I am a dead enemy of Nazism! I will certainly not perform in Berlin!"

Huberman paces the floor in deep thought.

"We will write him back, Ida, for the last time, and we will end the letter with this sentence: 'Herr Furtwängler, the Germans have become animals!'"[2]

"Broni," Ida says softly, "perhaps you should publish your refusal letter to Furtwängler in the newspapers. It will show other musicians that you stand strongly against Germany's laws and practices. It might encourage them to refuse to participate there as well."

"I would do that, Ida, but Wilhelm asked me specifically not to publish this correspondence, and I agreed."

When Wilhelm Furtwängler reads Huberman's reply, he frowns and shakes his balding head.

Germans have become animals? Is this truly what Huberman thinks of us?

He sits quietly, digesting his friend's harsh words.

When Berta walks into the room, she looks at him and asks: "Are you unwell, Wilhelm?"

"No, Berta," he says. "Not ill. Just humiliated. I finally understand what is behind Hitler's narrow-minded measures. This is not only anti-Semitism," he tells her, "but the rejection of any form of artistic, philosophical thought, the rejection of any form of free culture."[3]

Berta gives him a handful of opened letters. "I hate to tell you this, Wilhelm. But most of the other Jewish artists you invited to perform in Germany have also refused."[4]

Furtwängler feels defeated. He drops his head into his hands and exhales loudly.

"Berta, musical life in Germany is going to the dogs! How I detest the National Socialists' cultural policy, the complete 'aryanization' of art, the labeling of Jewish and nonconformist artists as degenerates, and the demands that art must serve the people, the state, and the race!" he shouts.[5]

"True art should never be used for political purposes! *L'art pour l'art!* Art is only for the sake of art itself."

"Do you now regret your decision to stay in Germany?" Berta asks, placing her hand gently on his shoulder.

"I simply tried to defend the autonomy of art against the encroachment of politics," he answers. "Instead, Berta, I find myself collaborating with the Nazis, giving them prestige through my artistic platform."

"You did what you thought was right," Berta says.

"I threatened not to cooperate, to quit, to cancel scheduled performances, but I conformed, Berta, and although I refused to join the National Socialist Party, I signed their contract and promised to stay."

Berta says nothing.

"Now I am miserable," Furtwängler says under his breath, "and criticized by the world's musicians. My life and music are controlled by political madmen."

CHAPTER 47

The Publication

Huberman was one of the greatest musicians I have ever come across. Right or wrong, mine is not altogether an eccentric impression: a long line of artists has testified to his towering stature as an artist, violinist, and man, including such vastly different musical character types as Brahms, Toscanini, Bruno Walter, and Furtwängler.

Hans Keller[1]

"I cannot believe Furtwängler did this!" Huberman tells Ida as he reads the newspaper *Neue Freie Presse.* "He asked me not to publish our correspondence regarding my refusal to perform in Germany, and then *he* publishes our private conversation!"

"Broni, he has also published this article in several other newspapers."

"His argument for me not publishing my letter of response to him isn't valid anymore," Bronislaw says.

"I will prepare a copy of your refusal letter to send to the *New York Times,* Broni."

"Ida, think of the fifteen million Jews worldwide that are all desperate. One part of them is afraid to further degrade the situation of their fellow believers by protesting, and the other part is afraid that their business relations will deteriorate. I believe my letter will give support and hope to a lot of these people scattered throughout the world."

everal weeks later, after the *New York Times* publishes Bronislaw Huber-man's refusal letter to Furtwängler, he receives comments from all over the world.

Some letters from rabbis and musicians support his stance, telling him his name will go down in history, remembered for a long time because he stood up to Hitler's Germany. Other musicians claim they admire his courage and political stance, but they will not refuse an invitation to con-duct or perform in Germany, striving to keep art free from the influence of politics. More letters than not, remind him of *l'art pour l'art*.

Huberman receives a letter from Wilhelm Furtwängler harshly criticiz-ing him for publishing the article for the whole world to read. He tells Bronislaw he doesn't wish to speak to him again, but for the sake of art, he hopes the antagonism between them will one day end.

Bronislaw shakes his head. "Do you think the antagonism will ever end, Ida?"

Ida shrugs her shoulders. "I don't know, Broni, but I have another let-ter for you, an invitation to teach in Vienna, and make our home at a castle in Vienna, Schloss Hetzendorf. Are you interested in becoming the director of Vienna's Master Violin School, the Akademie für Musik und Darstellende Kunst?"

Huberman smiles, raising his eyebrows. "Only if you would like to live in a Viennese castle, Ida."

Her eyes beaming, she nods her head and grins. "Yes, Broni, that would be delightful."

CHAPTER 48

The Castle in Vienna

Ida Ibbeken was really the ideal partner for a person like Huber-man. He fell in love with her. . . . She was everything to him; she was a secretary and a cook, and she carried his violin and everything. . . . She was totally absorbed in what he did."

Tzvi Avni

Soon thereafter, Bronislaw and Ida travel to Vienna, accepting the new position and moving into the beautiful Baroque palace Schloss Hetzendorf. As they walk from room to room inspecting their new residence, Ida reveals bits of interesting history about the residence.

"Broni, did you know that in 1694, the Count of Thun built this castle as a countryside hunting retreat?" she asks. "Empress Maria Theresa acquired the residence in 1742. So many royals have lived here—Emperor Joseph the Second, Emperor Franz the Second, Empress Elizabeth Christine, Maria Carolina of Austria, and many more."

"It is a beautiful place to live and teach," Huberman says as he admires the decorated halls, polished wood walls and doors, marble gallery auditorium, and the colorful murals gracing the walls and ceilings.

"I can just imagine the centuries of elaborate balls and receptions here," Ida says, "of all the famous feet dancing on these floors under these sparkling chandeliers."

"Perhaps we can hold receptions of our own here, Ida."

After they tour the elaborate building, they walk through the gardens and parks that surround the castle. Red roses grow in fields of emerald-green grass extending as far as the eye can see.

Huberman enjoys directing and teaching at the Vienna Master Violin School. One of his most gifted students is young David Grunschlag, the boy he met in Vienna in 1927 when his father, Morris, brought him to audition.

"Only one thing mars this glorious experience," he tells Ida after several months of castle life. "It surprises me how the Viennese seem so indifferent to the pain and persecution of their city's Jews. I expect Germany's harsh anti-Semitism under Hitler, and their blatant public brutality and hatred of the Jews. But I did not anticipate this type of prejudice from the Viennese—the lovers of all things beautiful and cultural."

"It seems," Ida responds, "that bigotry and discrimination are spreading from Germany and seeping like sewage into the cities of Europe, including beautiful Vienna."

Bronislaw senses that the problems, and the persecution in Vienna and Europe, will worsen, becoming far more violent in the near future.

On July 25, 1934, at the chancellery building in Vienna, one hundred and fifty Austrian Nazis, dressed like Austrian soldiers and police officers, surround Austria's Ballhausplatz. Bursting inside, overwhelming and killing the unarmed guards, they seize the chancellery, intending to install a Nazi government in Austria.

The chancellor, Engelbert Dollfuss, hears the commotion and steps out of his office to take a look. A Nazi aims his weapon, and shoots Dollfuss twice, hitting him in the back and throat. He slumps to the floor, bleeding and begging for a doctor and a priest.

"You will have no doctor or priest," one of the Austrian Nazis says. "We want to watch you die a slow and painful death."[1]

Ida hurries down the castle halls and into the room where Bronislaw is practicing.

"Broni," she cries, "Austrian Nazis have killed the chancellor and taken over the Ballhausplatz! I just heard the news."

"I suspected it wouldn't be long before the Nazis tried to take over another country," he says. "Germany isn't enough for them. They want Austria, too!"

"What will happen, Broni?"

He shrugs. "Ida, unfortunately I am not a prophet. I cannot say. But we can surely assume that Jews in Vienna will suffer even more deeply now. I am astonished to see no press coverage of the increasing anti-Semitism here—the vandalism to their businesses, the naked violence against Jews on the streets."

"We must do something, Broni!"

"I've been thinking I can play a benefit concert," he says, "speak directly to the audience from the stage about the abuse, and give all the proceeds to benefit victimized Jews here in Vienna."

Vienna experiences many disturbances that target Jews in their city that year. Bronislaw and Ida work hard on the upcoming concert to provide aid for the disenfranchised and persecuted people.

"Broni," Ida says, "the people in this city refuse to help, or even publicize, the event. They seem unwilling to do anything to help us help the Jews."

"Then, Ida, we will promote the concert ourselves."

On the evening of the concert, Bronislaw is disappointed to see an unimpressive attendance at the Vienna concert hall. Even so, he plays from his heart. At the end of the concert, few people greet him or ask how they can help care for the Jews in their city. Bronislaw is stunned by the indifference of the Viennese to the suffering of their city's Jewish population.

When Bronislaw and Ida return to the Schloss Hetzendorf, the violinist shakes his head and sighs. "Ida, are we going back to the times of Dreyfus? Will no one—NO ONE—help the Jews?"

On the morning of August 19, 1934, Bronislaw reads the evening newspaper, then crumples it and tosses it in the trash.

"This is bad news, Ida," he says. "Germany's president, Paul von Hindenburg, has died. Adolf Hitler has just declared himself president and head of the army. This means he is now the absolute ruler of Germany."

During the next few weeks and months, Bronislaw and Ida watch Hitler's anti-Semitic campaigns hammer Germany with barbaric propaganda, showing Jews as aliens, degenerates, global connivers and conspirators, political and sexual predators who exploit the true pure Aryan Germans.

Almost weekly, Hitler's cruel discriminatory laws target Jews in every part of their lives—personal, business, professional—and they encourage gullible Germans to hate the Jews and treat them with increasingly unbridled hostility.

Germans are instructed to boycott all Jewish businesses and services, leaving well-established medical doctors, lawyers, teachers, and merchants without income.

Hitler strictly forbids music written by any Jewish composer to be performed in German concert halls, or even hummed or whistled on the streets.

With the creation of Dr. Singer's Kulturbund, an organization Huberman loathes, Germans can finally be free from the works of Jewish composers, musicians, and artists, as well as keep the Jews out of their Aryan concert halls.

Many supposedly Aryan Germans stay silent about the drops of Jewish blood running secretly through their own family's veins. They know that if their heritage is revealed, they will be shunned and persecuted, or worse.

Public humiliation and persecution of Jews becomes a common sight in German villages and cities. More and more Jews begin to mysteriously disappear from their homes and communities. Many Jews try to leave Germany, but emigration is difficult as many of the world's countries establish stricter quotas and refuse them entrance.

The German people, in large numbers, support Hitler, taking his anti-Semitism to heart, looking to the new Führer as the savior of their fatherland."

Bronislaw and Ida see how quickly the ideas of fascism are spreading across Europe like some deadly, infectious disease.

William Dudley Pelley, leader of the American Fascist paramilitary group the Silver Shirts, frightens Americans, warning them about opening their country's boundaries and receiving Jewish immigrants.

"If ungodly numbers of refugee Jews come over here," Pelley says, "somebody must support them. If they apply for work and support themselves, it means that an equal number of native American Gentiles must relinquish their present jobs, and either go on relief or join the breadlines."

More than thirty-seven thousand Jews are able to leave Germany, emigrating to the world's few hospitable countries willing to accept them. But with immigration laws so harsh, complicated, and unaccommodating, the majority of Jews must stay in Germany, trying to weather the horrific storm of fascism.[2]

In 1934, Bronislaw and Ida travel the world, performing everywhere except Germany. Each time they return to the Schloss Hetzendorf, they see greater social and political tensions, as well as deepening hatred and violence toward European Jews.

In Germany, Jews can no longer own land, have a pet, or date Aryans. They are prohibited from working as newspaper editors, cannot participate in any of the arts (except in the Kulturbund), and are not allowed national health insurance.

The Nazis establish the Hereditary Health Court, forcing sterilization of all people they deem inferior, Jews and Gypsies, as well as those who have genetic defects. They also pass laws that send the unemployed, homeless, beggars, and alcoholics to concentration camps.[3]

"I sense that within a short time, things will become much worse for all but so-called Aryans, in Germany and Europe," Bronislaw tells Ida. "Much worse."

"Can it get any worse, Broni?" Ida asks.

As Bronislaw sits down at his desk, he sees an open letter waiting for him on top of his mail.

"What's this?" he asks Ida.

"You've been invited back to play in Palestine."

"Ida, write them that I eagerly accept their invitation!"

"I thought you might, Broni," she says, smiling.

"And, Ida, I wish to bring my son. I want to spend time with him, and he needs to learn about his being Jewish, and about Zionism."

CHAPTER 49

The Return to Palestine

The Jews are a community that share a common fate, a community whose members share a lot of common bonds and characteristics.

Bronislaw Huberman

Bronislaw and Ida travel to Palestine in 1934, eager and excited to step again onto its soil. Bronislaw's son, Johannes, accompanies them, his first trip to the Middle East.

As he has on previous tours to Palestine, Huberman feels the deep kinship, community, and a sense of profound mysticism in the country. He hopes Johannes feels it, too. He has much to teach his twenty-four-year-old son in their three short weeks together.

When he arrives in Palestine, Huberman receives an enthusiastic welcome from the music-loving Jews. He watches them stand in long lines to buy tickets to his concerts. The atmosphere is festive, the adults and children surrounding him applauding and cheering his name.

"It's like a holiday!" he hears a young girl squeal.

Huberman stays for eighteen days, playing twelve sold-out concerts— five in Tel Aviv, four in Jerusalem, two in Haifa, and one in the agricultural settlement Kibbutz Ein Harod. Johannes sits in the front row of each concert, visibly admiring his famous father.

Some twelve to fifteen hundred people crowd into the concert halls to hear the performances. After the regular concerts, Huberman arranges workers' concerts, offering heavily discounted tickets, making it possible for them to experience the music. Eighteen hundred workers attend the discounted concerts, but still four thousand must be turned away for lack of space.

After an evening concert for kibbutzniks and laborers at Ein Harod, Bronislaw tells his son: "Johannes, I have never encountered an audience anywhere in the world like this one. They are so receptive to the music, so genuinely understanding. I play here like nowhere else in the world."

Huberman pours his whole heart into his performances for the poorest citizens.

"It's wrong to presume that somebody less educated musically will be satisfied with a lesser performance," he tells Johannes. "For me, the only difference between the concerts for the well-to-do and those for the workers is the price of the ticket. I feel a special bond, a kinship with the people here. A kind of mysticism unites us, and seems to turn the individual into a national collective. I sense that happening here in Palestine."

Nowhere are these feelings more intense than in his concert for hundreds of farmers and laborers in the general assembly hall at Kibbutz Ein Harod. From the moment he begins playing, Huberman feels such a profound connection and love that he is certain he has never in his life played more emotionally or more profoundly. He is so moved by this audience and his experience there that he addresses them after the concert:

"Tonight I have experienced a feeling I have never in my life come upon. This sharing of music that occurred tonight, together, was not only to bring you and me pleasure, but to clarify to myself the feelings I have toward you, to express to you that I am with you in your feelings, your hopes, your troubles and struggles, your sacrifices, and your extraordinary achievements here in the Holy Land."

Bronislaw is so caught up in his emotions that he has to pause, to gather himself, before continuing. "I want you to know that I am with you completely, not just in the form which has been given to me to share: my musical expression."

For his deeply felt sentiments, the people show their gratitude with loud, long applause.

"My heart is full right now," he continues, "and I cannot say what I would like to say. Thank you for the feeling that you understand me, as I feel I understand you. Thank you!"

The violinist steps down from the platform, pushing back a tear. Ida comes toward him, whispering in his ear: "I am so proud of you, Broni."

"I feel at home here with my people, Ida, in this ancient land. Perhaps . . ." He stops and stares at Ida, turning the idea over in his head. "Perhaps it's the first time I have ever really felt at home anywhere."

"I understand, Broni," she says, tears forming in her eyes.

"I believe I am finally won over—I am becoming a true, and even an enthusiastic Zionist!"

"I knew it would happen, Broni!" Ida says.

CHAPTER 50

Mysticism in Palestine

*My sojourn [in Palestine] in 1934 provoked a fundamental change
in my attitude and interest in Palestine. All arguments or theories
are quite useful things as long as they are in accordance with life.
But as soon as there is a discrepancy between life and theory, then
I am too much of an artist not to bow first of all to life.*

Bronislaw Huberman

Ida notices something truly mysterious and beautiful being born in Huberman's heart while the two of them and Johannes tour Palestine during this third visit. Bronislaw seems to possess a new love and enthusiasm for this overheated country of sand, camels, and bugs.

"I am amazed at the progress and growth made here just since our last visit," he exclaims. "It seems that Palestine is developing so rapidly that centuries from now they will describe this time as if it were another biblical miracle."[1]

"I see it, too, Broni," Ida says. "I am glad we've been given this opportunity to come back."

"It is such an amazing land," Bronislaw says. "But the main source of inspiration in the Holy Land emanates from the atmosphere of mysticism of which everybody here, Jew or Gentile, feels the breath. The mysticism is born of the landscape, of the history, of the ideals in everybody's breast, of the miracles of the three religions represented here, of the hopes nourished and partly already realized by the Jews."

His eyes shining, he smiles, and continues:

"For most colonizing people, the countries they colonize are empty pages. But, Ida, for the Jewish people, Palestine is already a fully written book!"

A fter a brief tour of the Holy Land, a quiet rest by the banks of the Dead Sea, and a few awkward camel rides, Bronislaw finishes his work in Palestine, and they head back home.

As they travel, Huberman contemplates more deeply the issue of Zionism and of Palestine, as well as the failing Pan-European movement he has committed much of his life to.

"Ida," he says, after hours of quiet pondering, "I am a dedicated European, and I never was excited by the thought that the most European people of the world, the Jews, should move to an Eastern country."

Ida smiles, listening closely.

"But what I saw on this trip in Palestine makes me delighted. Nowhere else can one find such idealism, such enthusiasm. Sure, there are individual idealists everywhere, but a mass idealism, a collective idealism, exists in Palestine, and I believe it cannot be found in any other country," he says. "This is one of the reasons why I no longer see any incompatibility between my European and Palestine beliefs, though what I see in Palestine seems to be like a new and better Europe."

CHAPTER 51

The Decision

Can you imagine a pro-Jewish, pro-Zionist campaign more effective than the concert tour of a Palestine Orchestra? This will enhance the prestige of Jews all over the world.

Bronislaw Huberman

The night proves long as Bronislaw Huberman lies in bed and struggles to sleep. Feeling the chill of Schloss Hetzendorf's empty halls and huge rooms, he pulls the thick blanket up around his neck and stares into the darkness.

In his mind, he relives the exciting moments of his performances in Palestine a few days before, seeing the utterly delighted audience, hearing their cheers, applause, and calls for encores. He recalls his 1931 visit to the land, three years before, when he had first given thought to the local Jewish community's appetite for a great orchestra. He had dismissed the idea then, knowing that no top-notch, securely employed musician would be willing to leave a European orchestra to move to the desert. But now, since his recent visit to the Holy Land, with anti-Semitism increasing in Germany, and most of the German Jewish musicians no longer employed in orchestras, he realizes the situation has dramatically changed.

The dream of actually creating a new orchestra in Palestine, made up of first-class, German Jewish musicians, keeps him awake tonight, fanning the embers of an old fire and feeling it begin to glow anew in his heart.

"The timing, and the current abusive situation in Germany, might now make such an impossible dream come true," he whispers aloud. "Perhaps

Hitler himself has made possible an all–German Jewish orchestra in Palestine!"

He smiles at that thought as he closes his eyes and envisions the faces of the children and youths, adults and elderly, hungry for good music, striving to hear every note of every piece. Their faces, lined by years of labor and emotional strife, become softened, receptive to the timeless, invisible vibrations of music. In his previous trips to Palestine, he has noticed how music brings a much-needed rest to the hearts, minds, and spirits of these people.

Bronislaw ponders deeply throughout the night. He contemplates the mysterious mysticism in the air and the lush countryside of the Holy Land. He reflects on the people of Tel Aviv, Jerusalem, and Haifa, the kibbutzniks of Ein Harod and he remembers how everyone loved and appreciated the soul-healing qualities of music. A new energy, excitement, and sense of purpose grab hold of him, preventing him from sleep but kindling his heart and mind with the fire of new possibilities.

Long before dawn, Bronislaw rises, dresses, and sits at his kitchen table, jotting down notes about his new plan for an orchestra. Ida joins him.

"Good morning, Broni," she says, pouring his coffee. "You seemed restless last night. Did you get any sleep?"

"It doesn't matter, Ida," he says, not looking up from his notepad.

She pauses, looking at his face. "Broni? Are you okay?"

"Please sit down, Ida! I have something important to share with you."

Ida sits with eyes wide as Bronislaw tells her his new dream. She senses an alertness in him she seldom sees after he spends a long sleepless night.

"Ida," he says, "the rise of Hitlerism in Germany and Europe has dealt the death blow to our Pan-European movement. It has failed, and is no longer a goal we can reach. But I feel it is the perfect time to create the orchestra in Palestine. It will give German musicians salaried jobs, and deliver them and their families from Hitler's abuses."

He continues with excitement: "In addition to the new orchestra, we could establish a music school, taught by the orchestra's musicians. A school for children in Palestine will teach them the basics of music, as well as the rich music of their ancestors. This will ensure that the classical tradition of music will live on in Palestine for many generations to come."

"You are serious about creating this orchestra, Broni?"

"Yes, Ida. I am."

Not wanting to sound discouraging by bringing up the mountain of obstacles that stand in the way of realizing his dream, Ida says nothing.

Bronislaw leans toward her, taking her hand and squeezing it with excitement. "The time is right, Ida. It was impossible three years ago, or even last year. But things have changed. It is possible now!"

"Broni," she says slowly, carefully choosing her words, "you must realize that it will involve an immense amount of work. You cannot possibly handle more work right now with your concert and teaching schedule. This would be an incredible challenge, even if you were doing nothing else. And I must admit, I would worry about your health."

"Ida, I understand your fears and reservations for my plan and for my health. But I *must* do this. It has suddenly become so clear to me that with Hitler firing the best musicians in Germany, this is the perfect opportunity to give this wonderful audience in Palestine a first-class orchestra, and to give unemployed German Jewish musicians a job! But, even more important, this new orchestra will make a strong statement, raising a fist, not a gun, against the horror of Nazism, fighting against Hitler with the only weapon Jews have—their music. I will do this, Ida, and I will begin right away!"

Ida licks her lips, pressing them together.

"Ida, we must go to work on this immediately. Anti-Semitism in Germany is growing so rapidly. I sense the day will come when no Jew will be safe there. Many have been trying to leave, but they have no money to travel and few places to go. Most countries in the world have closed their doors to Jewish immigrants."

"Ida, can you imagine a pro-Jewish, pro-Zionist campaign more effective than a concert tour of a Palestine orchestra? This will enhance the prestige of Jews all over the world!"

After a while, Ida speaks. "Yes, Broni. I can see it, too. I believe you have made up your mind about this new orchestra and 'rescue mission' for the Jews in Germany."

"Yes, Ida, I have. Surely, if orange trees can grow in the desert, and a sand dune can become a city, there can also be a symphony orchestra in Palestine."[1]

"Then, Broni, no matter what it demands, or the hard work involved, I will make *your* dream *my* dream, and strive to help you make it come true."

CHAPTER 52

The Magnificent Obsession

*Because of the German barbarity, Palestine is provided with an
otherwise unimaginable opportunity to create a cultural institution
that's destined to serve as a model to the rest of the world.*

Bronislaw Huberman

Over the following weeks, the magnificent obsession of a new orchestra
and music school in Palestine grips the violinist's heart and soul. He begins
contacting his friends, fellow musicians, leaders in Jewish government, and
the colleagues he has come to know through the Pan-Europa movement.
He shares his idea, and asks for their help to make it a reality.

"I, too, am a Zionist," one friend tells him. "I believe we must somehow
get German Jews to Palestine—for their safety, and for the well-being of
their families. But create an orchestra? Is that really necessary and needed
at a time like this?"

"Yes!" Bronislaw responds. "Can't you see—to beat the world campaign
of anti-Semitism, it's not enough to create material prosperity in Palestine.
The symphony orchestra, as I imagine it, will be perhaps the first and
easiest step toward reaching the highest aim of Jewish humanity."

Bronislaw continues: "Heartbreaking attempts have been made by these
Jewish artists to find chairs in the orchestras of other countries, but except
for a handful, they are still without jobs, or even means of subsistence.
Think of all these excellent musicians in Germany. Just imagine the kind
of orchestra we could create if we could bring the best of them to Palestine.

It would be an orchestra that could compete with the greatest orchestras in the world!"

After hearing his idea, every listener, without exception, responds: "This will be a huge undertaking, Bronislaw, requiring much hard work, a very large financial commitment, support from influential people around the world, and musicians willing to take such a risk. To get permanent certificates for the musicians to immigrate to Palestine, you'll need approval from the Jewish Agency. Do you think you can actually do this, Bronislaw, with so many barriers to overcome?"

"Yes," he says with confidence. "I will start by making a substantial personal donation, and I will give a series of benefit concerts. I will also begin to ask people around the world, Jews and interested Gentiles alike, to donate to this cause."

"But, Bronislaw," a musician friend objects, "are you not using art for political purposes by depending on your fame as a violinist, and establishing an orchestra to help Jews escape from Hitler? Do you no longer believe in *l'art pour l'art*—art for art's sake only?"

"No, I do not," Bronislaw says. "I have descended into the deepest depths of my soul to find the hidden link between my impulse toward art and my impulse toward political action. And I have made a huge discovery. The true artist does not create art as an end in itself. He creates art for human beings. Humanity is the goal."

"This is not the same Bronislaw Huberman," many of his friends say.

"It's true," he says. "I am not that same man of many years ago!"[1]

"Do you think Palestine is ready for your vision, Bronislaw?"

"I traveled to Palestine for concerts in 1929, 1931, and this year, 1934. Each time I visit the country, I am amazed by the progress the people have made since my last visit. This progress covers all fields of life—education, art, science, nutrition, and the tremendous growth of the farm settlements."

Bronislaw continues: "In 1931, I had the vision of a symphony orchestra worthy of these wonderful audiences. In '31, however, it seemed a long road to achieving this goal. But with an irony only possible in a world being torn apart, it was Hitler who made this possible by firing Jewish musicians from their jobs in orchestras all over Germany. As a result of their joblessness and increasingly desperate situation at home, I now believe the Palestine symphony is achievable!"

"Surely, Bronislaw, creating and maintaining this level of orchestra in the Middle East will depend on nothing less than a . . . a . . . miracle!"

"Then I will believe in miracles!" Huberman says with great gravity.

Huberman is able to solicit help from many people who believe in his orchestra building and rescue mission. Others offer their support and assistance because they are deeply troubled by Germany's increasing persecution of the Jewish community. But the money needed to pay for the musicians to travel to Palestine, receive an acceptable salary, secure an adequate shelter for their families, as well as provide instruments, music, and a decent concert hall, is far above Huberman's personal resources. However, that doesn't stop Bronislaw Huberman from working and dreaming about his new all-Jewish orchestra and school.

CHAPTER 53

The Lawless Years

In reality, it is not a question of violin concertos, nor even merely of the Jews; the issue is the retention of those things that our fathers achieved by blood and sacrifice, of the elementary preconditions of our European culture, the freedom of personality, and its unconditional self-responsibility, unhampered by fetters of caste or race.

Patrick Harris

Bronislaw Huberman continues to teach at Vienna's music school as he and Ida make plans to establish the new orchestra in Palestine. They work with a sense of urgency, always aware of Hitler's new and more devastating abuses of German Jews. They also wonder when Hitler will close the borders, refusing Jewish residents the right to leave the Fatherland. They know that on any given day, their rescue operation could be stopped without warning.

They must also raise a huge amount of money and find trusted people to manage the new Palestine Symphony. Bronislaw plans to select the new orchestra's seventy musicians by holding auditions in Germany, recruiting only the finest and most skilled musicians.

But first, he must go to Palestine and meet with Jewish officials, most importantly, David Ben-Gurion, head of the Jewish Agency. Before he can move forward, Bronislaw must get his approval and secure Ben-Gurion's promise of permanent certificates for the emigrating musicians.

uberman takes a hiatus from his duties in Vienna and journeys to
Palestine. There he meets with Hebrew University's new chancellor,
Dr. Judah Magnes, an ardent Zionist dubbed the "Professor of International
Peace."

"Dr. Magnes," Huberman explains, "I, too, have become a Zionist.
I have an idea I want to discuss with you."

"Yes, Mr. Huberman. I am happy to hear you are now 'one of us.'"

"Dr. Magnes, I want to start a new orchestra in Palestine, composed
mostly of German Jewish musicians, who, as you well know, are experiencing horrible anti-Semitism in their home country. This plan will enable
them and their families to escape German persecution, to start a life with
a salaried orchestra position here, and, at the same time, it will be a major
step in the building up of Palestine's cultural life and economy. And we
will start a music school taught by the orchestra musicians to educate Palestine's children and preserve our rich heritage of music. To have a chance
of doing all this, I need your help."

"I like this plan!" Magnes says. "Rescuing Jewish musicians from an
anti-Semitic Germany to bring music here."

Magnes seems deeply thoughtful for a moment, then turns to Huberman and says, "I've always considered myself a pacifist. But with Hitler's
growing cruelty toward Jews in Germany, I could actually support the idea
of a war to stop him."

Magnes leans toward Bronislaw. "You know that Palestine already has
an orchestra."

"Yes, I know. But it's a poor one. Jews here in Palestine have such a deep
passion for music, they deserve a world-class orchestra."

"Dr. Magnes, I've learned that you are highly respected here, and people will listen to you. I need your help and support in this endeavor. And
we greatly need financial backing."

"I understand, Mr. Huberman," Magnes says. "I know a number of wealthy Americans who are horrified by the Jews' plight in Germany. They might be willing to donate money."

"I myself have seen the generous hearts of Americans," Huberman states.

"Yes, they can be quite benevolent. And as you well know, your name and fame will draw financial backing like a magnet from many people around the world."[1]

B ronislaw Huberman sits in the Palestine office of David Ben-Gurion, telling him about the new orchestra and requesting hundreds of permanent certificates to allow Jewish musicians to emigrate to Palestine.

Huberman knows Ben-Gurion cares little for music, and will not see the benefit of building the culture as part of the future Israel. He has been warned about the leader and thus, he has first garnered support from Magnes and Tel Aviv's mayor Dizengoff before he meets with him.

"Mr. Huberman," Ben-Gurion asks, "do you understand what we are trying to do here in Palestine?"

"Of course. You are inviting Jews to settle here to build a foundation for the establishment of a Jewish state," Huberman says.

"And if we are to create a national home for Jews, and gain political independence, the immigrants we need are hard workers—engineers, farmers, builders, and men for our military," Ben-Gurion explains.

"I believe creating the *culture* in Palestine is equally important as building homes, farms, businesses, and the armed forces," Huberman says. "An all-Jewish world-class orchestra will help build the state socially and economically, preserving the heritage of European music and bringing Palestine and Jews prestige around the world."

"Mr. Huberman, we welcome Jewish immigration, and it has grown considerably since 1933. We've made incredible progress in our settlements. I will consider your proposal and get back in touch with you."

The meeting ends abruptly. Huberman leaves Ben-Gurion's office feeling discouraged. He realizes that the man is not in the least bit interested in bringing European musicians to Palestine. But a lot of others in power do support his idea, and Huberman is banking on that.

B ronislaw continues to travel the world, performing in order to raise money for the new orchestra and planning trips to audition and recruit Germany's most highly skilled musicians. He hires some trusted musicians to help him with the auditions, and seriously considers resigning his teaching position in Vienna. The new rescue mission has taken first place in his life.

CHAPTER 54

Germany's New Laws

In 1935, the laws came out, the Nuremberg Laws. That was the first time you knew where you stood legally . . . before it was all guesswork. You could meet a Nazi in some office and he could exterminate you, or you could meet a Nazi that was very human and he could help you. . . . Before 1935, before the laws came out of Nuremberg, you swam your way through. . . . You know, there was [sic] no regulations. The laws of Nuremberg was the first, ah, form, legal shape where you knew where you stood.

Peter Gaupp, 1935, a half Jew who referred to the time
between 1933 and 1935 as the "lawless years"[1]

In early September 1935, Adolf Hitler is restless. He decides the time is ripe to impose more restrictions on Germany's Jews.

"We must make new and stricter laws for the protection of German blood and honor," he tells Bernhard Lösener, his desk officer for racial law in the Reich Ministry of the Interior. "Tell Pfundtner and Stuckart to write the legal language of these new laws. Have Dr. Gerhard Wagner join us, too. We will present these new laws at the Nuremberg party rally in two days."

"My Führer," Lösener says, "two days is not enough time to write new laws that will impact millions of people. We need far more time."

Hitler slams his fist on the table beside him. "Two days!" he shouts.

When Wagner, Pfundtner, and Stuckart arrive, they all begin taking furious notes while Hitler speaks.

"With these new laws," the Führer says, "we will further ostracize all Jews from German society. We must remove these parasites from our fatherland."

"Who exactly do you consider a Jew?" Dr. Wagner asks.

"This is a difficult question," Hitler says. "After so many years of German Jewish assimilation, how shall we decide?"

"I suggest the racial laws not only apply to full Jews, but to all half, quarter, and one-eighth Jews," Wagner says. "Surely the *Mischlinge*, the partial Jews, are more dangerous than the full Jews. With their mix of German and Jewish blood, these enemies of the state will have the intelligence and skill of Aryans."

"I must think on these racial laws," Hitler says. "In the future, we must forbid any sexual relations or marriages between Aryans and non-Aryans."

"A good idea, my Führer," Wagner says. "I believe we must also consider any Aryan who has married a Jew, as well as their children, to be inferior, un-German, and—"

"I can see problems with this arrangement," Lösener interrupts. "I fear disastrous social repercussions if we brand as Jews our highly decorated half-Jewish Great War veterans. And many Jews in Germany are distinguished supporters of the party."

"This is a problem," Hitler says. "One that will not be easily solved."

"These Jewish war heroes and party supporters *feel* German. They have publicly rejected Judaism," Lösener says. "The suicide rate will climb drastically if we label them as Jews. And if we treat half Jews as full Jews, we will lose about forty-five thousand soldiers in our armed forces. We cannot afford that!"

"When we need them for the security of the state, we will make use of them," Hitler says.

"The Jews in Germany are already considered the *Untermenschen*, the subhumans," Pfundtner states. "Aryans no longer shop in Jewish stores, and all their stores are marked with the yellow Star of David, and have *Juden* written on the windows. We have placed SA men outside the Jewish shops to forbid any Aryan from entering."

"Our plan to bankrupt Jews and cripple their businesses is working well," Stuckart says. "And to further isolate them from Aryan society, Jews must now sit in designated seats on buses, trains, and park benches."

"Yes," Hitler agrees. "Good. Good. And Goebbels is teaching our Aryan schoolchildren to avoid interaction with and contamination from Jewish children. We must keep our blood pure and untainted."

"How will we enforce these new laws?" Stuckart asks.

"Punishment will vary according to the offense," Hitler says. "We will punish violators with hard labor, imprisonment . . . or worse."

After hours of discussion, Hitler closes the meeting with these words: "These new laws seem far too humane to me. Should this legal attempt fail to regulate the Jewish problem, then we will hand over this problem to the National Socialist Party for a final solution."[2]

Bronislaw is astonished when he hears that Hitler has passed a new set of laws that will further alienate and persecute German Jews.

"Do you know what this means?" he asks Ida. "These anti-Jewish laws will make daily life even more difficult for Jews. Soon they will be outcast from every part of German society."

"What more can that madman do to the Jews?" Ida asks.

"It's not just the Jews, Ida. They are also arresting homosexuals, Roma, and Jehovah's Witnesses, imprisoning them in special municipal camps."

"What are they to do?" Ida asks. "Since most countries are unwilling to admit the Jews who want to leave Germany."[3]

"I don't know, Ida. What do other victims of ethnic cleansing do? Where can they go? They have few choices."

ithin a few weeks, Huberman receives a cable from David Ben-Gurion stating that the Jewish Agency has approved permanent certificates for Huberman's orchestra musicians and their families to immigrate to Palestine and remain as permanent residents. Huberman is overjoyed by the good news.

"There is no stopping us now!" he tells Ida.

CHAPTER 55

Realizing the Obstacles

*Bronislaw Huberman, by nature, found spending money quite
hard. There's no way he would have spent the amount of time and
money on the project that he did, without being obsessed by it. It
was all that preoccupied his every waking moment.*

Patrick Harris

At home in Vienna, in the autumn of 1935, Bronislaw puts his head in Ida's
lap and enjoys an invigorating head and neck massage.

"I needed that, Ida," he says. "I am feeling overwhelmed and exhausted
these days."

"You've got to slow down and rest more, Broni."

"There is so much to do, Ida. Now that we've received the promise of
permanent certificates, we must begin auditioning musicians. We have no
time to waste, as things in Germany become more dangerous every day."

"Broni, what I wonder is will German musicians see the *real* threat to
their safety, and be willing to move their families to Palestine? Many of
them have deep roots in Germany, going back many generations, and you
know that Jews have grown used to the anti-Semitism that's been in Europe
for hundreds of years. Sometimes it's bad, sometimes it's not so bad, but
it's always there. Many people say that these Nazis will not be in power
long, and things will get better."

"I have a terrible feeling, Ida, that this time is different, and it's going
to be very bad for Jews. I must convince them that Germany isn't a safe
place for them."

"Palestine is not such a safe place either, Broni. The Arabs and Jews are constantly fighting each other."

"Palestine seems far safer right now than Germany, Ida. I believe that with permanent certificates in hand, they will realize they must leave Germany."

"We have so much to do, Broni. I fear you are still facing overwhelming obstacles we don't even know of."

Bronislaw smiles thinly. "That's why I need you, Ida, and your wonderful head rubs!"

With the help and recommendations of Dr. Judah Magnes, Huberman contacts a lengthy list of wealthy Americans. He also contacts Zionists in London and starts organizations in major cities of the world to raise money from their Jewish residents. Ida assists him full-time, typing letters, making telephone calls, and arranging his travel schedule to meet with American donors who are sympathetic to the mission.

"Ida," he tells her every day, "I feel we must do this work quickly. If we don't hurry, we may find the German and Palestinian borders closed, allowing no one to leave or enter. The British already consider that the number of Jewish immigrants to Palestine is growing too fast. More than sixty-one thousand Jews immigrated from Germany, and elsewhere in Europe, this year alone, and the British administration responded by allowing less than one-third of the quota the Jewish Agency has requested for this year."[1]

"If Palestine closes its borders, thousands of Jews will be stranded in Germany, as well as our future musicians," Ida says.

"You are right, Ida. The Arab High Committee is already very nervous, and at any moment could demand that the British block all immigration of Jews to Palestine. These problems and obstacles are always on my mind. That's why we must work immediately and diligently."[2]

CHAPTER 56

The Need for Immediacy

We Jews are everywhere subject to attacks and humiliations that result from the exaggeration of nationalism and racial vanity, which, in most European countries, expresses itself in the form of aggressive anti-Semitism. The Jewish national home [Palestine] is not a luxury, but an absolute necessity for the Jewish people.

Albert Einstein[1]

Bronislaw pays close attention to the rapidly changing situation in Germany. He continues to publicly protest, but on a much larger scale, Germany's increasing anti-Semitism and persecution of Jews. He writes dozens of letters to international officials and newspaper editors, trying to warn the world of the threat of heightened violence and a coming war. He sends out urgent calls to influential leaders who he hopes will promote peace, as well as Zionism, stating that:

"I firmly believe that Palestine will, in a short time, be the first country where the human humiliation of a culture, limited only to one class or section, will disappear. It will be the first country where we shall witness the miracle of an entire community culture."

Albert Einstein, Huberman's friend from the Pan-Europa movement, also eagerly and publicly protests against Hitler, fascism, Jewish inequality, and racism. His letters and articles appear in newspapers around the world.

By speaking out so publicly, Einstein has become one of Hitler's top enemies. When the prominent scientist and his wife moved to the United States, an American friend warned them: "Your safety in America depends upon silence, and refraining from attendance at public functions . . . in the long run, your safety here depends on your discretion."[2]

But Einstein doesn't listen. He, like Huberman, and many other respected world citizens, continues to protest loudly against Jewish persecution, criticizing countries that have closed their doors to Jewish immigration and advocating a growing and stable Jewish community in Palestine.

Einstein calls for peace and equality among Jewish and Arab residents in Palestine. He, like other Zionists, worries that Palestine is a powder keg, the fuse already lit, threatening to blow up at any second. He knows that resident Arabs in Palestine could impede Jewish immigration, and ban the sale of land to immigrating Jews. Einstein, Huberman, and others sense that the situation in Palestine is becoming more tense and troubled.

D uring the winter months of 1935, Bronislaw and Ida talk with influential world leaders, raise money, and audition prospective musicians.

At the end of the year, they return to Palestine, where they are welcomed warmly by the people. Huberman gives eleven recitals and one chamber-music concert, and meets with a number of people who pledge their support for the new orchestra.

As he expects, he receives some opposition from the musicians employed in Palestine's small existing orchestra.

"I knew we'd have some friction," he tells Ida. "The orchestra members in Palestine fear these new recruits will take their jobs and make their orchestra obsolete."

"Broni, a new orchestra, consisting of Europe's finest musicians, may, indeed, put them out of work."

"I don't want that to happen," he says. "I will talk with them. Perhaps the two orchestras can work together in some way."

While in Palestine, Bronislaw arranges a time to meet with officials from the existing orchestra. They invite him to rehearse with them and hear some of their players individually.

Huberman takes the conductor's baton, and with diminishing patience, he tries to work with them. But it proves deeply frustrating. He returns to the hotel disenchanted.

"This existing orchestra plays at such a low level," he tells Ida. "And I am very disappointed by its inadequate management."

"So, the existing orchestra is useless to us?"

"I fear so, Ida. There are a few possibilities among the players, but only a few. When the time comes, I will have to see what I can do for the rest of the players. They might find employment playing chamber music, or playing in movie houses, coffee shops, and synagogues."

CHAPTER 57

Recruitment

The Jews are exposed, as a minority among the nations, not merely to external danger, but also to internal ones of a psychological nature.

Albert Einstein[1]

Huberman travels throughout Germany during the beginning of the new year 1936, auditioning German Jews, offering only the best players positions with the new orchestra. He is not able to attract nearly enough first-class musicians in Germany, so he decides to expand his search to other countries, where he senses Jewish musicians will soon also be at risk from the Nazis—Polish Jews, Czech Jews, and Austrian Jews. At each audition, Huberman is troubled by his inability to offer positions to lesser musicians who are desperate to leave.

"We cannot bring all of Germany's unemployed Jewish musicians to Palestine," he says. "If the orchestra is to be first class by the world's standards, then we must select only the finest, most experienced performers. In art, there can be no mercy and no compromise. But I hate to leave anyone behind who wishes to go."

"I know, Broni. It's very difficult."

Dr. Kurt Singer has worked hard building the Kulturbund in Germany. He is thrilled that the organization is strong and growing, providing work and cultivating the artistic and scholarly interests of Germany's Jewish population. Already organized in forty-nine German cities, the group now has more than seventy thousand Jewish members.

When Singer hears that Huberman is creating a new orchestra in Palestine, and actively recruiting Germany's best Jewish musicians, he begins to worry about the musicians in his Kulturbund. He also learns that Wilhelm Steinberg, his Kulturbund conductor in Frankfurt, is helping Huberman audition and recruit musicians from the organization. Steinberg, a highly talented Jewish pianist, violinist, and conductor, began his remarkable musical career at age thirteen and, by age twenty-nine, rose to be the music director of the Frankfurt Opera. He was fired by the Nazis in 1933, and restricted by the German Party to playing only in the Kulturbund.

"Stop being Huberman's spy!" Singer tells Steinberg. "We don't want to lose our best musicians to Huberman's new orchestra. We need them to stay in the Kulturbund!"[2]

As several of Dr. Singer's musicians show interest in joining the new Palestine Symphony, Singer tries to persuade them to remain with the Kulturbund.

"Your position here is secure. Herr Goebbels sponsors us and assures you permanent employment.

"Close your ears to Steinberg and Huberman's offers," he chides his musicians. "You are safe here. I have a good relationship with the Nazis, and I can protect you. And, after all, we have no way to replace our Jewish musicians here in Germany, so we need you."

Preferring to wait out the Nazi strife at home, most of the players choose to trust Singer, and when approached by Huberman or Steinberg, the majority of them choose to stay in Germany with the Kulturbund. Nevertheless, Singer becomes so incensed by Huberman's attempts to poach his players that he turns against any Kulturbund musician who even expresses interest in the Palestine Symphony.

Kurt Singer is misguided," Huberman tells Ida. "His musicians refuse to even talk with us."

"They need to believe in Singer, who believes the party will keep its word," Ida says.

"He is delusional!" Huberman shouts. "If Singer thinks the Nazis will keep any of their promises to Jews, he's living in a fantasy world!"

Some of the best musicians in Germany turn down Huberman's invitation to join the new orchestra.

"We believe this crisis in Europe is only temporary," they tell him. "It will blow over, and everything will become normal again."

"Germany may never be 'normal' again," Huberman tells them. "I sense Hitler will impose more and more restrictions upon Jews, even harsher than the Nuremberg Laws. It will get worse and worse. No one will be safe, not in Germany or Europe."

Many respond that they won't immigrate because they refuse to leave their extended family members behind, so Huberman returns again and again to the Jewish Agency, asking for more certificates. In spite of his efforts, the families of some musicians still refuse to leave their homes in Europe.

Other musicians want desperately to leave Germany, but refuse to go to Palestine, which is hot and seems a cultural wasteland to them.

"We want to go to beautiful places in the world, to established orchestras where we can make much more money than you are offering us in Palestine."

"That sounds fine," Huberman tells each one. "But few countries except Palestine are willing to allow German Jews to enter. You'll end up right here in Nazi Europe."

Huberman is aware that most of his words are falling on deaf ears.

Things begin to change, however, as months pass, and Huberman continues to audition and recruit musicians across Europe—from Warsaw, Prague, Budapest, and many more cities. As racial persecution continues to grow in Germany, becoming more dangerous and violent, seeping like sewage into all parts of Europe, Jewish musicians become more fearful for their lives and think seriously about leaving their homes. As the tide of anti-Semitism becomes more ominous, Huberman is besieged with requests from musicians who beg to become part of the new orchestra and receive certificates to Palestine. Many of the players, however, are subpar, and Huberman has certificates for only seventy musicians and their families. Frustrating and painful as it is, he must turn away the less skilled musicians.

Huberman seems to have some prescient inner clock about the increasingly mindless violence against Jews in Germany. His intuition pushes him to speed up his pace, knowing time is running out. But major obstacles still loom. A vast shortfall of funds still needs to be addressed, and they must find and audition musicians all over Europe to fill the many empty chairs in the orchestra sections. They must also attend to hundreds of necessary legal and organizational details in order to start an orchestra thousands of miles away in a desert outback.

Ignoring his own needs and brushing aside Ida's concerns for his health, Bronislaw spends every waking hour working toward the dream. He sleeps less and less. He becomes so depleted that he comments that he "is on the other side of a nervous breakdown." But he has far too much to do to succumb to it.

CHAPTER 58

1936: The Year of New Beginnings

From my point of view, the catastrophe in Germany has created
the best conditions for the founding of a fine orchestra.

Bronislaw Huberman

During the first days of the new year, Huberman travels to Germany, and with the help of colleagues, he auditions many talented musicians. One exceptional violist is a lovely young woman named Dora Loeb.

"You play beautifully, Fräulein Loeb," Huberman tells her, inviting her to join the new orchestra.

"You are asking me to move to . . . to Palestine?" she asks, wrinkling her face and frowning.

"Yes, fräulein. I am offering you an opportunity I cannot extend to many musicians. You are an exceptional violist, and your talents are greatly needed in Palestine."

"I'm not sure, sir, that I . . . I want to go to the Middle East. I have a large wonderful family here in Germany. I would become quite homesick if I left and traveled so far away. Anyway, Dr. Singer has asked me to join the Kulturbund, and I am inclined to accept his invitation in order to stay in Germany."

"I understand," Huberman says intently, "but I want you to listen to me carefully, Dora. Germany is changing rapidly, and anti-Semitism is becoming increasingly dangerous. Yes, you have parents and grandparents here, but you are young and gifted, and I'm certain they want you to have the rich life in music you have in front of you. That is the most precious gift they can give you. If you wait until life becomes unbearable here, you might not be able to escape at all. I am offering you a way to leave now, while you still can."

For the next several days, Dora Loeb struggles with her decision, weighing the advantages and disadvantages. Finally, won over by Huberman's words, and the tearful support of her family, she makes the decision to accept Huberman's offer. Huberman acknowledges her courage in saying "auf Wiedersehen" to her family.

O ne afternoon in Germany, Huberman auditions a handsome, young German violinist from Hamburg, Raphael Broches. Impressed with his playing, Huberman invites him to join the orchestra.

"I am honored that you have invited me, Mr. Huberman. I have idolized you my entire life. I would like very much to accept," Broches says. "But I am working on my PhD degree here, and I hope to finish it before I leave Germany."

"Mr. Broches," Huberman says, "the choice is yours, of course. But I'm sure you have experienced, firsthand, the dangerous developments in Germany for our people. No one knows what's going on in these Nazis' minds, but I believe the day may come, without warning, when you'll have no opportunity to leave Germany. And if you stay, you cannot work, so a PhD is worthless here. I am offering you a way, with other like-minded Jews, to use your talent in a country filled with music-loving and culture-starved people."

Broches falls silent, as if pondering his decision. After a few moments, he puts out his hand. "Mr. Huberman, I understand and I accept your offer, but with the caveat that you will allow me to return to Germany to finish and defend my PhD dissertation when I need to?"

A serious look crosses Bronislaw's face. "This will be your decision. But I must express my reservations in advance, Mr. Broches. Let me say, returning to Germany at a later time could be inauspicious. Come to Palestine for our first season, and we can revisit this idea afterward. I promise I will not block you, though I will try very hard to convince you otherwise."

Huberman also meets Horst Salomon during his time spent recruiting in Germany. Horst is a highly skilled French-horn player, one of the best in Europe. He was once a part of the Berlin Philharmonic, but is now employed with the Jewish Kulturbund. He is also a champion weight lifter, and is scheduled to compete in Berlin's 1936 Summer Olympic Games. He plans to leave Germany immediately after the games, and has several job offers already.

When Huberman hears Horst play, he knows he is one of the best horn players he has ever heard and immediately offers him a first-horn position in the orchestra.

"I would very much like the opportunity to work with you, Mr. Huberman, to become a part of the new orchestra," he says. "I will be able to leave Germany immediately after the Summer Games. May I ask you, sir, would it be possible to provide passage for my parents to Palestine?"

"I will use all my influence to try to secure papers for your parents, too," Huberman says.

"May I also recommend my friend Heinrich Schiefer, a fellow player in the Kulturbund?" Horst asks. "Heinrich plays the trombone exceedingly well."

When Huberman meets with German Jewish trombonist Heinrich Schiefer, he is impressed with his playing and invites him to join the orchestra as well.

"I am already thirty years old," Schiefer tells Huberman. "If I go to Palestine and become part of your orchestra, I will be too old to return and play again in the Berlin Philharmonic when the crisis in Germany ends."

"I know it's a difficult decision," Huberman says.

Heinrich closes his eyes, staying silent for a moment.

"I accept your offer, Mr. Huberman, even if doing so means I must say good-bye to Germany forever."

I n spite of Dr. Singer's objections, Bronislaw and Steinberg continue to recruit musicians from the Kulturbund. While in Germany, he auditions a flutist, Uri Toeplitz, who plays with the Frankfurt Kulturbund. Uri was a mathematics and musicology student in Germany until 1933, when the universities in Bonn and Cologne became "aryanized," forcing him to withdraw. Huberman invites Uri to join the orchestra, and also to become a member of the orchestra's board.

They meet one afternoon in a local café, sipping coffee and talking.

"I want to know more about your new orchestra," Uri says. "Will you hire a permanent conductor or depend instead on guest conductors?"

"I have not decided, Uri."

"Have you chosen the maestro to conduct the opening concerts?"

"No," Bronislaw says, "I haven't."

"Well, Mr. Huberman, I don't mean to pry, but who would you like to invite?"

Rather than display his impatience with the intensely curious Uri, Bronislaw decides to indulge him.

"Arturo Toscanini," he says, smiling.

"Toscanini, sir!" Uri exclaims.

"Do you think Toscanini is not a good choice, Uri?" Huberman says as he plays along.

"Yes, of course he's a good choice! But, sir, Toscanini is the most famous conductor in the entire world!"

"Yes, I know, Uri, and that's exactly why I would choose him."

O n a trip to Hungary, Huberman meets eighteen-year-old violinist Lorand Fenyves, a student at Liszt Academy, a musician purported to be a wunderkind. He arranges the young man's audition at a Budapest hotel.

Lorand bows slightly as he walks into the small salon off the lobby and sees Huberman and several others, sitting on couches and chairs, pads and pencils in front of them.

"What will you play, Herr Fenyves?" Huberman asks.

"I am here, sir, because Professor Jenő Hubay suggested I come and play Bach for you."

"Ah . . . Bach," Huberman says, nodding for Fenyves to begin.

Fenyves lifts his violin, closes his eyes, and begins to play a partita. When he finishes, a moment of silence fills the room.

"You play beautifully," Bronislaw tells him. "I am very glad indeed Professor Hubay sent you to me to audition."

"*Audition*, sir?" Fenyves asks.

"Yes," Huberman says. "Perhaps you were not told. I am in Budapest to audition musicians for my new orchestra in Palestine."

"*Palestine?*" Fenyves asks.

"Yes, Lorand, I'd like to invite you to move to Palestine to join the Palestine Symphony. We are planning our opening season this fall. Will you come join me on this adventure that I promise will be one of the greatest journeys of your life?"

"Herr Huberman, I am overwhelmed by this honor. But, sir, I wish you had invited me earlier."

"Why is that?" Huberman asks.

"I have already signed a contract with the Göteborgs Symfoniker. I will be leaving shortly to go to Sweden."

"I know the Göteborgs Symfoniker, and if you decide to come with me, I will take care of everything to do with your contract with them. It's of no concern," Huberman says. "Why don't you think about my offer?"

That evening, Lorand Fenyves talks with his father about Mr. Huberman's invitation.

"I am interested, Father, in perhaps becoming a part of the new Palestine Symphony," Lorand says. "Mr. Huberman told me the orchestra plans to employ only Europe's finest Jewish musicians."

"No, son, you do not want to go to Palestine. The country is a desert without culture. Anyway, you must honor your commitment to the Göteborgs Symfoniker. Go to Sweden, Lorand, not to Palestine—of all places!"

"But this new orchestra sounds like an opportunity to build something, Father, and I would like to work with Mr. Huberman," Lorand explains.

"I want to see you and your sister far away from Budapest, Lorand. You are not safe here with violent Nazi youth squads preying on Jews. You will be safe in Sweden, and surely have a good life there. The orchestra is established. You can see to your sister's needs as well. Starting an orchestra in Palestine is a complete roll of the dice, my son. For all of his power and fame, even Huberman may not be able to do this. It's a gamble on your lives."

Lorand's father listens to his son and finally says: "If you want to go to Palestine instead of Sweden, I won't stop you. But I will insist that you convince Huberman to take your sister, too, or you both go to Sweden."

"But, Father," Lorand says, "Mr. Huberman invited me, not Alice."

"Alice is also an accomplished musician, Lorand. Huberman must hire her, too."

For the next few sleepless nights, Lorand wrestles with the decision to accept or reject the invitation. He decides to ask the opinion of Felix Weingartner, a conductor he greatly admires.

Without hesitation, Maestro Weingartner tells him: "Lorand, Huberman is forging a most brilliant image for his future project. I urge you to break your contract with the Göteborgs Symfoniker and to accept this unique opportunity to play with the best musicians of Europe."

"Herr Weingartner," Lorand says, somewhat surprised by the maestro's answer, "you are recommending that I break my contract with the well-established Göteborgs Symfoniker and become a musician in Palestine with an orchestra not yet created?"

"Yes, Lorand!" Weingartner says. "I encourage you to do just that, and to leave Budapest quickly before the violence and anti-Semitism grow even worse."

Lorand walks home, wondering if Huberman will agree to bring his sister to Palestine as well. He telephones Huberman.

"I accept your offer, Mr. Huberman," he says. "But with one condition."

"And what is that condition?" Huberman asks.

"My sister, Alice, who is four years older than me, must go to Palestine, too."

"I see," Huberman says. "Is your sister a musician?"

"Yes, sir. Alice plays the violin."

"We do not need another violinist, Lorand," Huberman tells him. "But we really need violists."

"Oh, no problem, Alice is also a violist," he blurts out.

"Oh, oh, I see," Huberman says.

Lorand sucks in his breath, holding it, and waiting for Huberman's answer. He knows he cannot go to Palestine with his father's blessing if Alice is not invited, too.

"Well, in that case, Lorand, we must take Alice with us to Palestine."

When Lorand returns home, he tells his father about his conversation with Huberman.

"I had hoped you would choose Sweden, Lorand," his father tells him. "But, son, you alone must make the decisions that will affect your life. I am happy you've arranged for Alice to accompany you. I will support you in this decision. At least Mr. Huberman will take you out of Hungary."

When Lorand tells his sister that Herr Huberman has offered her a position in the Palestine Symphony, Alice is speechless.

"Mr. Huberman wants *me* to come to Palestine?" she asks.

"Yes, Alice. He wants you to play the viola."

"The viola!" Alice laughs. "Lorand, you know perfectly well I've never played the viola in my life! You told Mr. Huberman I was a violist?"

"Yes, Alice," he says. "So I suggest you learn to play it quickly. We sail to Palestine this summer!"

CHAPTER 59

Time Is Running Out!

Italy and Germany [are] the most influential countries in Europe,
and all the rest of Europe [should] revolve around this "axis."

Benito Mussolini, 1936[1]

Bronislaw Huberman listens with alarm to the news of the ever-increasing persecution of Jews in Germany and the rapid spread of anti-Semitism throughout Europe. He resigns his teaching post in Vienna, enabling him to dedicate all of his time, energy, and resources to establishing the Palestine Symphony. Despite the fact that he is Jewish, the Viennese city fathers express deep regret upon hearing that Bronislaw Huberman, one of their shining beacons of culture, is leaving his prestigious teaching position in Vienna. The announcement appears in the *New York Times*, stating: "The news was received with dismay by the musical public of Vienna, where the violinist has been a popular idol for years."[2]

Huberman is able to focus his efforts to recruit musicians for his orchestra, traveling more widely and auditioning players in Austria, Czechoslovakia, France, Georgia, Italy, Latvia, the Netherlands, Russia, Switzerland, Croatia, Ukraine, and his birthplace, Poland.

For his Poland auditions, Huberman enlists the help of his friend Jacob Surowicz, a violinist from Warsaw he met in Palestine in 1929. To begin auditions, Jacob contacts Jewish members from the Warsaw Symphony, an orchestra that is 40 percent Jewish.

The evening before auditions in Poland, Huberman lies in bed, pondering the fairness of his recruiting decisions, since he personally knows so many of Poland's musicians.

"Jacob," he tells Surowicz the next morning, "in order to remain impartial and fair, I will turn my back when I listen to each player. Bring out the candidates without introducing them to me. I want to make sure my selections are based solely on musicianship."

One morning, during the Warsaw auditions, Surowicz brings an entire family of musicians to Huberman—a father and three sons. Without seeing or meeting any of them, Huberman is so impressed with their musicianship, that he invites all four to join.

It is only after the audition that Huberman learns that all four are from the same family.

"Such excellent musicians in *one* family!" he exclaims.

Pesach Ginzburg, the father, is a violist. His three sons, Bloeslaw, Alfred, and Łódź, are a violinist, a cellist, and a timpanist. Overwhelmed by the invitation to join the Palestine Symphony, Pesach tells Huberman he had explored the possibility of his family moving to Palestine in 1929, to flee the toxic anti-Semitism plaguing their orchestra at that time. But he was unable to find an appropriate level of musical employment there.

Speaking in Polish, and with great emotion, Huberman tells Pesach: "Mr. Ginzburg, our orchestra, and the Jewish community in Palestine, will benefit greatly from having you and your sons there. And, please know that I will arrange for each of you to bring your wife and children."

Pesach Ginzburg takes Huberman's hand in his, looking directly into his eyes.

"My family is most grateful to you, Mr. Huberman," he says. "We thank you for this opportunity. Anti-Semitism in Poland has been terrible for years, and it is getting worse. With the violence and threats growing, we are eager to leave Europe, and honored to follow you to Palestine."

Bronislaw is so impressed with the many musicians he hears in Poland that he recruits more players from Poland than any other country.

CHAPTER 60

The Growing Musical Hodgepodge

*I don't know whether the people in Palestine are aware of it: for
me the main aspect of the orchestra is not the local Zionistic one
[and] neither that of charity. It is the outlook of the prestige of the
Jewry of the world, and of its cultural defense against the igno-
minious lies of Hitlerism, which counts most for me.*

Bronislaw Huberman

After many auditioning trips throughout Europe, Huberman has managed
to recruit only fifty-three suitable musicians of the seventy he needs for the
orchestra. All the players, as well as their family members, begin to sell
their houses, cars, furniture, and other possessions, making plans to sail to
Palestine early that summer.

Huberman makes a list of the orchestra chairs he needs to fill. He records the recruits' names and the instruments they play. The list has filled
up steadily, but not quickly enough. Knowing autumn's opening concert
date is rapidly approaching, he must redouble his efforts to fill the seventeen remaining chairs with the top-flight players he needs to realize his
vision.

For new recruits and their family members, Huberman applies for individual permanent certificates, and arranges living accommodations in
Tel Aviv. Already, the potential exiles number in the hundreds.

Huberman invites several of his master students from the music school
in Vienna, violinists David Grunschlag and Henry Haftel, who will both
ultimately sit in the coveted first-chair violin position.

Austria is still two years from the Nazi invasion, so there was as yet no urgency for David to get his family out of Vienna. Huberman offered to try to obtain certificates for his parents, but they had teenaged daughters to look after, pianist Rosi and Toni, so they chose to stay in Vienna.

One evening, Huberman notices Ida sitting by the parlor fireplace, smiling and shaking her head.

"What amuses you, Ida?" he asks.

"I was just thinking about the new orchestra, Broni. You have put together a remarkable and unimaginable hodgepodge of people, a most unusual mixture of the world's finest musicians!"

"What do you mean, Ida?"

"Think about it, Broni. You have twenty concertmasters—heads of sections, first-chair players—from orchestras all over Europe. I am discovering through my correspondence with them that many of these musicians have exhausting demands and extraordinarily large egos. I believe that trying to manage them all together might become quite challenging."

"Yes, Ida! I know what you mean. No symphony in the entire world has so many first-chair players filling so many positions in the orchestra. They will surely be difficult, but I can only imagine the quality of sound our string section will produce. They will be the envy of orchestras all over the world!"

"Also, Bronislaw, consider that the musicians speak different languages. Some will, no doubt, have difficulty communicating with each other. And no one speaks a word of Hebrew, even though they are moving to Palestine!"

"I'm sure they will all manage in German," he responds. "Ironic, isn't it, that they flee Germany's madmen only to speak her language in the Holy Land!"

Huberman laughs. "Still, I see what you mean, Ida! 'Hodgepodge'— that's a good word for the new orchestra."

CHAPTER 61

The Manager

There are moments one never forgets. This was one of them. A small man, dark, with graying hair, spoke shyly, almost nervously, feeling for his words, of things that are part of cultural history. A man quite unassuming, simply dressed in grey flannel trousers and a tweed jacket of warm brown. He was Bronislaw Huberman, perhaps the greatest living master of the violin. . . . I was overwhelmed by the simplicity of greatness. I basked in the warmth of a man too big to "show off."

from the *South African Jewish Times*[1]

Heinrich Simon, the Jewish head of the German newspaper *Frankfurter Zeitung*, a paper founded three generations before by his grandfather Leopold Sonnemann, is a lifelong friend of Huberman. After Hitler comes to power, Heinrich stays in Frankfurt for eighteen months, then gives up his job, escaping to London.

Huberman travels to London, and the two men meet at the Hyde Park Hotel. Enjoying the view of the park before them, they reminisce about their past experiences.

With enthusiasm, Huberman shares with Simon his dream of an orchestra in Palestine.

"This orchestra will play a triple role," he says. "First and foremost, it will hold up a fist against Nazism for the entire world to see! Second, it will give the struggling, pioneer country of Palestine an opportunity to hear first-class music. And third, it will absorb the best of the refugee artists who have been ousted from their posts by the Nazi racial laws. These musicians will also teach at the music school we plan to establish."

"Your idea has much merit, Bronislaw," Heinrich says.

"I have recruited two good friends to help me with the responsibility in Palestine," Huberman says. "A top lawyer in Jerusalem, Mr. S. Horowitz, and Lieutenant Colonel F. H. Kisch, former head of the Jewish Agency."

"It is obviously vital for your project to have such able leadership, Bronislaw."

"But, Heinrich, I need someone to carry out my artistic policy."

"Who did you have in mind?" Simon asks.

"You, Heinrich. I have *you* in mind. I want you to move to Palestine and supervise this endeavor for me."

Simon blinks his eyes several times, hesitating before he speaks.

"Bronislaw, you know I am not a Zionist. But I've always been a conscious Jew, and keenly interested in the efforts to revive the ancient homeland. I've had a longing to see Palestine myself, but I have never traveled to such a remote place."

"I know that, Heinrich," Huberman says. "But I know you, and I know you can do this. Just think of it. You, in Palestine, with the world falling apart in Europe."

"I must admit, having a hand in developing a refugee orchestra in the Holy Land is extremely interesting," Simon says, staring into the distance as if in deep thought. Huberman says nothing, and watches his old friend's face carefully.

After several moments, Simon puts out his hand to Bronislaw. "I don't have to think about it, Bronislaw. I'll do it!"

Within weeks, Heinrich Simon leaves London and sets sail in a small French vessel on the Mediterranean, the first lap of his voyage to Palestine. Stopping in Italy, he again meets with Huberman, and is anxious to hear more about the new orchestra. They walk up and down the beautiful hotel gardens on the slopes of the Pincio.

"Modern Palestine is young and vital," Huberman tells him. "And despite being thousands of miles from Europe, in the hearts of these pioneer people, the hunger for good music is astounding. I know they eagerly await the creation of this orchestra. Palestine will have one of the finest orchestras in the world. It will be Hitler's gift to the Jews." Huberman laughs. "How strange are the workings of fate!"

"Do we have a place in Tel Aviv to rehearse and give concerts?" Simon asks.

"Not yet. I have been too busy to attend to it. But it needs to be taken care of immediately."

"I will begin that search when I arrive in Palestine," Simon says.

That evening, Huberman gives a concert at the Augusteo. From his complimentary box seat, Simon is reminded how much the Italian people love his old friend's playing. The Augusteo is so crowded, Simon notices, that people who could secure no other seats are crouched uncomfortably on wooden benches under the orchestra, listening with awe and delight to the music.

One week later, Simon stands in the prow of a ship, jostled by excited young immigrants and trembling old men as each catches his first glimpse of Mount Carmel.

When the anchor drops in Haifa, Simon meets a group of customs officials who chatter in Hebrew like magpies. He feels excited to step into Palestine for the first time.

CHAPTER 62

The Maestro

A driven artist who strove for relative objectivity in performance, Toscanini was beloved by audiences for his thrillingly authoritative accounts of the standard operatic and orchestral repertory—even as he was feared by musicians who . . . [often] suffered his storied wrath.

David Mermelstein, *Wall Street Journal*[1]

By early February, Huberman knows he must find a conductor for the opening season. He wants to invite Toscanini, but feels he has waited far too long for the maestro to schedule a performance that is set to take place in a few short months.

"I have an important decision to make—the conductor for the opening season," Bronislaw tells Ida.

"And who are you considering, Broni?"

"You know perfectly well, Ida. Just one person, Arturo Toscanini. If he accepts, that will send a powerful anti-Hitler, anti-Fascist statement to the whole world."

Ida says nothing.

"Do you think Toscanini will decline, Ida?"

"How can we know, Broni?"

"I can think of several reasons why he would decline. Toscanini is the most famous conductor in the world! He is booked for years in advance by the very best orchestras, paying him absolute top dollar. That's why. So even if he wants to come, he has legions of obligations to fulfill, concerts around the world. Why would a man be willing to cancel everything and come to the middle of nowhere to lead an unknown, untried orchestra of immigrant Jews that can hardly afford to pay him?"

Huberman stops, tapping his foot in frustration.

"Also remember that Toscanini is seventy years old. Can he physically handle the long trip to Palestine, as well as the heat and weeks of nonstop performances in different cities?"

"That is certainly a consideration, Broni."

"Unfortunately, I can think of more difficulties, Ida. Toscanini will, no doubt, want to bring his wife, and we will have to provide them with expensive accommodations. He is accustomed to the finest hotels and the most lavish meals. Where in Palestine can we house them comfortably, and in an elegant fashion?"

Ida shakes her head.

Bronislaw remains quiet for a long time, rubbing his chin.

"Ida, we should invite the maestro in spite of the obstacles."

Ida smiles when he tells her his decision. "Broni, he might surprise us, and say yes."

"I agree," he says. "We will face each obstacle, one at a time."

Bronislaw writes Toscanini, asking if he might come to his home to discuss a musical matter that will have a far-reaching cultural and political impact.

As he tries to sleep that night, Huberman recalls Toscanini's well-known feelings about fascism, how he received a beating rather than agreeing to play Mussolini's Fascist anthem, how he canceled his contract for the 1933 Bayreuth Festival, publicly rejecting Hitler's personal request.

This is a man who may surprise us. This podium will give him an opportunity to make a bold, worldwide statement against Fascism.

Bronislaw is gambling that Toscanini believes that art and music no longer transcend the affairs of state, and that music must, and can, be called upon to serve political agendas.

CHAPTER 63

In the Meantime

Cruelty impresses. Cruelty and raw force. The simple man in the street is impressed only by brutal force and ruthlessness. Terror is the most effective political means.

Adolf Hitler[1]

Hitler continues to use dictatorial power and raw brutality to control Germany, rewarding friends who support him and punishing those who do not. Nazi rulers show no compassion in their treatment of Jews and others they consider subhuman. Calculating and cruel, German leaders unleash malicious treatment upon non-Aryans, with no accountability or fear of retribution. Jews sense that at any time, their homes could be raided, searched, and ransacked, their family members beaten, arrested, and imprisoned. Gestapo agents are everywhere, watching and listening, encouraged to find anyone hinting of disloyalty to Hitler's government. Swastika flags, by law, must wave above German homes and businesses. Jews live in terror. Friends betray each other and trust no one, not even their closest family members. Rumors run rampant in Nazi Germany, often costing a father his job, a family their home, and a neighbor her life. Failure to give the *Hitlergruß*, the Nazi salute, expresses opposition, often bringing punishment. Everyone is afraid, slow to resist, and frightened into obedience.

The Jewish musicians who previously thought Nazism, if given enough time, would blow over, have started to change their minds. Many who declined Huberman's auditions for the orchestra try to find him, now asking to fill chairs in his orchestra, hoping to find a way out of Germany with their loved ones.

As fascism and fear spread out from Germany, Jewish musicians across Europe contact Huberman, hoping to be considered, hoping to escape the approaching horror.

Huberman has a strong sense that another war is coming, and that the world once again will explode with violence. Visions of the coming apocalypse send chills down his spine. He feels deeply that things will get worse still for Jews. The clock ticks on his project.

I n the early weeks of 1936, Heinrich Simon travels to Tel Aviv and begins his search for a building to host the summer rehearsals and the opening concerts in October. But few buildings in the city offer him any promise. Most are too small, too dilapidated, or unavailable to rent or buy. He continues the search, sharing the pressure Huberman feels, combing the city for a suitable structure to use by summer. As frustration mounts, he is taken to a rough area he's never visited in Tel Aviv. After spending an entire day there, Simon telephones Bronislaw.

"I can find no place suitable for us," he tells Huberman. "The only possibility I have found is a building in the port area, called the Levant Pavilion, which was part of the International Fair in North Tel Aviv. But it's a real mess."

"How many people can it seat?" Huberman asks. "How much construction will be needed to make it work for us?"

"We could probably seat twenty-five hundred to three thousand people," Heinrich says. "But the building is in very bad condition, greatly in need of repair. Sections of the roof are missing, and birds have nested inside it. Rain has badly damaged the interior. Only a few rows of the auditorium are equipped with seats, the rest will require folding chairs. Also, as it is near the port, noise from the docks could present a problem."

"This is not good news, Heinrich. Have you checked the hall's acoustics?

Where are the front doors located? That makes a tremendous difference in the quality of a performance."

"I don't know," Heinrich says. "But I do know we will need much time and money to make the needed repairs. But, Bronislaw, I don't see any other choice. The Levant Pavilion is available. What do you want me to do?"

"Take it!" Bronislaw tells him. "Call a contractor, hire construction workers, buy building materials, and do whatever you must to ready it for the summer rehearsals. If you will take care of the Pavilion, Heinrich, I can remain in Europe, auditioning. We still have many chairs to fill."

Pushed out of the Berlin Philharmonic, horn player Horst Salomon spends his days preparing his body to compete in Berlin's Summer Olympic Games. Daily, he lifts weights, squats and bends over the bar. With the strength of Samson, his deltoids rippling, the muscles of his body pushed to their limit, he is determined to win weight-lifting gold for Germany.

Horst's parents have already packed their belongings, hanging on to the possibility Huberman expressed to Horst that they could travel to Palestine with their son after the Olympic games.

Horst is in the best physical shape of his life. His hard work has paid off and he has been accepted, his participation in the Olympics confirmed. But in early February, he is completely blindsided, devastated by the cruelty of the German authorities. When he receives a letter from the German Olympic Committee, he expects to find instructions for the competition. But as he reads the message, his body sinks to the floor.

That evening, Horst tells his parents the news. "I have been forbidden to participate in the Berlin games. The committee has canceled my place in the weight-lifting competition. They are allowing only the racially superior and pure-blooded Germans to participate, and it's come to their attention that I am of the Jewish race."

"Only Aryans can represent our fatherland at the Olympics?" his mother cries.

"Yes, Mother. Only blond-haired, blue-eyed, pure Germans can honor *my* fatherland."

Horst smashes the wall beside him with his fist, leaving a deep imprint. "For the first time, I look forward to leaving Germany."

CHAPTER 64

The Maestro Responds

What have you, "real Germans," done to rid Germany and humanity of this disgrace against an entire defenseless minority?

Bronislaw Huberman

When Arturo Toscanini receives Huberman's letter asking to meet him face-to-face, he invites him to his home on the island of Lago Mara, Italy.

On Saturday, February 22, 1936, when Ida and Bronislaw arrive at the Toscaninis' home, a servant shows them into the parlor, where the heavy-set and formidable wife of the anti-Fascist conductor orders tea, waiting with them for Arturo to come downstairs.

The maestro soon arrives, showering Bronislaw and Ida with an enthusiastic Italian welcome. He listens attentively as Bronislaw shares his feelings about and vision of a first-class, all-Jewish orchestra and school in Palestine.

"Maestro," Huberman asks, "will you come with us to Jerusalem, Tel Aviv, Haifa, Alexandria, and Cairo, and stand up with me against fascism by conducting in front of the whole world this Palestine Symphony of immigrant refugee Jews in its opening concert season this October?"

Toscanini is silent. Raising his eyebrows, he looks deeply into Bronislaw's eyes. Then he jumps to his feet, shouting: "Yes! Yes! Yes! I will most certainly do this! It is my duty to fight for the cause of artists persecuted by the Nazis! And to stand up against fascism for the whole world to see! I will stay as long as it takes, Mr. Huberman, and conduct this series with your Jewish immigrants.[1]

"And, Bronislaw," he continues. "I will conduct the Nocturne and

Scherzo from Mendelssohn's *Midsummer Night's Dream*! And why?" he shouts. "So the music of the Jew Felix Mendelssohn will again be played by German Jews for the world to hear!"

The maestro watches Ida's mouth drop open and her eyes grow wide. Bronislaw laughs out loud, stands up, and claps his hands.

"It is the duty of everyone to fight and help in this cause according to one's means!" Toscanini shouts, his eyes ablaze with fire.

"You, Maestro, have made me a very happy man!" Huberman says. "And, sir, I apologize for the shortness of time. I didn't think you would be free."

"Oh! Bronislaw!" he says, waving his arms in the air. "I am certainly *not* free! But I will cancel all the concerts necessary in order to conduct your new orchestra in the fall! And do not be concerned about finances. I will pay my own expenses, and conduct without charge—as a gift to you, your musicians, Palestine, and especially to Adolf Hitler!"

"Thank you, Maestro!" Huberman says, grasping Toscanini's hand, a rare wide smile covering his face. "This will be an historic moment in the struggle against Nazism, and in the building up of Palestine, for Jewish people everywhere!"

Bronislaw immediately announces Arturo Toscanini's acceptance, producing newspaper headlines the world over.

"Maestro Arturo Toscanini is willing to conduct the inauguration concerts in Tel Aviv, Jerusalem, and Haifa," he tells his staff, musicians, and crowds of clamoring newspaper reporters.

"This support by the greatest living conductor, Arturo Toscanini, a non-Jew, makes me particularly happy," Huberman exclaims. "It will enable me to lead this institution in the same spirit with which I have been fighting and working in Europe for many years."

Huberman asks Ida to type a letter to David Ben-Gurion, director of the Jewish Agency in Palestine.

"Tell Ben-Gurion that Toscanini has accepted my invitation," Huberman says. "Remind him of the great importance of this undertaking, the prestige Toscanini's involvement will bring to the Jewish National movement, as well as the help it will give to, and the money it will provide for, Jewish musicians made destitute by Germany's anti-Semitic policy. Also, inform him that Toscanini's concerts will bring in money for Palestine from the tourist traffic."

Bronislaw stops his dictation and spends a moment in thought.

"I want Ben-Gurion to know that we plan to make the orchestra independent of any financial support from the Jewish Agency. But tell him we need his assistance with the musicians' emigration expenses when they arrive in Palestine with their families. Let him know the Zionist bodies in Germany are willing to help, and suggest that he request the Zionist Federation to offer financial assistance as well."

CHAPTER 65

The Letter of Protest

*Divide each problem into as many parts as possible; that each part
being more easily conceived, the whole may be more intelligible.*

Descartes, *Discourse on Method*

The funds come in slowly but steadily in the first weeks of 1936, people
around the world sending large and small contributions in their effort to
support the creation of the orchestra. But even though the coffers are filling, the cash is still much less than needed.

One evening during dinner, Bronislaw and Ida discuss ways to raise the
much-needed money for the musicians' salaries, their transportation, and
accommodations.

"Ida, donations are coming in too slowly. I have concerns, I do."

"How much do we need, Broni?"

"Our deficit is over one hundred thousand dollars," he says. "How
disappointing it would be to have all the certificates promised to us, the
Levant Pavilion under construction for completion by summer, our musicians selected, packed, and ready to travel, Arturo Toscanini scheduled for
our opening concerts for no fee, and yet not have enough money to launch
the Palestine Symphony."

Shaking his head and frowning, Huberman continues. "Ida, we've come
too far to allow this dream to fail. Too many people are depending on us.
We must bring in more money. I have to give more benefit concerts and
find more donors," he says.

"Broni, you are already near the edge of physical and mental exhaustion. You will put your health at risk if you try to do more."

"What else can I do, Ida? We simply must raise more money."

After a few minutes of silence, Bronislaw tells her his idea. "Ida, let's go back to the United States. We will plan a tour across America, giving concerts in every major city. I will call on the American Jewish community to dig deeper. They have helped so much already. They must give more. I believe they will."

"I will make the travel and hotel arrangements, Broni," Ida says, and walks silently to the next room.

Bronislaw closes his eyes, taking a deep breath, allowing it to escape slowly.

"This is our last chance," he says aloud. "They must give more. They must."

Calling in favors from connections made over a lifetime in music, and meeting with Jewish leaders in New York, Chicago, and Los Angeles, Huberman schedules a nonstop series of fund-raising luncheon speeches, one-on-one meetings, cocktail-hour presentations, and benefit concerts of all sizes, starting at New York's Carnegie Hall. He covers every available venue America has to offer. The unprecedented schedule calls for sixty concerts in eighty days, traveling by bus and train across the United States, each stop a fund-raiser for the Palestine Symphony.

Ida packs multiple suitcases and a trunk, and prepares the double instrument case that Bronislaw designed to carry his four expensive Tourte bows and both of his violins, the beloved Stradivarius that he's played since childhood and his Guarneri del Gesù.

After the long, exhausting trip, Bronislaw and Ida arrive in New York City and immediately begin fund-raising. By day, Bronislaw addresses groups of people in social clubs, colleges, and churches, explaining his dream and asking for help. At night, he plays in concert halls, church and school auditoriums, and, of course, major performance halls. He speaks from the stage at every stop, telling the story of the Palestine Symphony and seeking donations for his dream.

People do respond in every city, in every state, and more than fifteen thousand additional dollars are deposited in the orchestra's bank account. They are still eighty-five thousand dollars short, but the tour is not over.

While in the States, by reading the daily newspapers, Bronislaw watches the unfolding events in Europe closely, becoming greatly distressed when he hears of the escalation of violence Jews are suffering in Germany. He is horrified when he learns of the large number of *non*-Nazi German intellectuals allowing the persecution to take place right under their noses, neither standing up to protect Jews nor publicly addressing the blatant oppression. It seems there is no one in Germany speaking out against Hitler.

Deeply frustrated, Huberman writes a long open letter to Britain's *Manchester Guardian*:

"To the editor," he dictates to Ida as she types. "Sir, I shall be glad if you will print the following 'open letter,' which I have addressed to the German intellectuals.

"Since the publication of the German racial ordinances, a document of barbarism, countless people have been thrown in gaols and concentration camps, exiled, killed, and driven to suicide. What have you, 'real Germans,' done to rid Germany and humanity of this disgrace against an entire defenseless minority?"

As Bronislaw continues to dictate the letter, his voice becomes louder and his face redder with anger and indignation.

"Before the whole world I accuse you, you non-Nazi German intellectuals, as those truly guilty of all these Nazi crimes. And, of this despicable breakdown of a great people, a destruction that shames the whole white race. It is not the first time in history that the gutter has reached out for power, but it remained for the German intellectuals to assist the gutter to achieve success. Germany, you people of poets and thinkers, the whole world, not only the world of your enemies, but the world of your friends, waits in amazed anxiety for your word of liberations."

Ida posts the letter that afternoon, and she and Huberman wait anxiously to hear the world's response when the *Manchester Guardian* publishes it.[1]

CHAPTER 66

The Announcement in the New York Times

I have learnt the lesson that has been forced upon me . . . that I am not a German, not a European, indeed perhaps scarcely a human being . . . but I am a Jew.

Arnold Schoenberg,
a Jewish-German composer and teacher[1]

In late February, the *New York Times* publishes the story that Arturo Toscanini will conduct the first concerts of the Palestine Symphony.

"Toscanini to Conduct New Orchestra of Exiles in Palestine," the headline states.

"Conductor Accepts Invitation for Opening Symphony in Tel-Aviv in October—Declares It His Duty to 'Fight' for Cause of Artists Persecuted by Nazis."

Bronislaw receives scores of telegrams and letters from the world's political leaders and supporters, each congratulating him on his excellent choice of conductor, each convinced Toscanini's acceptance will make an important political statement about Hitler and fascism.

Traveling throughout the States, Huberman rides the wave of enthusiasm, using the opportunity to write articles that American and international editors are thrilled to publish.

"Every concert we perform," he writes, "when broadcast to the world through the new Palestine radio, will be an eloquent accusation against the barbarism of the Hitler regime.

"It is this platform," Huberman continues, "that attracted Toscanini to accept my invitation to conduct the first concert tour at the end of October, helping me fight and work for a spirit of international understanding and brotherhood in Europe."

When Wilhelm Furtwängler hears that Toscanini has accepted Huberman's invitation to conduct the opening season of his orchestra of Jewish refugees, he begins to tremble. Pacing the floor, he tries to gather the courage to face Goebbels and the Führer with the sensational and politically catastrophic news.

"My Führer," Furtwängler says softly when they meet, "I have very bad news to—"

"I already know about Toscanini!" Hitler shouts, his face turning scarlet and his hands balling into tight fists. "He refuses our invitation to conduct at Bayreuth, yet he accepts Huberman's invitation to conduct that . . . that orchestra of filthy Jews!"

The Führer pounds his fist on the table beside him, each strike louder, harder, and more violent than the one before.

Not knowing what to do and feeling a knot of fear rising in his throat, Furtwängler swallows hard, bows slightly, and backs slowly out of the room.

In New York City, nightclub fiddler Julian Altman slips into his scruffy tuxedo and spits on his hands to smooth his short brown hair. Grabbing his violin, he scurries through the backstreets of the busy city, stepping into a small nightclub located near Carnegie Hall. He waits in the wings for his signal to play for the few customers sitting in dark corner booths.

When he pulls the bow across the violin strings, producing some music, it evokes little attention from the smoking, drinking customers.

A petty thief, when not locked up in one of the city's jails, Julian plays his fiddle at church gigs, small nightclubs, and on busy street corners, trying to make enough money to feed and shelter himself, his wife, and his aging mother.

As usual, he arrives home late, a few coins richer, a few drinks drunker.

Huberman wakes early, dresses, and meets with as many wealthy Jews in New York as he can, pouring out his heart to each one, describing his dream, and depleting more of his energy with each telling. Each day is different.

Some people pledge to send money, but fail to follow through. Others listen to his entire plea silently, and then refuse to help. Some schedule an appointment but cancel at the last moment or just fail to show up. And some write a check, but usually a small one.

Huberman rushes from meeting to meeting, trying to fill each day with engagements. Late each night, after a concert and fund-raising pitch, he collapses into bed, his stomach upset, his head pounding, and his muscles aching, but determined to work even harder the next day.

"You are heading for a breakdown," Ida warns him. "But I'm proud of you, Broni. You are becoming a public symbol of protest. Your articles and speeches are appearing in newspapers across the world!"

"My public outcry is having little effect, Ida. Few listen, and even fewer seem to care."

On February 27, Bronislaw practices for an hour and goes to bed earlier than usual.

He kisses Ida's cheek. "I'm going to try to sleep. The Carnegie Hall performance tomorrow night makes me nervous."

"Rest well, my dear Broni," Ida says. "You have forty-one more concerts in the next fifty-eight days."

Conductor Wilhelm Furtwängler, who, despite many options to work elsewhere, stayed in Germany, conducting for Hitler and his Nazi commanders. Though he never joined the Nazi party, the enmity he created by conducting the Berlin Philharmonic right up to 1945 would haunt him the rest of his life. © *Bittmann / CORBIS*

Huberman and Wilhelm Steinberg at the Ramleh Airport. December 1936.
Courtesy of the Murray S. Katz Photo Archives of the IPO

Toscanini and Huberman attending a rehearsal at the Levant Fair Hall
during the preparation for the first concert. December 1936.
Courtesy of the Murray S. Katz Photo Archives of the IPO

Renovation of the original Palestine Symphony concert hall. December 1936.
Rudi Weissenstein, The PhotoHouse

Conductor Wilhelm Steinberg
prepares the orchestra before
Toscanini's arrival. December 1936.
*Courtesy of the Murray S. Katz Photo Archives
of the IPO / Photographer: S. Sebba*

Hungarian born, Lorand Fenyves,
age sixteen, in a publicity photograph
taken when he graduated from
the Franz Liszt Academy of Music.
Courtesy of the Fenyves and Reichard families

Dov Ginzburg, tympanist of the Palestine Symphony and later the Israel Philharmonic
Orchestra, clowns for the camera to demonstrate the sometimes difficult conditions under
which the orchestra had to play. *Courtesy of Gina Ginzburg Tavor*

The enigmatic first conductor of the Palestine Symphony, Arturo Toscanini.
© The Estate of Robert Hupka, 2015

A billboard advertisement for the first Tel Aviv concert on December 26, 1936.
Courtesy of the IPO Archives

The Palestine Symphony with Maestro Toscanini. December 1936.
Rudi Weissenstein, The PhotoHouse

Toscanini and Huberman embrace after the first concert. December 1936.
Rudi Weissenstein, The PhotoHouse

Huberman and orchestra members after the first concert
on December 26, 1936, celebrating at the Kaete Dan Hotel in Tel Aviv.
Courtesy of the Murray S. Katz Photo Archives of the IPO

Huberman and Toscanini on a hot day at the beach in Tel Aviv.

Huberman arriving to play a concert in Edison Cinema in Jerusalem
with a chamber orchestra of players from the Palestine Symphony.
Courtesy of the Murray S. Katz Photo Archives of the IPO

Huberman with children of Kibbutz Ein Harod. December 1938.
Courtesy of the Murray S. Katz Photo Archives of the IPO

Carnegie Hall flyer for a Bronislaw Huberman recital.
Carnegie Hall Archives

Raphael Broches, violinist with the Palestine Symphony, circa 1936–37.
Tragically, he went back to Germany and disappeared in the Holocaust.
Müller-Wesemann Collection / IGDJ Bildarchiv

Violist Dora Loeb at the home of physiologist Dr. Bruno Kisch and his wife, contralto Ruth
Kisch-Arndt in Cologne, Germany. They provided shelter and safety from the Nazis for Ms.
Loeb, but could not dissuade her from returning to Germany. She was murdered in a German concentration camp. June 1939. *Courtesy of Dr. Arnold I. Kisch*

The next morning, February 28, 1936, Julian Altman's mother makes breakfast for herself and her son. Over scrambled eggs and dry toast, she says: "It says here in the paper that that famous violinist, ah . . . Bronislaw Huberman, is playing at Carnegie Hall tonight. You should go and hear him, Julian. He might inspire you to practice more."

"I may do that, Mother," he says, attempting to smile. He tears the concert announcement from the paper and stuffs it into his pocket.

CHAPTER 67

The Concert at Carnegie Hall

Everywhere in the world, music enhances a hall, with one exception: Carnegie Hall enhances the music.

Isaac Stern[1]

The limousines of New York line up at the front of midtown Manhattan's Carnegie Hall, the world's most prestigious venue for classical music.

The women's jewel-studded evening gowns, rings, and necklaces catch the chandeliers' lights, filling the room with a rainbow of sparkles in the ornate and celebrated home of the New York Philharmonic since 1892. Several thousand music lovers pass through its terra-cotta and brownstone entrance on this night, some climbing, with great effort, the one hundred thirty seven steps to sit in the top balcony.

Ida and Bronislaw arrive early, slipping into the Fifty-Sixth Street stage entrance.

Ida straightens Bronislaw's bow tie. She gently touches his face, frowning when she notices dark circles under his eyes and the paleness of his complexion.

"You look very tired, Broni," she says.

"Yes, Ida, I am exhausted."

Ida opens his double violin case, handing him the Stradivarius and one of the Tourte bows.

"No, Ida, tonight I will play the Guarneri for the Franck and, after the intermission, switch to the Strad for the Bach and Beethoven."

Ida gently places his beloved Stradivarius into its case, giving him the Guarneri del Gesù.

Settling into a grand tier box seat, Ida greets Huberman's guests, who sit beside her and wait for the concert to begin. The houselights dim. She feels great love and pride as she watches Bronislaw walk out on the stage and bow to the audience. She delights in the loud, spontaneous applause as New Yorkers welcome him to their city and great concert hall.

When the applause fades and the hall grows quiet, the virtuoso violinist nods to the pianist to begin. After she plays a brief introduction, Bronislaw holds his head high, lifts the Guarneri to his chin, and begins to play the Franck Sonata.

The audience listens attentively to the sonata's sweetly reflective Allegretto ben moderato. After the first movement's long piano and violin introduction, the Allegro follows, a turbulent second movement.

After Bronislaw finishes playing the third movement, Ida quietly leaves her seat to join him backstage during intermission.

When she arrives, she discovers the door partially open. She walks inside, and her eyes immediately focus on the open violin case. Putting her hand on her heart, she freezes, staring at the empty place where the Stradivarius should be.

"No!" she shouts.

Dashing downstairs, she waits in the wings while Bronislaw completes the Franck, takes his first bow, and exits.

"The Stradivarius has been stolen, Broni!" she whispers in his ear as he comes offstage, her hands trembling, her voice shaking.

Ida watches in horror as Bronislaw's face turns ashen, paler than before the concert, as if drained of all blood.

"Call the police, Ida," he says. "I must finish the concert."

Struggling to breathe, her heart pounding, she alerts the authorities. Returning to her seat and sitting motionless, she watches Bronislaw reappear on the stage.

At the end of the concert, Ida joins Bronislaw in his dressing room. He sits down in a chair, lowers his head, and holds it between his hands.

"Broni!" she says, kneeling by his chair, "I am so sorry. I don't understand what happened."

A valet rushes into the dressing room. "We have called the police, Mr. Huberman," he shouts. "They are looking for it. They will find it, sir."

Ida concentrates on the valet's face. He lowers his eyes, his face turning pink.

"I'm so sorry about this," he says, avoiding her inquisitive gaze.

Suddenly Bronislaw jumps to his feet, his face blood-red, his expression instantly, drastically transformed.

"It is my own fault, Ida," he shouts, stomping his foot. "I should have known better than to leave the Strad in my dressing room! How could I have been so utterly stupid?"

Ida puts her arms around his shoulders, trying to calm him as she watches his emotions shift from violent rage to deep sorrow, back and forth, verbally scourging himself as well as the criminal who stole the instrument.

"The thief must be stupid!" Huberman shouts, bending down and looking at the bows still stored in the double violin case. "A smart thief would also have taken these expensive Tourte bows! The bows are not only valuable, but easy to sell, with no danger of arousing suspicion! The Strad is too well known. It cannot be sold on the open market."

"I am so so sorry, dear," Ida whispers again. "I know how you treasured that violin. I am sure the police will recover it, Broni."

"Let's leave now, Ida," Bronislaw says, his face and body appearing dog-tired and defeated. "I am beyond exhausted."

Ida and Bronislaw leave Carnegie Hall and return to their hotel room. They stay in close contact with the New York police all night as the whole city searches for Bronislaw Huberman's irreplaceable Gibson Stradivarius.[2]

CHAPTER 68

Mourning the Loss

One slot in the case held the Gibson Stradivarius, named—like many Strads—for an early owner, George Alfred Gibson, a prominent English violinist. The second slot held an equally precious violin made by Antonio Stradivari's Cremona colleague, Giuseppe Guarneri.

Joshua Bell[1]

The next day, February 29, Huberman waits impatiently to hear word of his violin's recovery. He grieves profoundly over the loss, fearing it is gone forever, possibly already sold to a secret buyer in some New York City back alley. He tries to put the theft behind him, but cannot. The burglar's sneaking into his private dressing room, putting his hands on the delicate Stradivarius, and whisking it away haunts him in his nightmares. Several times each day, he and Ida contact the police, hoping, yearning, for some word about the violin. But they learn nothing.

Julian Altman hides the violin at home in his bedroom closet, hoping his mother won't find it. When she goes to bed, and he is alone, he takes the instrument in his hands, running his fingers along its honey-stained wood. He grins, widens his eyes, and shakes his head in amazement.

"Such a beautiful violin, and now it's mine!" he mumbles.

Digging through a crowded bathroom cabinet, he finds an old bottle of black shoe polish. Coat after coat, he rubs the ebony polish on the

Stradivarius's ancient Cremona wood, covering it with layer upon layer of thick black lacquer. Soon he has completely concealed the beauty, majesty, and identity of the three-hundred-year-old violin.

In the midst of deep and constant mourning, Bronislaw tries to busy himself for the sake of the new orchestra, playing scheduled concerts and speaking with everyone who will listen to him explain his dream. He and Ida cross the country from coast to coast, trying desperately to raise more money.

"I am weary, Ida," Huberman finally admits. "I have met with hundreds of people, played numerous concerts, written letter after letter begging for money, and we are still eighty thousand dollars short of our goal. I can't do this much longer. My head is exploding. My body aches. My stomach is a painful mess. I can't eat or sleep. I am already on the *other side* of a nervous breakdown."

"I have been worrying about your health, Broni. You've worked much too hard in a very short time. But you've done what you can do, everything humanly possible to raise the money. You must stop for a while, rest, and protect your health. Perhaps we should postpone the orchestra's opening season, holding it in a year or two instead of this October. The postponement would give us more time to raise money, recruit musicians, and refurbish the Levant Pavilion."

"No, Ida," he says. "We cannot postpone the opening concerts. The timing is right, and everything is in place. If we wait, we might have the money but we might forfeit everything else. We must continue to move ahead. The opening concerts must happen in October."

Broni," Ida says, after reading the day's mail, "we've received a letter from Sir Arthur Wauchope, the British high commissioner in Palestine. He wants to thank you for informing him of Toscanini's acceptance of the invitation to conduct the orchestra. He offers his continued support and plans to attend the opening concert in Palestine."

"Wonderful!"

"Sir Arthur also congratulates you on your 'splendid' work.

"And, Broni," she adds as she unfolds the daily newspaper, "the *New York Times* has another article this morning about Toscanini and the orchestra, with the headline 'Toscanini Decides to Do Mendelssohn—Selects Composer Barred by Nazis for Concert in Palestine by German Exiles.'"

"The maestro's personal jab at Hitler!" Bronislaw chuckles.

"Broni, listen to this: 'Arturo Toscanini has decided to include music by Mendelssohn on his first program with the new Palestine Symphony, which he will conduct in Palestine next October. Mr. Toscanini's choice of the Nocturne and Scherzo from Mendelssohn's *Midsummer Night's Dream* was considered significant, since the Palestine Symphony is to be composed principally of outstanding German instrumentalists who have been denied the right to work in Germany.'"

"I hope Wilhelm Furtwängler, as well as the Führer, read this article," Huberman says.

When Adolf Hitler learns that Toscanini will be conducting Mendelssohn at the Palestine Symphony's opening concert season, he orders Goebbels to tear down the bronze statue of Felix Mendelssohn that stands prominently in the front of the Leipzig Gewandhaus, the city's old opera house.

"Destroy all the other statues of Jewish composers in Germany, too!" he demands.

The next morning, Ida receives a letter from Arturo Toscanini. She takes it to Bronislaw unopened.

He holds the letter in his hand for a moment and takes a deep breath.

"Ida, I am not expecting a letter from Arturo. I hope he's not ill, or must, for some reason, cancel," he says.

He opens the letter, reads it, and smiles.

"Arturo tells me he received a letter from Albert Einstein, expressing his admiration of Toscanini for agreeing to conduct the October concerts in Palestine.[2]

"What a relief. I am glad to know that Albert knows about the orchestra, and Toscanini's acceptance to conduct it," Bronislaw says.

"Isn't Professor Einstein living here in the States, Broni?"

"Yes, he lives in Princeton, New Jersey," he says.

Ida raises her eyebrows. "Broni, do you think Professor Einstein might help us raise the money we need?"

"I could never ask him, Ida."

"But, Broni, Einstein left Germany in protest of Nazism, he worked closely with you in the Pan-Europa movement, and he is an ardent Zionist as well as the most famous Jew in the world. He plays the violin, and loves music. I think he will be happy to help."

"But, Ida, so many people ask him for personal favors. And I've heard his wife, Elsa, is ill. I don't want to bother him."

"It might just be the last resort available to help launch the orchestra, Broni."

Huberman pauses and looks at Ida.

"You may be right, Ida. He *is* the most famous Jew in the world. That could mean a lot."

CHAPTER 69

Einstein's Idea

We are all aware that this orchestra, with the aid of universal broadcasts, international festivals in Palestine, and tours to foreign countries, will have a more immediate appeal and effect in the world than any other cultural institution in Palestine, no matter how important and successful it be in the long run.

Bronislaw Huberman

Bronislaw writes a letter to Einstein, apologizing in the first sentence for being one of those people who wish to use his good name. He explains the opportunity Palestine offers for a cultural institution like the orchestra and school, and asks to meet with him. A few days later, he receives an invitation to Princeton from the famous scientist.

Einstein himself warmly welcomes Bronislaw and Ida to his Princeton home. Bronislaw notices how much the physicist has aged since he last saw him, his gray hair curling wildly around his ears and neck and his sad beagle eyes drooping even more than before, appearing almost comical.

"How is Mrs. Einstein?" Ida asks as they sip tea in the small study filled with books on the desk and floor and papers stacked high on each piece of furniture.

"She is very ill," the professor says. "She suffers serious heart trouble."

"I am so sorry, Professor Einstein," Ida says.

"Thank you, Ida. I will give her your regards."

For the next few minutes, Bronislaw and Einstein talk about old times, the Pan-Europa movement, and Zionism. When the conversation turns to Germany, Einstein shakes his head and frowns.

"It hurts me to see such persecution of our people, Bronislaw. I cannot sleep fearing what this madman Hitler will do. But I know we share these feelings. You are here for another purpose. Tell me more about this orchestra of yours."

"Albert, as you know, all of the Jewish musicians in Germany are today either unemployed or eke out a miserable existence in the Kulturbund orchestras and theaters. Not only is German barbarism responsible for this, but to the same degree, the delusions, chauvinism, and political-economic ignorance of many governments outside Germany."

"Yes. I see that, too," Einstein says.

"It is a phenomenon which, I believe, is unique in history; that an empire should wantonly destroy its own culture has happened before, but the unique fact is that neighboring countries do not at once grab these victims of barbarism and open wide their gates to the most outstanding personalities in public, artistic, and social life."

Quietly smoking his pipe, Einstein listens closely to his guest.

"Albert, we are trying to create an orchestra of the highest European standards in a tiny country in need of an orchestra, made up of musicians in need of a home," Bronislaw says. "We have recruited most of the musicians, we are refurbishing the Levant Pavilion in Tel Aviv to use as a concert hall, the Jewish Agency has offered the musicians and their family members permanent certificates, and with Toscanini's acceptance to conduct, we have everything in place, except the necessary funds. During the eighty days of my sojourn in the United States, I have played, or will play, sixty concerts, raising tens of thousands of dollars toward the formation of the orchestra."

Bronislaw continues: "We also need funds to establish a music school for children. I believe it is vital for the future of a Jewish state to cultivate music education, which will lead to enhancement in all spheres of culture. The new orchestra's musicians will teach at the academy."

"So you intend to have a country full of musical prodigies, Bronislaw?" Einstein asks, and grins.

"Well, Albert, not exactly. We want to make sure each young musician has mastered several instruments, not just one."[1]

"I think a first-class orchestra with Jewish musicians in Palestine, as well as a serious music school, will be an invaluable contribution to the uplifting of the country, to music culture in general, and to the German refugee problem," Einstein says.

The professor pulls a small calendar from a desk drawer. "Bronislaw, let's find an evening when we can host a dinner together, perhaps at the Waldorf Astoria in New York City. I believe we can count on New York's wealthy Jews to attend this dinner and support the Palestine Symphony and school."

Bronislaw smiles, looking first at Einstein and then at Ida. He notices tears fill Ida's eyes.

"This is wonderful, Albert," he says. "I thank you on behalf of the hundreds of Jewish musicians, and their families, now suffering Hitler's abuse."

On Saturday, March 7, 1936, Ida opens the *Manchester Guardian* and notices that the British newspaper has published Huberman's letter in full. She wonders if his words, harshly condemning Germany's non-Nazis who stand by and allow the Nazis' abuse of the Jews, will create sympathy and support from readers or simply be ignored.

Her answer comes soon, as she and Bronislaw receive little response to the article from the world's slumbering masses. She feels disappointed that so many people seem not to care that European Jews are suffering persecution under Hitler, but she isn't surprised. She recalls the benefit concert Huberman gave in Vienna to aid Hungarian Jews, the Vienneses' refusal to help promote it, and the embarrassingly low attendance. She suppresses her hurt and anger, staying busy with preparations for the upcoming Einstein dinner, scheduled for March 30 at the Waldorf Astoria.

During the month of March, Bronislaw and Ida learn that Hitler has ordered his troops into the Rhineland, aggressively breaking the terms of the Versailles Treaty that Germany signed after the Great War, in 1918.

"German military forces have entered the demilitarized zone in the Rhineland," Bronislaw tells Ida as he reads the morning newspaper. "Hitler is taking a huge gamble by ordering his troops to reenter the Rhineland, and purposely violating the Treaty."

"Surely, German leaders know the world will regard their actions as an act of hostility," Ida says.

"An action that will certainly threaten world peace," Bronislaw says. "This is the type of military aggression that leads to war. France or Britain will intervene and stop them. Clearly."

In Berlin, Hitler meets with his generals. "We have thirty-two thousand soldiers and armed policemen stationed in the Rhineland," he tells them. "If France shows a hint of taking a military stand against us, we will retreat."

"France is suffering such internal political crises right now," a general tells Hitler, "my bet is they will not respond."

"With our troops marching into the Rhineland," Hitler says, "this has been the most nerve-racking forty-eight hours of my life."[2]

Hitler and his generals watch closely France's response as German troops violate the Versailles Treaty. But neither France nor any other European country does anything to stop them.

"If France had marched into the Rhineland," Hitler later admits, "we would have had to withdraw with our tails between our legs."[3]

CHAPTER 70

The Dinner

This touring orchestra, made up of exiled refugee Jews from all over Europe, will be representing all of us, standing up with fists raised high against Nazis in the struggle against intolerance in all its forms. Not with machine guns and tanks, but with music. Our music.

Bronislaw Huberman

On March 30, New York's elite, dressed in glamorous clothes and jewels, crowd into the city's elegant Park Avenue Waldorf Astoria, one of the nation's most popular and lavish hotels. They fill the spacious grand ballroom, hundreds of Jewish men and women smiling, greeting each other, and finding their reserved seats at the tables.

One by one that evening, they meet Bronislaw Huberman and Albert Einstein. With great excitement at seeing the famous men, the diners exchange pleasantries, basking in their good fortune to be able to attend this important evening.

After the reception and dinner, Professor Einstein officially welcomes the guests and introduces Huberman, inviting him to speak. The guests stand to honor Huberman as he approaches the podium.

"Good evening. I play the violin," Huberman says, and smiles, receiving jovial laughs from the audience who know very well who he is. "For the past two years," he says, "I have had the dream of creating a new orchestra in Palestine. I have been impressed by the wonderful audiences I found in Palestine, feeling that they deserved a first-class orchestra."

The guests respond with polite applause.

"The other end of my vision came from Mr. Hitler in 1933," Huberman says. "When the greatest orchestral musicians in Germany were dismissed and made homeless, I had my idea completed.

"People have asked me: 'How will the orchestra reflect on the Jews in the world at large?' I believe it will provide an objective proof to the world of the injustice of the present German regime in choosing professional competence on the basis of race rather than on merit. The orchestra will offer a great opportunity for the Jew to show that, as a group, he is eminently fitted to provide for the world the highest quality of music."

The audience shows support with strong applause.

"When I plucked up the courage to approach Arturo Toscanini, our greatest conductor, to inaugurate the orchestra, he agreed in two minutes . . . canceling all his conflicting engagements. Toscanini's support of the orchestra constitutes a historical mark, both in the struggle against Nazism and in the upbuilding of Palestine."

The dinner guests rise simultaneously, clapping wildly.

Einstein stands and makes his way to the podium, shaking Bronislaw's hand.

"Fine people of New York," Einstein says, "the creation of the Palestine Symphony is a great contribution to the German Jewish refugee problem, and to music culture in general. My support for Bronislaw Huberman and his project is absolute, and I know that, under Mr. Huberman's direction, a great and powerful orchestra will come into being."

Einstein turns his head, looks at Huberman, and continues.

"Please know that whatever we do for Palestine, we do for the honor and well-being of the whole Jewish people.[1]

"Our Palestine struggle is for Jews everywhere, not just for those who settle in the homeland.[2]

"I call on you now to dig deeper than you have before, perhaps deeper than you have ever dug, and lend your most generous support to my friend Bronislaw Huberman. Please help us establish this new orchestra and children's music school. Palestine will be a center of culture for all Jews, a refuge for the most grievously oppressed, a field of action for the best among us, a unifying ideal, and a means of attaining health for the Jews of the whole world."[3]

By the end of the evening, with excitement and generosity, the dinner guests have pledged the needed eighty thousand dollars, the amount necessary to close the deficit on the budget.

Bronislaw and Ida express their deepest gratitude to Einstein then depart, returning to their hotel room. They spend the rest of the evening contacting the orchestra's musicians, supporters, and staff with the good news: "With the help of Professor Einstein, we have succeeded in collecting substantial financial backing from American Jews for the orchestra. We now have the necessary funds. Prepare to sail to Palestine within the next six weeks!"

"It's finally come true," Bronislaw tells Ida. "A world-class orchestra of exiled Jews in Palestine, created in record time, conducted by Arturo Toscanini; this is the answer to Hitler's persecution."

That night, Huberman sleeps more soundly than he has in years. He still mourns the loss of his Stradivarius and hopes somehow to recover it, but the evening's festivities, and the complete funding of the orchestra and music school, bring him unusual joy.

CHAPTER 71

A Fitting Home

Everything is new, new, new here. There is no past; only the present and the future exist. . . . Tel-Aviv is a fitting home for our refugee orchestra.

Heinrich Simon[1]

During the first days of April, Bronislaw and Ida make plans for the musicians and their families to sail to Palestine. Heinrich Simon travels to Europe to report on the many endeavors he is supervising in Tel Aviv to prepare the way for the musicians' arrival.

"Bronislaw, if the workers can continue at this pace, without interruption, they tell me the Pavilion can be finished by October, in time for our opening concert season," Heinrich says. "With all the enthusiasm among the people there, however, I wonder if the hall will be large enough to accommodate everyone who wants to come."

"What final work needs to be done?" Bronislaw asks.

"Mainly the roof," Heinrich says. "We've run into problems. The roof is tin, and lined with beaverboard, a flimsy material made of wood fibers and wastepaper pressed together into panels. It's not the sturdiest stuff for a roof and ceiling. The contractor suggests we tear it off and build a new roof, using stronger materials. But I told him to simply patch it. We have neither the time nor the workers, materials, and money to rebuild it and have it ready for summer rehearsals."

"Palestine has heavy rainfall during the late fall and winter," Bronislaw says. "Is there any risk the roof will not hold up?"

"The workers think it'll be okay," Heinrich says. "They added more nails to make the beaverboard more secure. Right now, Bronislaw, we need to turn our attention to the poor acoustics and lighting problems in the main hall."

"I trust your judgment, Heinrich. Do what you think is best and most needed."

"For the concerts scheduled after Tel Aviv," Heinrich says, "we have reserved the Edison Theater in Jerusalem. It's not in great shape, but will do. We have also secured Haifa's Armon Theater, a modern cinema. Not ideal, but the best we can find."

"Heinrich, have you considered where we will hold the workers' concerts? These are just as important to me as the main ones. Also, I would like to explore inviting the Arab population as well."

"We plan to rent large warehouses and factory structures as well as a few open fields in Hedera, Pardess Hanna, Rehovoth, Nathania, and Pet-ach-Tikvah. I think you'll be pleased."

"Good," Bronislaw says. "You mentioned that the people in Palestine are excited about the concerts. How are they responding to Maestro Toscanini's coming to conduct?"

"You can't imagine the excitement. The news of Toscanini coming to Palestine has created a syndrome they call Toscanini fever. Some say he will never actually come. Others believe that if the maestro does come, he will leave after the first rehearsal. At least one person has told me that Toscanini should not step into such a dangerous situation, that with the Arab problem he will not be safe there."

"I, too, am concerned about his safety," Huberman says.

"People in Palestine seem ready to storm the orchestra offices as soon as we put tickets on sale," Heinrich says. "They tell me they are willing to forgo their last morsel of bread rather than be without a seat at the opening concert. Some are already asking employers to pay them in concert tickets instead of shekels."

With only a few weeks remaining before the musicians leave their homes in Germany and Europe, Ida confirms the musicians' reserved passages on trains and ships, double-checking the list of passengers in order for Ben-Gurion and the Jewish Agency to release the necessary certificates. Ida also reconfirms the modest apartments she has reserved near the Levant Pavilion, rooms close enough for the musicians to walk to rehearsals.

"Broni," she tells him, "everything is coming together nicely. But we still can find no appropriate place in Tel Aviv to house Maestro Toscanini and his wife."

"I will make this a priority for Heinrich," he says. "My biggest problem is finding the rest of the musicians we need. We still have empty orchestra chairs. Many applicants are applying, but so few are good enough. And we're only a few months away from the opening. This is a big dragon to slay, Ida."

When Heinrich returns to Tel Aviv, he begins the difficult search for a wealthy family with a large comfortable home who is willing to move out during the October concert season so that the Toscaninis can occupy their domicile while he's in Tel Aviv. For the concerts in Jerusalem, Heinrich reserves the presidential suite at the King David Hotel for the maestro and his wife.

Part 5

CATASTROPHE!

Another feature of Palestine life is the continuous state of alarm in which everybody is more or less living there. Most people in Europe and America who hear about that state of permanent emergency, deplore it.

Bronislaw Huberman[1]

CHAPTER 72

The Untimely Death of the Dream

The Arabs found rioting to be a very effective political tool. . . .
Arabs were afraid of being displaced by Jewish immigrants. To stop
the disturbances, the [British] commissions routinely recommended
that restrictions be made on Jewish immigration. Thus, the Arabs
came to recognize that they could also stop Jewish immigration by
staging a riot.

Jacqueline Shields, "Pre-State Riots: Arab Riots of the 1920s"[1]

Suddenly and without warning, on a warm morning in April 1936, the
rumbles of Arab discontent over Zionist advances in Palestine explode in
Nablus, a city controlled by the British Mandate of Palestine since 1922.
The uprising in Nablus or, as the two-thousand-year-old biblical city was
called, Shechem, catches Jewish settlers by surprise. Bands of Arabs riot,
attacking Jewish families with bullets, bombs, and swords. Haifa, a city
north of Tel Aviv, erupts simultaneously with fierce fighting between Arab
and Jewish farmers and shopkeepers.

Since 1933, Jewish immigration to Palestine had tripled. For years,
Palestinian Arabs protested the British Mandate government's authority
over them as well as Britain's immigration policy, claiming that the British
supported limitless Jewish immigration to Palestine. The British stonewalled
them, unresponsive to their pleas. In protest, the Arab League called for a
general strike. When the British continued to ignore their requests, the
Arabs finally took action, resorting to bloodshed.

The violence spreads quickly into a full-scale revolt, leaving Arabs as well as Jews dead, railways destroyed, and homes and businesses burned to the ground.

Britain ships twenty thousand troops to Palestine. They respond to Arab rioters with military force. The vicious hostilities mushroom among Muslim, Jewish, and Christian Palestinian leaders and clerics.

Several days after the Palestine hostility breaks out, Bronislaw is in his bedroom getting dressed to audition a musician. Ida comes in, handing him a telegram from his lawyer, Mr. Horowitz, in Palestine.

Scanning the telegram, Bronislaw learns the severity of the Arab revolt—too volatile, too dangerous. Horowitz tells Huberman it's impossible to go forward in the present environment, that everything must be delayed. Huberman's legs feel suddenly weak. He sits down hard on the edge of the bed. Closing his eyes, he says nothing, shaking his head slowly from side to side in disbelief.

That afternoon, another telegram comes, this one from David Ben-Gurion. He tells Huberman that he can no longer honor his promise to provide permanent certificates for the musicians and their families.

When Bronislaw reads the telegram to Ida, she wraps her arms around his shoulders and cries.

"Ida, I will *not* let this dream die!"

Bronislaw watches as the aggression in Palestine escalates through the month of April. It seems clear that the violence is not going to slow down anytime soon. He spends many hours in his chair, staring into space, trying to hold on to his dream.

Bronislaw and Ida contact the musicians, supporters, donors, and everyone associated with the orchestra, and report the devastating news. One by one, the orchestra recruits respond. Some cancel their participation in the group entirely, and some decide to wait to see what will happen in the near future. Bronislaw receives telegrams and letters from the recruits, most of them deeply upset over the disruption of their plans and others describing the hardships they face in Germany and Europe. All the musicians worry about finances, since they will not be receiving paychecks that summer.

Bronislaw receives a desperate letter from horn player Willi Wolf Sprecher, one of the many new orchestra recruits who have already sold all earthly possessions in anticipation of a paying job in Palestine that summer. He tells Huberman that he has moved his family out of their apartment in Saarbrücken, Germany, and they are living in the tiny, cramped home of his wife's parents. With no source of income, he must depend on his in-laws for board and bread, a situation that is becoming more difficult every day. When he asks for urgent help, Huberman writes him, assuring Sprecher that the delay does not affect his pledge to create the orchestra.

"I feel such a huge responsibility for the members of my orchestra," Bronislaw tells Ida. "I hate to put them through this, but it cannot be helped. I want them to know that I intend to keep my promise of the orchestra and their jobs."

The orchestra's plans come to a standstill while Huberman waits for word from Palestine. In time, he realizes there will be no rehearsals in that country beginning in September, no opening concert on October 18, 1936, and perhaps no new orchestra at all.

Heinrich Simon tells architect Oskar Kaufmann to stop the renovations on the Levant Fairgrounds Pavilion. The workers put away their hammers and saws and pick up weapons instead, in the effort to defend their families.

Though they were previously promised, David Ben-Gurion will not even discuss the possibility of issuing permanent certificates to the musicians now, the documents that would allow them into Palestine.

Britain sends more troops to the Middle East, trying to suppress the warring between Arabs and Jews, but with little success.

After receiving word from Huberman, Toscanini cancels his travel arrangements, sad to think he will no longer be conducting the opening concerts.

"I will create the best orchestra in the world in Palestine, even if it kills me!" Bronislaw tells Ida. He feels the pressure in the pit of his stomach, making him nauseated and anxious.

Ida takes his hand in hers. "We can do nothing now, Broni, but wait," she says.

Throughout the months of spring, the uncontrollable violence in Palestine boils hotter, spilling into the scorching summer, destroying homesteads and devouring people—Arabs, Jews, and Christians.

Palestinian Arab settlers continue to demand cessation of Jewish immigration, the sale of land to Jews, and the establishment of an Arab national government. Negotiations between British, Arab, and Jewish leaders fail to bring resolution, much less a full day of peace. The arson, bombings, murders, and massacres continue as the British struggle to restore some semblance of order.[2]

In the darkest days of early summer, a depressed and discouraged Bronislaw wakes one morning with the first encouraging seed of hope planted in his heart since the Arab revolt began in April.

"The orange blossoms in Palestine are growing, about to bloom, and burst into fruit," he whispers.

He envisions the multitudes of Arab orange groves that cover Palestine, trees bearing millions of perfect round oranges that will soon hang heavy from their branches, ripe and ready to harvest.

"Perhaps . . ." he says aloud. "Just perhaps . . ."

He bolts out of bed, anxious to tell Ida his developing new plan.

"Ida, in previous revolts, I remember vividly how the fighting stops by the first of October so that Arab farmers can harvest their oranges. Most of their income depends on picking and selling those oranges on time."

Bronislaw telephones Heinrich Simon, instructing him to reschedule rehearsals to start the first of November and to reschedule the opening concerts for the end of December.

"Arab farmers can't riot and pick oranges at the same time," he writes. "We will not allow the orchestra to die because of this revolt!"

"But, Bronislaw," Heinrich says, "what about Maestro Toscanini?"

"I will ask him to come in December instead," Bronislaw says.

"And what about the certificates, Bronislaw?"

"I'll reason with David Ben-Gurion," Huberman says. "We'll see what can be done."

"Bronislaw, I have had to stop the construction on the Levant Pavilion. With the fighting, we cannot find workers. They've taken up arms. But perhaps, when and if the fighting slows in October, we can begin the renovations again."

Heinrich pauses, then continues. "Of course, Bronislaw, you know about the rains that come in November and December. The storms will, no doubt, slow down the construction. We might not be able to finish the Pavilion in time for the December concerts."

"Heinrich, my friend, this new plan is a gamble on many fronts. Delays in construction are just another one—one that you must manage. But, I believe, if the orchestra has any chance at all to survive, we must go forward in absolute faith."

With the rescheduling decision made, Bronislaw travels to Toscanini's home in Lago Maggiore. Upon hearing the new plan, Toscanini agrees to make himself available, promising with enthusiasm, to appear in Palestine to conduct the series of concerts.

Bronislaw learns from Ida's conversations with the musicians that they, too, will strive to survive through the summer until their passage to Palestine can be arranged in the fall.

But Bronislaw knows the plan cannot go forward unless Ben-Gurion guarantees the Jewish Agency's issuing of permanent certificates to the musicians in November.

Immediately Bronislaw contacts Ben-Gurion in Palestine, explains his new plan, and asks for the permanent certificates.

After much delay, back-and-forth negotiations, and what seems to Huberman like stalling, Ben-Gurion finally responds with a definite no. He will not provide permanent certificates to the musicians and their families.

"Mr. Huberman, we can no longer afford to send you our precious permanent certificates," Ben-Gurion tells him. "We now have very few of them to give out, and we must use them to bring permanent workers and builders to Palestine, not your high-minded, cultured musicians. We need robust men with strong backs who will get their hands dirty and work to build our country. Your cosmopolitan musicians will step into Palestine, feel the heat and bugs, see the sand and camels, and rush back home to civilized Europe."

"Perhaps in October," Ben-Gurion says, "we will be able to offer you *temporary* certificates. But permanent certificates are now out of the question."

Bronislaw raises his voice in frustration. "This is not acceptable!" he shouts, his face blood-red, his heart pounding. "I cannot have my musicians give up European positions and break up their households without securing their full rights to Palestine. I would rather give up the whole business than deal with temporary labor permits. We will not come to Palestine with only temporary status. You promised us permanent certificates, and I expect you to keep your promise! You are going back on your word!"

But Ben-Gurion refuses to change his position. He will give no permanent certificates to Bronislaw Huberman's musicians.

Two opposing wills of hardened steel collide. Both men are Polish-born lions, intractable in their goals. Bronislaw Huberman, an artist of the first rank, molded by politics, wants to bring European culture to Palestine, to protest Nazi persecution of Jews, and to save Jewish lives. David Ben-Gurion, with a Zionist heart, is dedicated to a single goal of creating the State of Israel with workers, farmers, and engineers, decidedly not musicians from Europe.

At the end of the blunt conversation, Bronislaw slams down the receiver, shouting to Ida: "That liar! Without permanent certificates, our orchestra is dead!"

CHAPTER 73

Effort and Sacrifice

I have been moving heaven and hell to establish a first-class orchestra in Palestine! The Jewish Agency promised certificates for the musicians, but now they are looking for ways out of the agreement. It seems that three years of effort and sacrifice have come to nothing.

Bronislaw Huberman

Determined to keep the new orchestra afloat, Bronislaw Huberman the musician-statesman becomes Bronislaw Huberman the warrior. He has made a commitment to the project, people are depending on him, and he will not settle for temporary status for his European musicians.

He spends an entire morning sitting in a chair, contemplating his next move to get around Ben-Gurion's unwavering will.

Huberman asks Ida to book his passage to London for the next day, where he will seek an appointment with the president of the World Zionist Conference, Chaim Weizmann. If Ben-Gurion will not cooperate, he'll go over his head.

Huberman knows that Weizmann is a music lover, a highly cultured man who will be able to see clearly the benefits of a world-class orchestra in a future Israeli society. He also knows that Weizmann, who made vital contributions to the Allied war effort in the Great War, is highly respected and politically well connected in London.

Huberman's fame serves him well, and making an appointment with Weizmann does not prove difficult. Weizmann, it seems, is well aware of

Huberman's efforts over the previous years to create the orchestra. He welcomes Bronislaw into his study in Hempstead for their meeting.

Bronislaw explains the orchestra's dilemma, the need to postpone the opening concert dates, and David Ben-Gurion's refusal to give his musicians the permanent certificates he promised them.

"It seems that three years of effort and sacrifice have come to nothing," Bronislaw tells him. "Thus I come to you, Dr. Weizmann, asking that you prevent this fiasco."

Listening intently to Huberman over the course of a long afternoon, Weizmann finally responds: "I can say, Mr. Huberman, that I fully support your remarkable dream. I see its benefits both in the here and now in Europe and Palestine, and in the future hoped-for state of Israel itself. And I promise you now that I will make all inquiries with those I know here in London, and in Tel Aviv, to see what can be done to help you fulfill this dream. But," he concludes, "with the uproar in Palestine right now, I can make you no promises."

Bronislaw thanks him and returns home to Ida. Together, they begin the long wait for word from Weizmann.

Weight lifter and French-horn player Horst Salomon misses participating in the Summer Olympic Games in Berlin when, on August 1, four thousand athletes from forty-nine countries gather to compete in 129 events.

Adolf Hitler has constructed a new sports complex for the event, one that covers 325 acres and includes four individual stadiums, all draped in Nazi banners and swastikas.[1]

Not a sports fan, Hitler had been uninterested in the whole idea of hosting the Olympics. But Goebbels had convinced him to agree, telling the Führer they could exploit the Olympic festivities, advancing the Nazi cause, both inside and outside of Germany.[2]

More than four million tickets are sold to people around the world, sports fans eager to attend the games. During those two weeks in August, Hitler soft-pedals his anti-Semitic agenda, removing anti-Jewish signs and slogans from the city's streets, seeking to present Germany as a peaceful, tolerant country. He also rounds up Germany's bums, winos, and male prostitutes from the streets, sending them to Dachau or Sachsenhausen for six months of rehabilitation.

America, Great Britain, and France threaten to boycott the games, in protest against Hitler's racial policies, but their threats prove empty. They all decide to participate.

All "non-Aryan" athletes, like Horst, are excluded from representing Germany in the games, with the exception of two token Jews.

Hitler himself opens the eleventh Olympiad. As he arrives at the stadium, Richard Strauss conducts an orchestral fanfare written by Richard Wagner. Thousands of German spectators cheer, saluting and honoring the Führer as he strides to his highly visible seat at the head of the stadium.[3]

Hitler is popular with some Americans, including the American hero-pilot Charles Lindbergh, a special guest of Hitler's who sits in an honored place right beside him during the Olympic Games.[4]

Hundreds of thousands of spectators watch as team after team of athletes marches into the stadium. One lone runner carries the relay torch, a flame originating from the site of the ancient games in Olympia, Greece. Germany's "Aryan" athletes, most of them blue-eyed blonds with finely chiseled bodies, seem to suggest a mythical link between Germany and the culture of classical antiquity. The ceremonies are filled with elaborate public spectacles and rallies, record-breaking athletic feats, and German hospitality.[5]

During the choreographed pageantry and competitions, Horst sits at home in Berlin, his head in his hands, his heart crushed. He learns that Germany's heavyweight Josef Manger wins the gold medal in weight lifting, representing and honoring the Fatherland. Germany's other Aryan weight-lifting contestants—Rudolf Ismayr, Eugen Deutsch, Karl Jansen, and Adolf Wagner—win medals of silver and bronze.[6]

Horst, like the rest of Huberman's musicians, waits at home for notifications about the orchestra plans. He is anxious and ready to leave Berlin, the city of his birth, along with its Nazi brutality. He eagerly anticipates playing his horn in the new symphony orchestra for the music-loving people of Palestine.

Time slows down, and the hot summer days pass miserably, as Bronislaw, Ida, and everyone connected to the orchestra wait for word about the permanent certificates. Huberman keeps abreast of the situation in Palestine through daily telegrams reporting the continuing conflict and escalating violence and predicting no end in sight.

"Too much time has passed," Bronislaw tells Ida. "Dr. Weizmann is having no success securing our permanent certificates."

While they wait, Bronislaw receives a telephone call from Meir Dizengoff, the mayor of Tel Aviv.

"Mr. Huberman," the mayor says, "we understand that you are planning your orchestra's concerts for the end of December. I'm calling you as a courtesy to let you know we have recently placed a new tax on all concert tickets sold in Tel Aviv."

Bronislaw looks up to the ceiling and presses his lips together tightly.

"An entertainment tax?" he asks, his face beginning to flush, his voice becoming firm.

"As you know," the mayor continues, "we have no income tax in Palestine, and the budget of the government is financed by indirect taxes. Therefore we must charge you, yes, an entertainment tax on the sale of tickets."

Bronislaw takes a deep breath, trying to keep his temper in check so he can properly and politely answer the mayor.

"If our audiences must pay taxes on the tickets they purchase, it will make tickets too expensive, and sales will significantly decrease. Must I remind you, Mayor Dizengoff, that the orchestra's entire financial support comes from ticket sales? I advise you, in all seriousness, that I will not relent in this point!"

"But, Mr. Huberman . . ."

Bronislaw continues, his voice growing louder: "Either the Tel Aviv township will withdraw this egregious demand on the orchestra, or you will have to give up the orchestra completely! I will retire from the whole project."

"But, Mr. Huberman, this is essential—"

"Mayor Dizengoff, you must affirm to me *now* that no tax will be charged on these tickets. I have not driven myself, and the whole world, crazy over the past months and years in order that the Tel Aviv municipality should enjoy tax benefits."

"This is not my rule, Mr. Huberman, but the—"

"If you proceed with this demand, I will consider it an absolute vote of no-confidence. I will not continue my negotiations on this subject!"

Bronislaw abruptly ends the conversation. He hopes he has heard the last words on the subject from Mayor Dizengoff and the Tel Aviv municipality.

Bronislaw hears nothing from Chaim Weizmann. He waits impatiently, his anxiety increasing as each day passes without a word. He often feels discouraged, but remains determined to succeed, no matter what it takes.

On Tuesday, August 11, he receives a highly unusual and surprising telephone call, not from Weizmann but from the British Mandatory high commissioner, Sir Arthur Wauchope.

"Mr. Huberman," Wauchope says, "I understand you wish for the British Mandatory government of Palestine to allow you permanent certificates for Jewish musicians from Europe to immigrate to Palestine to form a new orchestra."

"Yes, Sir Arthur," Huberman says, explaining at length, and in detail, his dream.

Sir Arthur pauses for a long time before he speaks.

"I deeply appreciate what you are proposing, Mr. Huberman. But I must take some time to consider your request."

Bronislaw thanks Wauchope for his interest and consideration. The British high commissioner again promises to consider his request and ends the conversation.

Bronislaw takes a deep breath and smiles. He is amazed at receiving a call from Sir Arthur himself, and the call renews his hope.

"Ida," he says, "I am sure Sir Arthur's attention to this matter is a direct result of my plea to Chaim Weizmann. I suspect Weizmann himself might have approached the British prime minister with my request."

"Broni, if for some reason Sir Arthur denies your request, can you appeal to someone in a higher position?"

"No, Ida," he says. "There is no one else in a higher position to consult. This is the end of the line."

CHAPTER 74

The Message

Palestine has needed a symphonic orchestra, there is a consuming thirst for the music that possesses the Jews in Palestine to a greater extent than any other people in the world.

Bronislaw Huberman[1]

As the days pass with no further word from Sir Arthur Wauchope about the permanent certificates, Bronislaw is sleepless with anticipation.

Cables and letters of invitation pour in from around the world, asking him to perform in concert halls.

"Do you want me to accept or reject these invitations, Broni?" Ida asks.

"Accept them, Ida. We need the money for the orchestra. But keep December and January open for the concerts in Palestine and Egypt."

"You are so determined to create this orchestra, aren't you, Broni? You are making definite plans without knowing if you will have the permanent certificates."

"Yes, Ida, I am." He smiles thinly. "Faith, Ida. We must have faith."

The Olympics in Berlin end on August 16, and life in Germany returns to its horrible normal. The signs announcing "Jews Are Unwanted Here" reappear on store and restaurant windows and in city parks. Cruel anti-Semitic depictions of Germany's Jews grow more common and more dehumanizing.

The musicians, suitcases packed, wait to leave Germany and sail to Palestine. On September 7, Germany imposes a 25 percent tax on all Jewish assets. Hitler renovates a camp fifteen miles northeast of Berlin and reopens the concentration camp Sachsenhausen, filling it quickly with thousands of political prisoners.

That month, Bronislaw and Ida learn that Tel Aviv's mayor, Meir Dizengoff, has died.

As the October temperatures begin to drop in Europe, Bronislaw and Ida anticipate the oncoming winter months. He has planned to begin rehearsals, with Wilhelm Steinberg conducting, in early November, preparing for the concerts in late December. But time is marching on with still no word about the permanent certificates. As each day passes, he watches developments in Germany escalate, and senses another European war is inevitable.

One evening, Bronislaw feels faint. He lies down, places his hand on his head, and groans. "Up to now, Ida, I have been on the edge of a nervous breakdown. But now I am in its very center."

Bronislaw and Ida stay in contact with the musicians over the long days and weeks. They wait, packed and ready to leave, in Berlin, Warsaw, Vienna, Paris, Prague, Rome, Stockholm, Zagreb, Leningrad, Wiesbaden, The Hague, and other European cities.

Finally, after long days and sleepless nights filled with anxiety, Bronislaw receives a call from Palestine. Sir Arthur Wauchope has made the decision to bypass the Jewish Agency and Ben-Gurion completely, and to issue Huberman seventy "Extraordinary Use" permanent certificates to the British Mandatory state of Palestine, for use by his sole discretion. Huberman's eyes fill with tears of relief and joy.

"The Palestine Symphony rises from the dead!" he shouts to Ida. "We are going to Palestine!"

During the early days of October, Huberman's musicians, along with hundreds of their family members, board ships and head for Palestine. The Jewish refugees sail across the Mediterranean to the Middle East with their wives and children in tow, bringing as much of their family belongings as they are allowed. Most of them are tearing up deep family roots, and though they are profoundly relieved to be escaping a world of anti-Semitic intolerance, they are extremely anxious to be making this lengthy exodus toward an unknown new life.

Family by family, they pour into Haifa's port. Heinrich Simon meets them there, loading them into buses and taking them to Tel Aviv.

Heinrich chuckles quietly as the cultured, sophisticated Europeans, wearing citified-looking hats, fashionable suits, and polished shoes, step into Palestine's sand and see camels milling around them. Their mouths drop open, and their eyes grow wide.

"They look as if they have arrived on another planet," Heinrich says to the bus driver. "I'm glad they didn't arrive in the summer, when the heat and humidity are so high you could sweat standing in the shade!"

"Culture shock," the driver says, grinning. "I see it all the time."

"The weather is cooler now," Heinrich says, "but I'm hoping they can survive November and December's heavy rains."[2]

Heinrich moves the people quickly into the buses.

"We need to hurry to make it to Tel Aviv before curfew," he tells them.

After a bus ride, they arrive in Tel Aviv. Heinrich escorts them to the row of rented apartments near the Levant Pavilion and provides everything they need for the night.

A team of local physicians meets the new arrivals in Tel Aviv, should any of them need medical attention.

Just as Huberman predicted, the fighting begins to slow as Arab farmers lay down their weapons, suspending the violence in anticipation of October's orange harvest. For the first time since April, Palestine experiences a much-needed respite from the intense rioting and bloodshed.

During the month of October, as the rest of the musicians travel from Europe to Palestine, Huberman remains in Europe, day by day auditioning Jewish players who now yearn to leave Europe. He continues to look only for the very best musicians, but the increasing numbers wishing to audition is a constant reminder of the worsening situation for European Jews. Huberman is painfully aware he cannot bring them all.

He finalizes his invitation to the Kulturbund conductor Wilhelm Steinberg, and much to Kurt Singer's chagrin, Steinberg leaves Frankfurt and immigrates to Palestine, eager to begin work preparing the orchestra in advance of Toscanini's arrival.

Part 6

THE DREAM
COMES TRUE!

Hold out, dear soul, your Palestine Symphony is sure to be the foundation of something great, that will ring through the history of musical culture of the nations. May God bless all your Jewish national and universal strivings.

J. Wassilevsky

CHAPTER 75

The Rehearsals

In reality, it is not a question of violin concertos nor even merely of the Jews; the issue is the retention of those things that our fathers achieved by blood and sacrifice, of the elementary preconditions of our European culture, the freedom of personality and its unconditional self-responsibility unhampered by fetters of caste or race.

Bronislaw Huberman[1]

At the start of November 1936, Heinrich Simon greets returning construction workers at the Levant Pavilion. They have come to finish the renovations halted by the recent Arab uprisings. Simon knows they must work quickly to complete the Pavilion in time for December's concerts.

Heinrich also welcomes conductor Wilhelm Steinberg, exhausted from his trip but excited to begin work with the musicians. Together they lay the groundwork for six intensive weeks of rehearsals before Toscanini's arrival on December 20.

Thirty-seven-year-old maestro Wilhelm Steinberg stands at the podium, baton in hand, the new orchestra members before him. He speaks to them loudly, trying to talk above the noise of the rain beating on the tin roof, the workers hammering and sawing, and the seamen laboring in the shipyard next door. He speaks in German, the one language most of the players from across Europe have in common.

"We have much work to do before December twentieth," Steinberg shouts. "We will rehearse separately in sections, as well as together with the full orchestra."

For many hours each day, Steinberg leads rehearsals. He conducts nonstop with one section and then the next—strings, horns, and woodwinds—each working together in their own rooms, and then, to create a unified sound, all of them coming together as a full orchestra at the end of the day.

"Horst!" Steinberg shouts to Horst Salomon. "The horn section must play together. It's got to be a unified sound. Please. No soloists. Again!"

"Maestro," Horst responds, "we are doing our best. We only have one set of lips!"

Everyone laughs.

During rehearsal breaks, musicians corner Steinberg, telling him their problems and needs. Burdened by grievances, Steinberg meets with Bronislaw, who has finally arrived for the final weeks of rehearsals.[2]

"We have some issues," Steinberg tells Huberman. "The musicians complain they cannot rehearse with all the noise. The rain, the shipyard, and the construction workers are drowning out their instruments. They cannot hear themselves play!"

"I cannot control the weather, Wilhelm, or the shipyard's activities," Bronislaw says. "And the construction must be done if the hall is to be ready."

Steinberg continues. "We also have problems with rainwater. It pours through the seams in the tin roof, accumulating in the beaverboard, and dripping through the ceiling when wood fibers become saturated. The water is damaging instruments and soaking our sheets of music while we try to rehearse."

"The workmen are repairing the roof, Wilhelm. Until it is finished, I will provide umbrellas to keep the musicians dry."

"Bronislaw," Steinberg goes on, "the musicians also protest their low wages. They complain they are earning too little to feed their families."

"When I hired them, Wilhelm, I told them we could provide bread but not butter. Our budget is stretched to its limits. We will earn additional funds through concerts and ticket sales."

"I understand, sir," Steinberg says, rubbing his eyes as if he is worn out and weary.

"And, Mr. Huberman, at least one of the musicians, Dora Loeb, is homesick. She wants to return to Germany."

"I'm very sorry to hear that, but we cannot stop her," Bronislaw says. "I think, however, if she returns, she will put her life at risk."

Rain pounds the tin roof, dripping onto musicians who balance umbrellas between their necks and shoulders, struggling to play and stay dry. Several days later, Steinberg meets with Huberman again.

"We have another ongoing problem," he tells him. "In our orchestra, as I'm sure each of them has made you well aware, we have twenty string players who were concertmasters in their home orchestras—violins, violas, basses, and cellos. Every single one of them expects to be a first-chair player. And when they cannot, they complain and sulk like babies."

"Oh! The egos!" Bronislaw groans. "I've already discussed this situation with each of them. We are rotating the musicians, yes? Allowing each to play first chair when his or her turn comes?"

"Yes, sir," Steinberg says. "As we discussed. But now they *all* want to play first chair for the opening concerts. The ones that can't are miserable, and they let everyone know it! Especially *me*!"

"Can't you deal with them, Wilhelm? By the time Arturo arrives, they must be an orchestra with a single voice, not a bunch of individual egos."

"I know," Steinberg says. "They will be."

One day in mid-November, as Steinberg rehearses the entire orchestra together, he stops abruptly, puts his hand to his head, and closes his eyes. The musicians stop playing and watch him closely.

Saying nothing, he stands at the podium, his body exhausted, his head hurting, his patience gone. For a moment, he remains motionless, hearing the cacophony of hammers and saws resounding throughout the hall as the battery of workers struggle to complete the hall renovations in time for the opening concert.

He opens his eyes and looks at the musicians, their hair and clothes wet with rain, their shoes and pants caked with mud from the unpaved roads they walked that morning to get to the hall. He looks at their music, black ink streaming down wet pages, the notes, tediously copied by pen, disappearing.

Steinberg takes a deep breath and holds it. He recalls the well-known stories about Arturo Toscanini, his piercing eyes of fire, his fierce temper, his legendary impatience and harsh demands for absolute perfection.

"I will never have this orchestra ready for him!" he whispers between clenched teeth. "Toscanini will leave after the first rehearsal!"

Steinberg can no longer contain his building rage. His face turns red, his eyes widen, and his nostrils flare. And to the shock of all, the volcano inside him erupts, exploding with German fury.

"I cannot do this! It is impossible!" he screams.

He slams his baton on the podium and stomps out.

Bronislaw witnesses Steinberg's explosion. Racing to his side, he tries to calm him.

"I can't work like this," Steinberg tells him. "There's too much confusion and racket. It's *not* possible."

"We need you, Wilhelm," Huberman says, placing his hand on Steinberg's shoulder. "No one else can do what you are doing. Go home and rest. I will see what I can do about the confusion and noise."

The workers all over the hall are witnesses to Steinberg's meltdown. All have stopped working. Huberman motions for them to gather.

"Gentlemen," he says, "I appreciate your hard work. We cannot hold our concerts without your craftsmanship. But I must make a very large request."

Huberman clears his throat. "Would you be willing to work during the nights instead of during the days so my musicians can practice without the noise? I will pay you extra wages if you will do this."

The workmen put down the tools and go off to speak among themselves.

When they return, one of the workers speaks for the group. "Mr. Huberman, we will do the work at night. And we will have the concert hall ready in time. But we won't accept extra wages."

Huberman is amazed. "What do you want?" he asks.

"We all want season tickets for the concerts."

Overwhelmed, Bronislaw simply nods. "Thank you. Thank you."

The next morning, when Bronislaw, Steinberg, and the musicians arrive at the hall, rain still drops from the ceiling but the incessant noise of construction has stopped. As Steinberg ascends the podium, the entire orchestra stands and applauds. Huberman stands across the hall. When his eyes meet Steinberg's, he smiles, acknowledging Steinberg for taking a correct and necessary stand for control of the orchestra. He knows an important page has turned for both the conductor and for the orchestra.

That afternoon, Bronislaw asks Steinberg a curious question.

"Wilhelm, I strongly believe in the power of music to elevate thousands of hearts into harmonic unity. I'd like to propose that we invite Arab workers to attend the discounted workers' concerts. Will you and the musicians discuss this possibility? I will leave the decision up to you."

Steinberg later reports to Huberman.

"Yes, Bronislaw," Steinberg says, "we wish to invite and welcome them."

In Germany, a group of Nazis, following Hitler's earlier instructions, tear down the bronze statue of Felix Mendelssohn that stands in front of the Leipzig Gewandhaus, smashing it up and using the metal for scrap.

Mayor Carl Friedrich Goredeler protests the act, and resigns.

"Mendelssohn was a nonpracticing Jew, baptized a Lutheran, and fully assimilated into German society!" Goerdeler argues. "His music has long been a part of Germany's heritage."

His words fall on deaf ears. The party destroys statues of other Jewish composers, too, including Gustav Mahler, Arnold Schoenberg, Giacomo Meyerbeer, Ignaz Brull, and Karl Goldmark, insisting that although once greatly loved, these giants were Jewish, and intrinsically Aryan art should be undefiled by Jewish blood.[3]

CHAPTER 76

Troubles and Tickets

The Palestine Orchestra [is] the greatest achievement of the best Jewish musicians from Europe, and it [has] the potential of becoming one of the best in the world.

Jehoash Hirshberg,
Music in the Jewish Community of Palestine: 1880–1948[1]

Day after day, week after week, Bronislaw watches the musicians rehearse under the baton of Wilhelm Steinberg. They have scheduled sixty rehearsals in six weeks. The orchestra members are exhausted, but few complain. They know they must be ready for Toscanini.

In early December, the tickets go on sale. One hundred thousand people, from all over Palestine, storm the ticket office, desperate to buy tickets. Bronislaw calls the police to protect the staff, as demands for tickets swell. Officials try to control the crowds, but brawls break out, resulting in chaos. Some try to steal tickets, a few resort to blackmail. Those fortunate enough to have tickets hide them, guarding them like gold.

"I never expected *this*!" Huberman shouts to Heinrich above the noisy chaos. "We have room for fewer than three thousand people, not tens of thousands."

A worker runs up to Huberman, grasping a ticket. "I was prepared to forgo my last piece of bread," he says, "rather than be without a seat at the opening concert!"

Huberman and Heinrich are stunned by the demand for tickets. "Perhaps we should ask the construction workers to enlarge the hall before our next series," Huberman suggests.

Within two hours, every available concert ticket has been purchased, grabbed, or spoken for. Thousands of people are upset and angry that they must go home without tickets.

With every ticket sold, the hall renovated, the tin and beaverboard roof patched, and the orchestra thoroughly rehearsed, Bronislaw focuses on the upcoming arrival of Arturo Toscanini and his wife.

"Heinrich," he asks, "tell me again the maestro's travel itinerary."

"For the fourth time." He smiles. "Maestro and Mrs. Toscanini will fly to Milan, take a train from Milan to Brindisi, and fly from Brindisi to Cairo. After an overnight rest at the American Hotel there, they will fly directly to Tel Aviv."

"Make sure we have a doctor standing by in case Toscanini or his wife needs medical attention after such a long trip.

"And, Heinrich, for the concert itself, hire extra police to protect the diplomats and other prominent guests."

A few days before the opening concert, Bronislaw witnesses a feverish enthusiasm among the people in Tel Aviv. Everywhere he goes, people rush to him, exhilarated about the coming of Toscanini. A sense of excitement fills the city as crowds anticipate the opening night, calling Palestine the "pioneer of musical culture in the Near East."

In the days before the Toscanini concert, people again start referring to the frenzy as "Toscanini fever." The incredible enthusiasm seems more like psychosis. The big questions are how three thousand tickets can be distributed to the one hundred thousand people who so desperately want one.

Bronislaw hears about a woman in Tel Aviv who has just given birth to twin girls. In honor of Arturo Toscanini, she names one child "Tosca" and the other child "Nini."

Wilhelm Steinberg holds his last rehearsal on December 19, the day before Toscanini's arrival.

That night, he cannot sleep. He obsesses about each detail of the next day's rehearsal, handing over the baton to Toscanini, knowing this maestro will accept nothing short of perfection.

He lies in bed, his body trembling, his mind listing everything that must be done before the next day's rehearsal.

That night, Bronislaw and Ida stay up late, discussing the plans, activities, and all the unpredictable unknowns that morning will bring.

"Broni," Ida asks, "Wilhelm seems unusually nervous about meeting Toscanini tomorrow."

"I can imagine his anxiety," Bronislaw says. "He must feel tremendous pressure to impress Toscanini with his musicians, who have rehearsed together for only six weeks. And I'm sure he worries about Toscanini's temper.

"Toscanini makes heavy demands on his orchestras," Bronislaw says. "I hope he will be a bit more gentle with *our* musicians, realizing what they have passed through before coming here. Arturo is severe, but he is also beloved by musicians. Perhaps he has the right to be severe with them, because he is certainly severe with himself. To him, music is a *sacred* thing."

"Broni," Ida says, "I have another worry. With all the heavy rain, I am concerned about the stability of the roof. With all the water, I fear that the cheap tin and beaverboard might collapse."

"The workers feel the roof will hold, Ida. Surely they know better than we. I am more apprehensive about the hall's acoustics. Even with all the work done on it, this auditorium is far from adequate."

"Broni," Ida says. "I wish you were playing at the opening concert. I think people will be disappointed."

"No, Ida. I do not want to play. I want the *orchestra* to be the 'star' of the evening."

French-horn player Horst Salomon is also restless that night. He wonders if the others are as nervous as he is about playing for Toscanini. He rises from bed to practice one last hour before morning.

CHAPTER 77

Toscanini Fever!

*How shall I convey the magic of [Toscanini's] hand? Under it those
difficult passages do not exist. The music rises and falls, sings and
laughs, wrings our hearts, and causes our eyes to weep. We play as
we have never played before. . . . Tears stream down the eyes of
those of us to whom music is dearest. Here at last is our Eldorado—
oh, to be the instrument in the hands of the greatest master living.*

Thelma Yellin, a cellist in the orchestra[1]

On the morning of December 20, Bronislaw rises early to welcome Maestro
and Madame Toscanini to Palestine. The conductor's arrival creates uncom-
mon commotion, excitement, and in some cases, near pandemonium among
the people. The police try to restrain the hordes of people who line up to
see the Toscaninis as they land at the Tel Aviv airport. People push forward,
hoping to get a glimpse of the couple they regard as royalty. Bronislaw, Ida,
Tel Aviv officials, and a multitude of music lovers greet them as they enter
the airport pavilion.

"Welcome to Palestine!" Bronislaw tells the Toscaninis, trying to speak
loud enough to be heard above the cheers.

Toscanini smiles, waving his arms to greet the shouting people, seeming to relish the attention.

"Thank you for this enthusiastic reception!" he calls to them. He turns
to Bronislaw, his eyes wide with excitement: "Huberman! It seems as if
their *messiah* has finally arrived!"

"Come, Maestro, we will take you to your villa so you may rest from your trip," Bronislaw says, motioning the Toscaninis to a waiting car.

"No! No! No!" Toscanini shouts, as if fueled by the impassioned reception. "The musicians are at the hall now, yes? So, we go to the hall at once! Let's begin to rehearse!"

Wilhelm Steinberg and the musicians have been rehearsing since morning.

Steinberg stops the session when he hears Bronislaw and Toscanini enter the Pavilion stage door.

"He's here!" he tells the musicians, noticing the anxious and exhilarated expression on each player's face.

When the famed maestro steps inside, a sudden silence blankets the hall. No one speaks, as if to do so might ruin the sanctity of the moment. A few seconds later, the musicians quietly rise to their feet.

Wilhelm Steinberg trembles as he greets the great maestro and presents the orchestra to him. He is thrilled beyond words to finally meet him.

Tall and slender, Arturo Toscanini looks distinguished in his black waistcoat, his silver hair framing his stately Roman features. His eyes light up as he addresses the orchestra with a simple nod, saying *"Buongiorno."*

He mounts the rostrum, opens his own well-marked score on the podium, taps his long flexible baton, and says simply: *"I Brahms."*

As the orchestra plays, he listens intently.

"Oboe cantare, singen, trumpet piu forte," he says softly, nodding, gently encouraging individual musicians. The expression on his face changes often, moving from deep concentration to joy as he bids the performers to play to his liking.

"Piu piano, sht, sht, piano, piano, pianissimo," he says.

Satisfied with the skills of the orchestra, he says: *"Bene, andiamo avanti"*

(Let's move on) and leads them into the second movement. The rehearsal seems to go well, the musicians becoming visibly more relieved and relaxed as they appear to sense Toscanini's approval.

During the third movement, the Allegretto grazioso, Toscanini turns his full attention to the oboe, the instrument that carries the gorgeous solo line. He asks the oboist to repeat the melody over and over. Humming along with the music, Toscanini telegraphs body, hand, and eye signals to the young player, coaxing musical phrases from him beyond his previous best. Finally finding the sound that pleases him he says, *"Bene!"* The orchestra respectfully applauds their colleague.

B ronislaw sits in the front row in the hall, Steinberg and Ida beside him. He feels great pride as he watches the greatest conductor in the world lead his newly created orchestra. Bronislaw turns his head and smiles at Steinberg, whispering: "They are ready, Wilhelm. You have done very well."

Steinberg nods, smiling at Huberman.

But as the orchestra begins playing the last movement, Toscanini's expression suddenly turns sour, his eyes narrowed and focused.

"Tempo! Tempo" (Time!) he shouts, tapping the stand firmly with the baton.

The musicians stop. No one moves.

Toscanini's eyes grow wide, as if burning with anger and fire.

Bronislaw's heart skips a beat. He holds his breath, waiting to see what will happen.

"No! No! Terrible!" Toscanini screams, his anger visibly mounting, his arms flapping forcefully in all directions. He focuses his fiery gaze, stomping his feet, screaming out in every language he knows.

"Non Mozart, non Haydn, Rossini—Italiano—la precisione!" (Not Mozart, not Haydn, Rossini—Italian—be precise!) he screams, striking the stand with his baton, again and again. Bronislaw watches the outburst in horror. Steinberg places his hand on his chest as if having a heart attack. Ida seems bewildered, her jaw dropping in disbelief. The musicians sit stunned,

as if in shock. With faces frozen, they wait motionless for Toscanini's next command.

Rising from his seat, Huberman moves quickly to the platform. He puts his hand on Toscanini's shoulder and whispers into his ear.

"Maestro," he says, "the musicians have difficulty understanding Italian. Might you dance to the music in order to show them the feeling you desire?"

"Dance?" the maestro asks. "Ah, *si, danza! Danza!*" He grins suddenly, lifting his baton and signaling the orchestra to begin.

Bronislaw returns to his seat hoping the rest of the rehearsal will go smoother.

"What did you say to him, Broni?" Ida whispers.

"Since they have no language in common, I suggested another mode of communication," he says.

Bronislaw tries not to chuckle as he watches the conductor sway his agile body from side to side, raising his feet, tapping his toes lightly, dancing around the platform as if he has lost his mind.

The musicians seem surprised as they study the maestro's movements, watching him closely. Toscanini occasionally dances throughout the rest of the rehearsal, his temper tamed, the musicians appearing relieved, the color returning to the players' faces.

When the rehearsal ends, Bronislaw asks Wilhelm and Ida to take the Toscaninis to the villa where they are staying. Huberman talks with the musicians, concerned they might be upset or discouraged by Toscanini's intimidating outbursts.

"Do you understand what the maestro wishes?" Bronislaw asks.

"Yes, Mr. Huberman, we are starting to," someone says. "It's becoming clearer."

Day after day, Bronislaw attends each rehearsal, watching Toscanini grill the musicians, pushing them long and hard. Again and again, the maestro stops the orchestra abruptly, glaring at individuals with his fiery eyes, stomping his feet, flailing his arms, and screaming criticisms at the top of his voice.

Within moments after rehearsals, once Toscanini has gone, Bronislaw meets with his musicians, encouraging them and telling them stories he's heard about Toscanini. He tells them that the conductor once said that Bruno Walter and Furtwängler enjoyed conducting; "you see them smiling, almost fainting while they conduct. I, on the contrary, suffer like a woman giving birth!"

"To him, music is a *sacred* thing. He bleeds for it," Huberman says.

"Mr. Huberman," a musician tells him, "it makes us feel honored that the maestro deals with us so severely. We feel he is treating us as professionals, and that we are meeting his high expectations."

Lorand Fenyves stands up, his face beaming.

"Mr. Huberman," he says, "Toscanini is a magician! He doesn't simply *conduct* the orchestra, he *hypnotizes* us!"

CHAPTER 78

The Birth of the Palestine Symphony

Dec. 26, 1936, the inaugural concert of Palestine Symphony, is considered as one of the most important moments in the history of the Jewish state. I consider that day as the happiest day of my life!

Bronislaw Huberman

On Saturday morning, December 26, 1936, rain beats down hard on the roof of the renovated Levant Pavilion, growing heavier with each passing hour. Ida walks through the empty concert hall, filled with thousands of chairs in neat rows, and is pleased to see everything ready for the evening's opening concert.

She glances up at the ceiling and stops, a look of concern on her face. Water is soaking through the beaverboard, making brown spots on the ceiling. She watches the circles enlarge and darken, and she wonders if the roof's tin and beaverboard panels can withstand the storm and the accumulating water. She is worried when she steps in several small puddles on the floor, and finding a handful of rags, she wipes them dry.

When Bronislaw arrives at the hall, Ida points to the ceiling, showing him the expanding rings of water.

"Don't worry, Ida, it will hold," he says, and smiles.

Toscanini looks forward to the concert that evening.

"Since I set foot in Palestine," he tells Bronislaw, "I have lived in a constant state of elation of the soul. I am telling you that even today, Palestine continues to be the land of miracles."

The maestro rehearses the musicians that morning, suffering no outbursts of temper and pleased with their playing.

After the rehearsal, he returns to the villa to rest, rising before evening, dressing in concert tails, and waiting for the chauffeur to take him and his wife to the Levant Pavilion.

A s the Sabbath ends, Bronislaw watches thousands of Jews move toward the Levant Fairgrounds. When the doors open, a flood of people file inside, escaping the rain and claiming their seats. The hall fills up quickly with gentlemen dressed in tuxedos, suits, and ties, and women wearing brightly colored gowns and elbow-length gloves. They talk among themselves excitedly, smiling and waving programs at their friends as they wait for the concert to begin.

Above their heads, a few frightened sparrows fly around, swooping and twittering, adding to the air of festivity below.

Bronislaw greets the dignitaries, escorting them to the hall's front row, his recent allies and supporters as well as his antagonists and naysayers: Chaim Weizmann, David Ben-Gurion, Golda Meir, and a host of other high-ranking officials. He wishes Einstein could be here to rejoice in this evening. But Mrs. Einstein had died that week.

After everyone is seated, Bronislaw watches Sir Arthur Wauchope enter the hall with great ceremony, an accompanying Fire Brigade Band playing loudly the British anthem as the high commissioner walks down the aisle. Huberman greets Sir Arthur, thanking him for his part in making the dream come true.

With every seat filled, Bronislaw sees hundreds of ticketless people pushing through doors and squeezing through windows, eager to be present for this historic occasion. A loud commotion outside brings him to a window. He looks out onto hundreds more people, crowding the fairgrounds, surrounding the Pavilion. They hug the building, pressing their ears to the wall. They sit on the ground, kneeling beneath windows. In the near distance, he sees shabbily dressed immigrants standing on the Yarkon

River's shore, and Arab fishermen paddling rowboats to the water's edge, all hoping to hear the music.

A few minutes before the concert starts, Ida takes her seat. A frail, elderly man sitting behind her begins to cough. She turns around and asks: "Sir, do you need a glass of water?" He motions no with his hand and smiles, but continues to cough. Ida takes the handkerchief from the sleeve of her blouse and hands it to him.

Ida looks up at the ceiling. The dark wet circles have widened, a few drops of water falling through soggy sections. Taking a deep breath, she prays that the ceiling is stable and that the heavy rain will stop.

As she worries about the patched roof, she hears loud noises around and above her, footsteps, sounds of people climbing drainpipes and scurrying around on the wet roof.

"No!" she mumbles. "Not people on the *roof*! The ceiling will crash under all that weight!"

As the hall becomes quiet, the lights dim, and the musicians take their places, she swallows hard and squeezes her eyes shut. The man behind her is still coughing, at times appearing unable to catch his breath. Ida looks up at the ceiling. It seems to vibrate from the activity on the roof.

"It's too late," she mumbles. "I can do nothing but wait. And pray the roof won't fall."

From his seat, Bronislaw looks through a window, up to the sky, and sees a radiant full moon shining over Tel Aviv. His heart smiles.

He looks at his musicians. They wait for the maestro to take the podium as they anticipate playing their first concert in the Holy Land.

Lorand Fenyves, the brilliant young violinist from Budapest, catches Bronislaw's eye and nods. Lorand's sister, Alice, the newly trained violist, smiles at him sweetly. He sees Pesach Ginzburg from Warsaw, his three strong sons, Bloeslaw, Alfred, and Łódź, seated in the orchestra near him, and Horst Salomon, the Jew who was barred from the Olympic Games, seeming at peace, holding his horn.

Jacob Surowicz, David Grunschlag, Henry Haftel, Uri Toeplitz, and so many others are alive and well, here tonight under Palestine's full moon, free from Hitler and Nazi abusers, beginning their lives anew in the ancient land of their kin.

Something stirs deep within the violinist's heart. He tries to describe it: "Elation? Relief? Satisfaction? Realizing a dream, and working with others to fulfill it? Awe for music's power to transform human lives?

"Yes, all of these," he whispers.

As he looks at the faces of these seventy Jews he was able to pluck from the Nazis' talons, he struggles for the word that most defines his feelings. He smiles when the word finally comes to mind.

"Hope," he whispers. "Hope for *my* people. That is the word I feel."

He thinks with gratitude of Ida, Heinrich, Toscanini, Einstein, Wauchope, Weizmann, Steinberg, and all the world's helpers whose generosity, support, and sacrifice brought this orchestra into being, his impossible dream buried deep within *their* hearts as well as his own.

Everyone waits, inside and outside, faces aglow with excited expectancy as Toscanini appears and ascends the podium. The audience springs to its feet, welcoming the great maestro with booming applause and deafening cheers.

They quiet quickly when he taps his baton, calling the orchestra to attention. The first note they hear comes from Horst Salomon's French horn as he launches the inaugural concert with Carl Maria von Weber's *Oberon*.[1]

They watch the musicians lift their instruments, and filled with awe and reverence, the audience revels in the first notes of the first performance of the Palestine Symphony. After each piece, they respond with calls of *"Bravissimo! Bravissimo!"*

They watch Toscanini as he stands tall and confident at the podium, elegantly leading. Before their eyes, the baton becomes a magical wand calling forth sounds of enchanting beauty. The maestro seems younger than his seventy years as he conducts the *Oberon* Overture, the overture of *La Scala di Seta* by Rossini, the Second Symphony of Brahms, the *Unfinished* Symphony by Schubert, and the Nocturne and Scherzo from Mendelssohn's *Midsummer Night's Dream.*

As Ida listens, she anxiously eyes the ceiling. A few raindrops escape through the roof and fall on some heads below. But, lost in the music as they all are, the spectators seem unaware.

Ida relaxes, scolding herself for fretting, realizing the ceiling is bound to be safe, having been checked by the workers. Deciding not to worry about it anymore, she glances up at it one more time. She cannot believe what she sees. Gasping, she jerks her hand to her mouth. One of the panels is cracking, sending a small but growing stream of water to the floor. As if in slow motion, the break grows larger and larger until a man's foot punches through the beaverboard. One leg follows, and then the other, his limbs dangling precariously from the roof, over the heads of the audience.

"The ceiling is falling!" she wants to scream, warning the audience to run from the building. But she doesn't. She freezes, holding her breath, waiting in horror for the man to burst through the beaverboard, fall to the floor, and bring the whole wet roof down with him.

She hears a loud crash, and within her, her emotions explode.

No! No! Please, not the roof, not tonight!

She jerks her body around in the direction of the racket. The ceiling hasn't fallen, but the elderly coughing man sitting behind her has fallen onto the floor in a dead faint, his metal chair clanging as it hits the floor. He is sprawled on the ground and not moving, Ida's handkerchief still in his hand. Before she can jump from her seat to help him, ushers move in. As quietly as possible, they carry him from the hall.

Her body shaking, she takes a deep breath and tries to steady her nerves, glancing again at the ceiling. The legs are gone. A tarp is spread over the gap. She no longer hears footsteps above her, and assumes someone has safely removed the people and covered the hole.

With the roof seeming to be secure, Ida turns her attention to Toscanini, who conducts the orchestra with animated movements, the aging, handsome conductor visibly relishing this unique experience.

She thinks about the people from Cairo to London to America, listening to the concert as it is broadcast live around the world.

She can hardly wait to read the reviews in the newspapers, wondering how reporters in the audience will describe the ecstasy of this evening, the birth of an orchestra—an orchestra of exiles, a fist against intolerance raised high in the face of the Führer—with music, the only weapon they have.

Turning her head and looking at the man she has so long loved, Bronislaw Huberman, she remembers the young woman who once nursed him to health, his body and soul bruised and broken. She recalls the moment his car drove away, leaving the clinic forever, and how, at the time, she wondered if she would ever see him again. She remembers the waiting, the months her heart longed to be at his side. She smiles as she thinks of his unexpected call, the one in which he stated his love, and invited her to share with him his music and his life. She has shared his dream of an orchestra in Palestine, year after year, up to this very night, supporting him during all the highs and lows.

Even now, she thinks, *I share in the dream's fulfillment, in the beauty of music now filling this makeshift concert hall.*

The concert ends with thunderous applause, loud and long, the audience springing to its feet and calling for encores.

A woman turns to her friend and says: "I feel as if I am in Paris, London, or New York!"

Sitting beside her, a Tel Aviv correspondent from the *New York Times* jots on paper: "Both inside and outside the hall, a feeling of real ecstasy overwhelms the audience as the performance ends."[2]

A t last, Maestro Arturo Toscanini turns to the audience, bowing and showing his appreciation for their applause, joy written on his face, his arms reaching out to them with affection.

At that moment, a mob of photographers leaps from their seats, rushes to the platform, and thrusts cameras in the conductor's face. Toscanini tries to shield his face as they press their shutters and pop blazing flashbulbs in his eyes. Chaos envelops the conductor, who is temporarily blinded by the light.

He screams out in disgust, turning away, leaving the platform, escaping the photographers, and departing the hall through the backstage door.

He runs into the darkness, hearing the crowds call out to him wildly: "Toscanini! Toscanini!" They beg him to come back, to take additional bows, to allow them to express their gratitude.

Toscanini stops, listens to the continued pleas. But he will not return to the hall. He absolutely refuses to face again the brazen, disrespectful photographers.

S eeing the maestro exit the building and sensing he won't return, Bronislaw ascends the platform, motions for silence, a pause in the applause. He stands before the three thousand guests, and in a loud voice, he expresses his gratitude to the audience and to the musicians, thanking them for attending the inaugural concert of the Palestine Symphony. Then he explains Toscanini's abrupt departure, telling the audience that the maestro is exhausted and needs to rest.

Before he steps down, Huberman calls on the audience to "continue to stand for justice and liberty, and fight against intolerance and anti-Semitism in every way!" They respond with hearty applause, appearing to both congratulate him and express their gratitude.

⌒⌒⌒

L ater that night, back in their room, Bronislaw's eyes fill with tears. He looks at Ida and smiles.

"Nothing could describe the concert tonight, except the word *divine*," he says softly. "This has been the happiest day of my life."

Unable to hold back her own tears, she allows them to flow freely.

Bronislaw takes her hand in his, holding it gently.

"We did it, Ida!" he whispers.

He shakes his head in disbelief and looks deeply into her eyes.

"My lovely Ida, we *really* did it."[3]

EPILOGUE

The Rest of the Story

*I am convinced that Huberman's life and work must be recalled to
as large a number of people as possible. Indeed, Huberman deserves
not only such a short essay, but a complete biography.*

—Helmut Goetz, writing on the twentieth anniversary of
Bronislaw Huberman's death, November 1967[1]

After the highly successful inaugural concert on December 26, 1936, the
Palestine Symphony, conducted by Arturo Toscanini, performed (as well
as discounted workers' concerts) in Tel Aviv, Jerusalem, and Haifa. Before
Toscanini's departure from Palestine and the final performance on January
5, 1937, more than fifteen thousand people had attended rehearsals and
performances. In the green room after the last concert, Bronislaw recalled
that Toscanini had a melancholy expression on his face, and said: "Oh,
Huberman! I am so sad to leave this wonderful audience. I must come back.
I feel I must come back!"

The Arab revolt of 1936 plagued the new orchestra until it ended in
1939. Six hundred and thirty people were killed, and some two thousand
were injured during the fighting.[2]

On November 19, 1938, Huberman performed as a soloist with his
orchestra for the first time.

During World War II, the orchestra performed before the Allied Forces
(1942–44) in a concert in the western desert for soldiers of the Jewish
Brigade, as well as giving 168 concerts for Allied troops.

On May 14, 1948, when Israel officially became an independent state, the orchestra played the national anthem, "Hatikvah" (The Hope). On that day, forty-four of the founding musicians still remained with the orchestra. David Ben-Gurion changed the orchestra's name to the Israel Philharmonic Orchestra (IPO). The IPO, often referred to as "Israel's most treasured cultural possession," served as the new country's foremost cultural ambassador, carrying the joy of music and the message of peace around the world, bringing much pride to Jewish people everywhere.

During the Arab-Israeli War of 1948, following Israel's declaration of independence, the orchestra played numerous concerts under the baton of twenty-nine-year-old Leonard Bernstein. Henry Haftel remembers: "The people in Jerusalem were without water or food, but we played before packed houses . . . playing during a war is the most exciting thing you can imagine. You feel that you are taking part in a very special effort, keeping the morale of the people high through your art."

For the next twenty years, Bernstein conducted the Israel Philharmonic Orchestra, making it one of the most famous in the world.

The orchestra played seventeen concerts during the Sinai campaign in 1956, and five more concerts during Israel's Six-Day War in 1967. During the 1973 Yom Kippur War, the orchestra performed before Israeli Defense Force soldiers from the Golan Heights to Sinai.

In 1982, the orchestra celebrated "Huberman Week," commemorating Bronislaw Huberman's birth one hundred years before.

A few years later, they celebrated the one-hundredth anniversary of Arthur Rubinstein's birth, the pianist who was Huberman's childhood friend and played with the orchestra many times.

In the orchestra's sixth decade, it embarked on its first tour to Poland, performing in the country where the majority of people were massacred in German death camps. During this tour, they proclaimed: "We are here, and the Jewish people, its culture and heritage, cannot be annihilated."[3]

The IPO performs concerts around the world and has become one of the world's finest orchestras, attracting many of the greatest conductors:

Leonard Bernstein, Zubin Mehta, David Robertson, Kurt Masur, Daniel Barenboim, and many others. Zubin Mehta has been the music director since 1977, and music director for life since 1981.

Huberman's dream for the orchestra, and for the musical training of Israel's children, continues to grow. In the orchestra's seventh decade, Zubin Mehta led the IPO in a historic concert, bringing five hundred Palestinian and Jewish children together in the concert hall. The program, named KeyNote, now includes more than twenty thousand youngsters annually, from kindergarten to university.

In 2016, the orchestra will celebrate its eightieth anniversary.[4]

Huberman described the Palestine Symphony as "an audience without an orchestra for an orchestra without an audience."[5] He often referred to the new orchestra as a miracle, a Jewish orchestra that was rescued from Hitler's persecution and assembled in the little country of Palestine. "I call this a miracle!" he said many times.

Bronislaw Huberman, after founding the orchestra, gave concerts throughout the world. At the end of an Australian tour, in 1937, when he flew to a remote airstrip in the middle of the desert to refuel the plane, he got out to stretch his legs. There was only one other plane on the isolated strip.

"Dr. Huberman, I presume?" he heard someone say. Turning around, he saw his childhood friend Arthur Rubinstein, standing behind him.[6] The two world-famous musicians from Poland would be friends for a lifetime.

Returning from a tour in Indonesia, Huberman's plane crashed near Palembang, Sumatra, killing four of the nine passengers aboard. In the accident, he broke the bone in his left arm, near his wrist, two fingers in his right hand, his shoulder, and a rib that punctured his lung. He was hospitalized for five weeks. After a difficult and painful recovery and much therapy, he was again able to play concerts around the world.

Huberman also played concerts to benefit various charities, including the Red Cross, a charity concert at the opera in Paris in January 1940, and a benefit in Cairo to help Anatolian earthquake victims.

In 1941, during World War II, Huberman became a United States citizen. He made another appearance at Carnegie Hall, playing under Bruno Walter, both donating their services to benefit the British American Ambulance Corps.

In the summer of 1942, he performed Mendelssohn before an audience of seven thousand at the Lewisohn Stadium in New York City, and the next year, he repeated the performance there for ten thousand people.

After the war, he toured Europe, spent six months at an Italian health resort, and returned home to Switzerland. Throughout the years, Ida Ibbeken stayed lovingly by his side.

In the early morning of June 16, 1947, with Ida beside him, Bronislaw Huberman passed away. Ida remembers it as the morning "his passionate heart ceased to beat, almost imperceptibly, and without a struggle, like a soft breeze, ended this struggle-filled life."[7]

No records were kept, but it seems most likely that between 1935 and 1939, Huberman saved the lives of almost one thousand Jews.[8]

An historian wrote: "Huberman is now viewed as a mythic figure from a golden age of violin playing. His playing of the Brahms concerto moved the composer to tears. . . . He collaborated with the finest musicians of his time, such as D'Albert, Friedman, Casals, Furtwängler, and Bruno Walter. Going beyond the province of a master musician, Huberman's tireless efforts to oppose Fascism and save an entire orchestra from the Nazis by creating the Palestine Symphony bespeak the heroism of a world figure."[9]

Ida Ibbeken spent the rest of her life in Israel, working on Huberman's archives, translating his letters, correspondence, speeches, and other material into several languages. She donated his archives to the F. Blumenthal Music Center and Library in Tel Aviv.

Bronislaw Huberman never again saw his beloved 1713 **Gibson Stradivarius** after it was stolen from Carnegie Hall on February 28, 1936.

Lloyd's of London compensated Huberman with thirty thousand dollars for his loss.

"The loss of my dear violin," Huberman stated in 1936, "on top of incessant pressure from this [United States concert] tour . . . I feel I am close to a breakdown. But cost what it may, I must go on."[10]

The violin surfaced fifty years later, in 1986. On his deathbed, Julian Altman confessed his crime to his wife, Marcelle Hall, revealing to her the violin's location. Hall gave the information to the police and received a reward from Lloyd's of London, the insurer, of two hundred sixty-three thousand dollars. Hidden inside the black-shoe-polished violin, she found yellowed newspaper clippings reporting the theft, dating back to 1936.

In 2001, American violinist Joshua Bell bought the Gibson Stradivarius from English violinist Norbert Brainin for nearly four million dollars. Bell plays the Stradivarius around the world, and on many occasions, has played it as guest soloist with the Israel Philharmonic Orchestra.[11] He performed the Oscar-winning score for the film *The Red Violin*.

Bell states: "The connection between the violinist and violin becomes almost like your soul mate. Some people compare it to getting married, finding the right instrument is probably harder than finding the right wife. So, it must have been devastating to [Huberman] to go back to [his] dressing room and find out that your soul, your voice is missing."[12,13]

In 1919, after Huberman granted his wife, German actress **Elsa Galafrés**, a divorce, she married Hungarian composer/conductor, Ernő Dohnányi, having given birth to his son Matthew in January 1917. Upon his urging, Galafrés gave up her singing and acting career, devoting all her time to the children, marriage, and home. After fifteen years, the marriage ended in divorce, and in 1949, Ernő Dohnányi married his third wife, Ilona Zachar. Dohnányi died in Tallahassee, Florida, in 1960.[14]

Elsa later wrote a book about her life with Bronislaw Huberman and Ernő Dohnányi: *Elsa Galafres: Lives, Loves, Losses*.[15] She died in 1977.[16]

Johannes Huberman, the only child of Huberman and Elsa Galafrés, born on December 19, 1882, was officially adopted by Elsa's second husband, Ernő Dohnányi. Johannes (John) married composer Barbara Pentland, and they had one child, a daughter, Joan Huberman-Payne, who met her famous grandfather one time at age three. Johannes became an engineer, and moved to Vancouver, British Columbia.[17]

Alexandra Goldman Huberman, Bronislaw's mother, is believed to have lived the rest of her life in the south of France, unsuccessfully seeking a titled gentleman to marry.

After the inaugural concert of the Palestine Symphony, on December 26, 1936, **Arturo Toscanini** conducted additional concerts with the orchestra in Tel Aviv, Jerusalem, Haifa, Cairo, and Alexandria.

"Since I set foot in Palestine, I have lived in a constant state of elation of the soul. I am telling you, that even today, Palestine continues to be the land of miracles," he said.[18]

After the 1936–37 concerts in Palestine, Toscanini told Huberman: "Oh, Huberman! I am so sad to leave this orchestra, these wonderful audiences! I must come back, I feel I must come back."[19] The maestro bought a piece of land in Palestine, and he and Huberman planted several memorial orange trees on it.

Toscanini returned once more in 1938 to conduct the Palestine Orchestra.

From 1937 to 1954, Toscanini led the NBC Symphony Orchestra in New York. His final performance, an all-Wagner program, took place on April 4, 1954, in Carnegie Hall. He died of a stroke on January 16, 1957, at his home in Riverdale, New York, just before his ninetieth birthday. In his will, he left his custom-made baton to his protégée, Herva Nelli. Toscanini was posthumously awarded the Grammy Lifetime Achievement Award in 1987.[20]

Albert Einstein became an American citizen in 1940, choosing to retain his Swiss citizenship as well. During the war, Einstein helped the U.S. Navy evaluate designs for future weapons systems. He became a member of the National Association for the Advancement of Colored People, and was active in the civil rights movement in the United States.

On April 17, 1955, while working on a speech to commemorate Israel's seventh anniversary, Einstein suffered an abdominal aortic aneurysm. Taken to the University Medical Center at Princeton for treatment, he refused surgery. Einstein died at the university medical center early the next morning—April 18, 1955—at the age of seventy-six.

During the autopsy, Thomas Stoltz Harvey removed Einstein's brain, apparently without the permission of his family, for preservation and future study by neuroscientists. Einstein's brain is currently located at the Princeton University Medical Center.

In 1999, *Time* magazine recognized Albert Einstein as its "Person of the Century."[21]

After the concert series in 1936–37 in Palestine, **Hans Wilhelm Steinberg** accepted Toscanini's invitation to move to the United States and become associate conductor of his NBC Symphony Orchestra. In the years that followed, Steinberg became music director of the Buffalo, New York, Philharmonic, the Pittsburgh Symphony (1952–76), and the London Philharmonic (1958–60).

Steinberg died in New York City on May 16, 1978, at the age of seventy-nine.[22]

Huberman's lifelong friend **Arthur Rubinstein** became one of the greatest pianists of the century. During World War II, he moved his family from

Paris to Beverly Hills, California. After the war, he performed around the world, including Israel, where he performed with the IPO. He became an American citizen in 1946 and moved to New York in the 1950s.

In his latter years, Rubinstein lost his eyesight. In April 1976, he made his final recording with the IPO: Brahms's First Piano Concerto, conducted by Zubin Mehta. Rubinstein died at age ninety-five, on December 21, 1982.[23]

The Polish violinist **Raphael Broches** and the German violist **Dora Loeb** were the only two members of the Palestine Symphony who decided to return to Germany after the 1936 inaugural concert series. Huberman had agreed to give Broches a leave of absence to return to Germany to finish his PhD, but tried unsuccessfully to make him understand the danger of his returning to Europe. Broche's research took longer than he had intended, and when he finally packed and prepared to return to Palestine, the Nazis blocked his exit. He later perished in the Treblinka extermination camp.

Dora Loeb, homesick for her family and miserable because of the weather in Palestine, could not be dissuaded from quitting her position with the orchestra. She promptly returned to Germany and joined the Frankfurt Kulturbund Orchestra. She played there until Hitler shut down the Kulturbund in 1941. She was deported to Riga concentration camp, where she disappeared, presumed murdered by the Nazis. Many players in the Kulturbund also perished in the Holocaust.

Lorand Fenyves's father died in Hungary in 1941, before Hungary entered the war. But Lorand was able to bring his mother and grandmother to Palestine. In 1940, he helped found the Israel Conservatory and Academy of Music. He formed a string quartet in Tel Aviv that for many years was the country's foremost chamber ensemble.

In 1957, Fenyves and his family relocated to Geneva, where he became the director of the Orchestre de la Suisse Romande and taught at the Conservatoire de Genève. He lived in Switzerland for eight years and then moved to Canada, becoming a Canadian citizen in 1963 and teaching at the annual Jeunesses Musicales summer school at Mount Orford, Quebec. He later took a teaching position at the University of Toronto.

He retired in 1983, worked with his association, the Banff Centre of the Arts, taught at the University of Western Ontario, and continued to perform around the world.

Lorand Fenyves died in Zurich, Switzerland, on March 23, 2004.[24]

His sister, Alice Fenyves, became one of the foremost music teachers in Palestine.

Horst Salomon and Huberman were not successful in getting Horst's parents out of Germany and to Palestine. His mother died of natural causes in Berlin after the war broke out. Horst's father and sister were most likely killed in Auschwitz. His brother managed to emigrate to England, and survived the war.[25]

Jacob Surovicz's son, Leopold, a pianist who fled Europe and illegally sneaked into Palestine aboard a ship in 1939, joined the orchestra in 1951. Leopold's son, Gabriel Vole, the third-generation member of the orchestra, a double-bass player, joined the orchestra in 1967, after serving in the Israeli Defense Forces.[26]

From 1936 to 1959, **David Grunschlag** served as first violinist, concertmaster, and occasional soloist with the Palestine Symphony and the Israel Philharmonic Orchestra. In 1959, at the request of Leonard Bernstein, he joined the New York Philharmonic on a European tour, and then joined the Philadelphia Orchestra, from which he retired in 1984.

In 1937, Huberman arranged for Grunschlag's father to come to Palestine, recruiting him as a trumpet player in the orchestra. The next year, Huberman was able to secure a permanent certificate for David's mother to enter Palestine, saving her from being sent to a Polish internment camp. In 1939, Huberman brought David's young sisters, the duo piano team Toni and Rosi Grunschlag, to London. The two young women had been stranded in Vienna. Rosi states: "When I think back what we endured during the thirteen months that we were with Hitler. It's amazing . . . I don't know if I could do that over again."[27]

Toni and Rosi became renowned duo pianists, eventually living in New York City and performing around the world into their old age.

David Grunschlag's daughter, Dorit Straus, worked with producer/director Josh Aronson to make a documentary about Huberman and the founding of the Palestine Symphony: *Orchestra of Exiles* (2012).[28]

In 2013, Ms. Straus retired from her position as worldwide fine art manager at the Chubb Group of Insurance Companies, and now spends her time as an independent consultant and an advocate for artists and the arts.[29]

"I can only say that I am here because of Huberman's efforts and what he did personally for my family. I owe [him] a debt of gratitude that I don't know how to repay."[30]

Henry Haftel was given responsibility for the orchestra during World War II, when Huberman couldn't get to Palestine. Haftel became the concertmaster, a leading player, and soloist, as well as the manager, director, troubleshooter, fund-raiser, and impresario of the Palestine Symphony.

On May 26, 1955, the Israel Philharmonic Orchestra gave a private concert for Pope Pius XII in the Vatican's consistory hall, the first time any orchestra from abroad had played privately for Pope Pius.

On that day, Concertmaster Haftel thanked the pope for the opportunity to play for him, adding: "The Jewish people are happy to express through music their gratitude for the help the Church gave to persecuted people. Our orchestra is composed of musicians from fourteen countries, most of them have suffered persecution," he pointed out.[31]

Uri Toeplitz became the orchestra's principal flutist, and served on the board, for the next thirty-five years. He died in Jerusalem in 2006.

Uri's son, flutist Gideon Toeplitz, born in Tel Aviv in 1944, led the Pittsburgh Symphony Orchestra from 1987 to 2003, and was listed for five years running by the *Pittsburgh Post-Gazette* as one of the "Top 50 Cultural Leaders" in Pittsburgh. He died in October 2011.[32]

Heinrich Simon served as the orchestra's manager for two years.

David Ben-Gurion became the first prime minister of Israel and is widely hailed as the state's main founder. In June 1963, he resigned as prime minister, and retired from political life in June 1970. He died in 1973 at his home in Kibbutz Sde Boker.[33]

Even though he died during the 1936 Arab revolts in Palestine, the first mayor of Tel Aviv, **Meir Dizengoff**, is remembered as a central figure in the birth of the State of Israel. The declaration of independence was made on May 14, 1948, in his former home, a simple stucco building now called Independence Hall. In 1909, Dizengoff and sixty-six families had come together on the shoreline, founding Tel Aviv. He also established the city's first municipal police force.[34]

When Israel became a state, **Chaim Weizmann** was chosen to serve as its first president, a role he filled until his death in 1952.[35]

~~~

Sir Arthur Grenfell Wauchope retired as the British high commissioner in Palestine in 1938, due to ill health. He died in 1947.

Kurt Singer led the Kulturbund in Germany until 1938. At its height, the organization employed two thousand Jewish artists and had seventy thousand audience members all over Germany.[36]

On November 9–10, 1938, Singer was visiting his sister in the United States and lecturing at Harvard University when his friend Ernest Lenart told him about Germany's *Kristallnacht*. Lenart urged Singer to stay in America, but he returned to Europe. In 1941, the Nazi Party dismantled the Kulturbund. Singer fled Berlin, but was captured by the Nazis and sent to Theresienstadt, where he died in January 1944.[37]

Wilhelm Furtwängler conducted the Berlin Philharmonic during most of the Nazi regime. In 1936, he was offered, and accepted, a position conducting the New York Philharmonic. But due to his alleged Nazi associations, the offer was rescinded. On February 7, 1945, he slipped into Switzerland. Furtwängler's war crimes trial began on December 11, 1946, the tribunal conceding that he played no part in the National Socialist organization. His "guilt by association," however, long troubled his career. In 1949, American sentiment again caused the cancellation of his position as conductor of the Chicago Symphony Orchestra. Furtwängler died on November 30, 1954, near Baden-Baden, West Germany.[38]

Richard Wolff, the first violinist of the Berlin Philharmonic, once stated:

"Furtwängler could have enjoyed a secure and comfortable life abroad during the dreadful years of the Nazi regime, but he felt it his responsibility to stay behind and help educate the younger German generation and to keep alive spiritual values in Germany in her darkest hour."[39]

⤛⤜

Adolf Hitler incited World War II, advocating Fascist policies that resulted in millions of deaths. Afraid of falling into the hands of the enemy, on April 30, 1945, Hitler committed suicide in his Berlin bunker. Berlin fell on May 2, 1945, and five days later, Germany surrendered to the Allies.[40]

In 1945, Lew Besymenski, a captain in Russia's military intelligence unit, found Hitler's personal collection of music, records he listened to privately. Stored in Moscow, the collection was discovered again in 1991. The one hundred records in the collection, marked *Führerhauptquartier*, included a collection of Russian composers, Peter Tchaikovsky, Alexander Borodin, and Sergei Rachmaninoff. Some of the well-worn records featured Jewish soloists, including violinist Bronislaw Huberman and pianist Artur Schnabel.[41]

Mrs. Winifred Wagner supported Hitler for a lifetime. After the collapse of the Third Reich, a denazification court banned her from the Bayreuth Festival. Still a committed Nazi and admirer of Hitler, she died in Überlingen, on the shore of Lake Constance, on March 5, 1980, at the age of eighty-two. Her body was interred at Bayreuth.[42]

In 1931, **Joseph Goebbels** had convinced Hitler to host the Olympics in Berlin and to use the worldwide event to promote Nazism.[43]

After Hitler's suicide, Goebbels became chancellor of Germany for one day before he and his wife, Magda, poisoned their six children and killed themselves in Hitler's Berlin bunker.[44]

Theodor Herzl, who died in Edlach, near Vienna, on July 3, 1904, was brought to the State of Israel in August 1949, where his body was reinterred on the northern slopes of Mount Herzl—named in his memory. His tomb lies on the crest of the mountain range overlooking the Judean Hills on one side and both old and new Jerusalem on the other.[45]

The First World War (1914–18) set the stage for **World War II** (1939–45), when Adolf Hitler and his Nazi Party rearmed Germany, signing treaties with Italy and Japan in their quest for world domination. During the Holocaust, Hitler murdered six million Jews in Nazi concentration camps as well as millions of others he deemed "undesirable."

During World War II, an estimated forty-five to sixty million people died worldwide.[46]

Bronislaw Huberman kept the handwritten note he received from **Johannes Brahms** at Vienna's Musikverein Hall, on January 29, 1896, for his entire life. It remained in the Huberman family, undocumented and unknown, for one hundred and eight years.

Later in her life, Joan Huberman, Bronislaw's granddaughter, recalled that the note was kept in her father's bedroom and was never publicly exhibited. On May 20, 2005, with Joan's consent, London's Sotheby's Musical Manuscript auctioned and sold the Brahms-penned note for 10,200 GBPs, ($17,136).[47]

The **Felix Mendelssohn statue**, once standing in front of the Düsseldorf Opera House and torn down by Nazis in November 1936, was replaced seventy-six years later, paid for by private contributions from more than two hundred Düsseldorfers.

"It is long overdue to restore Mendelssohn to his rightful place of honor in Düsseldorf," Bernd Dieckmann, a representative of the committee, said. "This barbaric act [by Nazis, in 1936] left a painful empty space in our city, which had not been filled."[48]

APPENDIX 1:

Original Orchestra Members Listed in 1936–37 Opening Concert

ARGENTINA:

Boris Rogoff, second violins. Philharmonic Orchestra Buenos Aires

AUSTRIA:

Felix Galimir, first violins. Leader of the Galimir Quartet and of the Vienna Concert-Orchestra
David Grunschlag, first violins. Vienna Concert-Orchestra
Heinrich Haftel, first violins. Vienna Concert-Orchestra
Alfred Lunger, first violins. Vienna Concert-Orchestra
Lotte Hammerschlag, violas. Leader, Vienna Concert-Orchestra
Renée Galimir, violas. Member of Galimir Quartet
Dr. Hans Levitus, clarinet. First Clarinet, National Theatre
Linz Gustav Totzler, tuba. Orchester-Verein, Vienna

CZECHOSLOVAKIA:

Szlomo Bor, second violin. Symphony Orchestra Prague
Oskar Heller, trombone. National Theatre Kosice
France Schulamith Silber-Chajes, first violins. Broadcasting Orchestra Paris
Ben Ami Silber, second violins. Broadcasting Orchestra Paris
Aszer Borochow, second violins. Orchestra Cortôt Paris

GERMANY:

Rudolf Bergmann, leader, first violins. Leader, Municipal Orchestra Wiesbaden; New Opera Hamburg

Basia Polischuk, first violins. Leader, Jüdische Kulturbund Berlin

Andreas Weissgerber, first violins. Germany (immigrated to Palestine 1933)

Klecki Mnasza, second violins. Gewandthaus Leipzig

Harry Blumberg, violas. Berlin String Quartet

Jacob Bernstein, violoncelli. Leader, Philharmonic Orchestra Stockholm; Leipzig Symphony Orchestra

Ary Schuyer, violoncelli. Leader, Frankfurt Opera and Museum Orchestra

Albert Katz, violoncelli. Leader, Leipzig Symphony Orchestra

Josef Weissgerber, violoncelli. Germany (immigrated to Palestine 1933)

Ernst Boehm, bass. Leader, Broadcasting Orchestra Cologne; Orchestra Jüdische Kulturbund Frankfurt

M. Salomon Engelsman, flute. First flute, Dresden Philharmonic Orchestra

Erich Toeplitz, flute. Orchestra Jüdische Kulturbund Frankfurt

M. Heinrich Zimmermann, clarinet. First clarinet, Orchestra Jüdische Kulturbund Frankfurt, Municipal Orchestra Wiesbaden

Horst Salomon, horn. First horn, Orchestra Jüdische Kulturbund Berlin

Wolf Sprecher, horn. Opera and Municipal Orchestra Saarbrücken

Mischa Rakier, trumpet. Dresden Philharmonic Orchestra; Municipal Orchestra Saarbrücken

Heinrich Schiefer, trombone. First Trombone, Orchestra Jüdische Kulturbund Berlin

Kurt Sommerfeld, timpani. Berlin Kulturbund Orchestra

GEORGIA:

Mordechai Pinski, bass. Professor at the Conservatory of Music in Tiflis (Tblisi, Georgia, today; in 1936, part of Russia)

HUNGARY:

Lorand Fenyves, first violins. Second leader, Budapest Concert-Orchestra and Budapest Philharmonic Orchestra
Alice Fenyves, violas. Budapest Municipal Orchestra
Dr. Laszlo Vincze, violoncelli. Leader, Budapest Concert-Orchestra
Tibor Silk, horn. First horn, Budapest Concert-Orchestra

ITALY:

Adolfo Farnesi, bass. Leader, Broadcasting Orchestra Rome
Hans Sachs, trumpet. First trumpet, Orchestra Municipale San Remo

LATVIA:

Israel Segall, timpani. Symphony Orchestra and Opera, Riga

NETHERLANDS:

Salomon van den Berg, oboe. "Residenz-Orchestra" The Hague
Louis Staal, clarinet. First clarinet, Haag'sche Symphony Orchestra
Josef Samson de Groen, bassoon. First Bassoon, Philharmonic Orchestra Groningen

POLAND:

Mieczyslaw Fliederbaum, first violins. Leader, Warsaw Philharmonic Orchestra
Jacob Surowicz, second violins. Leader, Warsaw Philharmonic Orchestra
Moszek Lewak, second violins. Leader, Philharmonic Łódź
Mosze Sztyglic, second violins. Warsaw Philharmonic Orchestra
Alfred Ginzburg, second violins. Warsaw Philharmonic Orchestra
Liftman Boruch, second violins. Opera Warsaw
Pelssach Ginzburg, violas. Leader, Warsaw Philharmonic Orchestra
Bloeslaw Ginzburg, violoncelli. Leader, Warsaw Philharmonic Orchestra

Abraham Wenger, bass. Leader, Philharmonic Orchestra Łódź

Leon Szulc, bassoon. First Bassoon, Vienna State Opera; Professor of the Warsaw Conservatory

Bronislaw Szulc, horn. First Horn, Warsaw Opera; Professor of the Warsaw Conservatory; Conductor of the Scottish Orchestra in Glasgow and the Łódź Philharmonic Orchestra

Zwi Feldmann, trumpet. Warsaw Philharmonic Orchestra

Michal Podemski, trombone. First Trombone, Philharmonic Orchestra Łōdž

Lodz Ginzburg, timpani. Broadcasting Orchestra Warsaw

RUSSIA:

Seew Mirkin, bass. Leader, Leningrad Philharmonic Orchestra (today's St. Petersburg

SWITZERLAND:

Dea Gombrich, first violins. Adolf Busch Chamber-Orchestra

CROATIA:

Jaroslaw Front, violas. Leader, Philharmonic Orchestra and Opera Zagreb (Yugoslavia in 1936)

UKRAINE:

Marek Rak, first violin. Leader, Lemberg Philharmonic Orchestra and Opera (Lemberg is now Lviv in Ukraine)

UNITED STATES:

Jacob Shumer, flute. First flute, Chicago Symphony Orchestra

Josef Marx, oboe. First oboe, Symphony Orchestra Dayton, Ohio; Broadcasting Station Cincinnati, Ohio

No Associations Given in Program:

Joseph Bernstein, first violins
Raja Berson, second violins
Selmar Chasin, second violins
Dora Loeb, violas
Chaim Bor, violas
Adolfo Odnoposoff, violoncelli
Chaim Bodenstajn, violoncelli[1]

APPENDIX 2

Officers of the Palestine Symphony

THE BOARD OF TRUSTEES:

Bronislaw Huberman, President

S. Horowitz, Deputy Chairman

Colonel F. H. Kisch, Treasurer

Israel M. Sieff, London

Daniel Heineman, Brussels

Robert von Hirsch, Basle

THE CHAIRMEN OF THE BRANCHES OF THE PALESTINE SYMPHONY ASSOCIATIONS IN TEL AVIV, JERUSALEM, AND HAIFA:

Paul J. Jacobi, Hon. Secretary

THE PALESTINE SYMPHONY ASSOCIATION:

Tel Aviv:

Mrs. S. Hoofien

Moshe Chelouche

S. Bruenn

Mr. Chelouche

Dr. E. Hurwitz

S. Bruenn

M. Kanyuk

Jerusalem:
S. Horowitz
S. Jacobs
K. Kronenberger

Haifa:
Victor Konn
Mrs. M. Katz
Dr. L. Mayer
L. D. Watts

The Management:
Dr. Heinrich Simon, General Manager
Shlomo B. Lewertoff, General Secretary

APPENDIX 3

Internet Extras

ARTURO TOSCANINI:

To view videos of Arturo Toscanini, please see these websites:

1. Toscanini's 1926 rehearsal:
   www.youtube.com/watch?v=A8GDjgzHuGE.

2. Toscanini's earliest Wagner recording, in 1932:
   www.youtube.com/watch?v=4S-glm9GSuo.

3. Toscanini throws a temper tantrum:
   www.youtube.com/watch?v=-F1__ELBbXc.

BRONISLAW HUBERMAN:

To view performances by Bronislaw Huberman, please see these websites:

1. *Nocturne Op. 9 No. 2* (Chopin):
   www.youtube.com/watch?v=ByhwHJ5nRv0.

2. *Romanza Andaluza*, 1929, with Siegfried Schultze playing the piano:
   www.youtube.com/watch?v=O9M3znlOA90.

3. *Ungarischer Tanz Nr. 1* (Brahms), 1932:
   www.youtube.com/watch?v=f-ILCC_sqVc.

4. Paganini: *La campanella*:
   www.youtube.com/watch?v=1Ouqa2L1OjM.

Wilhelm Furtwängler:

To view performances by Wilhelm Furtwängler, please see these websites:

1. Wagner, *Tristan und Isolde Vorspiel*, Berlin, 1930:
   www.youtube.com/watch?v=4o142b5plHc.
2. *Tristan und Isolde: Prelude*, Bayreuth, 1931:
   www.youtube.com/watch?v=8S2jb6py9fI.

Richard Strauss:

To view Richard Strauss's *Parsifal:* Act III, *"Nur eine Waffe taugt,"* Bayreuth, 1933, please see: www.youtube.com/watch?v=s6kPiXuoPoI.

Joseph Goebbels:

To view Goebbels making the speech, *"Rede über den Judenboykott,"* 1 April 1933, please see: www.youtube.com/watch?v=gRQHwKMgOYc.

Adolf Hitler:

To view Adolf Hitler's speech, "Triumph of the Will," in 1934, please see: www.youtube.com/watch?v=d0OtwfYahyg.

Joshua Bell:

To view Joshua Bell talking about the Gibson Stradivarius, please see: www.youtube.com/watch?v=r5aLHuk0PUU.

"Hatikvah":

To view Paolo Olmi conducting the Israel Philharmonic Orchestra, playing "Hatikvah," please see: www.youtube.com/watch?v=Bn4iVOt3OAE.

UNITED STATES HOLOCAUST MEMORIAL MUSEUM, WASHINGTON, D.C.

For more information about the Holocaust, please see: www.ushmm.org/.

ACKNOWLEDGMENTS

So many people were involved in writing this complicated story of Bronislaw Huberman, and we appreciate each one.

Our deep gratitude goes to our extraordinary book agent, Greg Johnson, President of WordServe Literary, FaithHappenings; Penguin Random House's Natalee Rosenstein, Robin Barletta, Allison Janice, and Pam Barricklow. Diane Dill and Nina Krstic who helped with the difficult job of locating copyrights and permissions; to encouragers and supporters, including Harlan Hobart Grooms, Alyce Elizabeth George, Rebecca Pounds George, Dr. Timothy George (Denise's husband), Dr. Christian Timothy George, the members of The Book Writing Boot Camp, and many others. A special thank you goes to Mrs. Willene Wyse (Denise's mother), who first recommended that the story be written into book form and encouraged the entire process. And to Maria Bachmann, Josh Aronson's violinist wife who encouraged him for three years in the making of the film, and then the long hours it took to co-write the book. Additional thanks to Dorit Straus, who brought Josh Aronson the story with the idea it should be a film.

An additional word of gratitude to: Dr. Arnold I. Kisch, Kathleen Sabogal, Thalia Fenyves-Reichard, Daphne Fenyves, Avivit Hochstadter, Gina Ginsburg Tavor, Joan Huberman Payne, Mark Huberman, Jeffrey Huberman, and the Library of Congress. The authors wish to credit the Felicja Blumental Music Center & Library, the Bronislaw Huberman Archive, Tel Aviv, Israel, for access to photographs presented on pages 1 (top), 2 (top right and bottom), 3 (top), 4 (top), 6 (top and bottom), and 8 (bottom) of the first photo insert, and page 6 (top) of the second photo insert.

NOTES

Prelude

1 Found at: Roy H. Schoeman, *Salvation Is from the Jews* (San Francisco: Ignatius Press, 2003), p. 245.

2 Quoted from: www.nizkor.org/hweb/people/h/hitler-adolf/hitler-1922.html. Accessed: Oct. 27, 2014.

Part i: A Son Is Born

1 Found at: www.goodreads.com/quotes/tag/childhood. Accessed: Sept. 17, 2014.

Chapter 1: The Boy

1 Found at: www.goodreads.com/quotes/tag/childhood. Accessed: Sept. 16, 2014.

Chapter 2: A Childhood Denied

1 Bronislaw Huberman, "Huberman Life and Lifestyle," in an address at the Concert Goers' Club, "The Artist in His Workshop," on Friday, May 19, 1911.

Chapter 3: Leaving Home

1 Comment made about B. Huberman by Noel Strauss. Found at: www.huberman.info/reviews/1940s/. Accessed: Jan. 11, 2015.

2 Found at: www.historyplace.com/worldwar2/riseofhitler/born.htm. Accessed: Dec. 19, 2014.

3 Found at: www.historyplace.com/worldwar2/riseofhitler/born.htm. Accessed: Aug. 2, 2014.

4 Schickelgruber was the name of Hitler's paternal grandmother. His father took the name of his supposed father—Hiedler or Hitler, before Adolf was born. Although it remains unproven, some scholars believe Hitler's father was half Jewish. Found at: www.theguardian.com/notesandqueries/query/0,5753,-57564,00.html. Accessed: Oct. 6, 2014.

Chapter 4: Concerts for Cash

1 From www.huberman.info/literature/books/galafres/. Accessed June 12, 2014.

2 Found at: www.nytimes.com/learning/general/onthisday/bday/0128.html. Accessed: September 22, 2014.

3 Found at: www.amazon.com/Rubinstein-A-Life-Harvey-Sachs/dp/0802115799/ref=pd_sim_sbs_b_3?ie=UTF8&refRID=05VNBBGWZ0CX318Z2MGZ. Accessed: Oct. 20, 2014.

Chapter 6: The Brief Education of Bronislaw Huberman

1 Found at: www.huberman.info/literature/interviews/etude_1912/. Accessed: January 4, 2015.

Chapter 7: The Great Joachim

1 Found at: http://pronetoviolins.blogspot.com/2011/01/huberman.html. Accessed: Oct. 20, 2014.

Chapter 8: The Aging Diva

1 Found at: http://en.wikipedia.org/wiki/Adelina_Patti. Accessed: Aug. 4, 2014.

Chapter 9: The Gift

1 Found at: http://books.google.com/books?id=oZFHRfnKtYIC&pg=PA1&lpg=PA1&dq=violins+of+Cremona&source=bl&ots=ugEEEpgBuE&sig=G0cjMj-P3BSDzKmDNw_QfMD9GhA&hl=en&sa=X&ei=PrfjU47YBaXhsASir4GoDg&ved=0CIgBEOgBMAg4Cg#v=onepage&q=violins%20of%20Cremona&f=false. Accessed: Aug. 8, 2014.

2 Found at: www.firstworldwar.com/bio/franzjosef.htm. Accessed: Aug. 7, 2014.

Chapter 10: The Old Composer

1 Found at: www.musicwithease.com/brahms-quotes.html. Accessed: Aug. 11, 2014.

2 During those years, a great debate ensued about the purpose of art. Most believed that art should be used only to glorify art, and should not be used for any other reasons.

James Abbott McNeill Whistler writes: "Art should be independent of all claptrap—should stand alone, and appeal to the artistic sense of eye and ear, without confounding this with emotions entirely foreign to it, as devotion, pity, love, patriotism, and the like. All these have no kind of concern with it." James Abbott McNeill Whistler, in his book, *The Gentle Art of Making Enemies*, published in 1890. Found at: http://arthistoryresources.net/modernism/artsake.html. Accessed: Sept. 5, 2014.

L'art pour l'art (art for art's sake) became a popular belief in the late nineteenth century. Oscar Wilde, like many artists and writers, believed that: "A work of art is the unique result of a unique temperament. Its beauty comes from the fact that the author is what he is. It has nothing to do with the fact that other people want what they want. Indeed, the moment that an artist takes notice of what other people want, and tries to supply the demand, he ceases to be an artist, and becomes a dull or an amusing craftsman, an honest or a dishonest tradesman. He has no further claim to be considered as an artist." (Oscar Wilde, *The Soul of Man Under Socialism*, 1891, in the *Pall Mall Gazette*. Found at: http://arthistoryresources.net/modernism/artsake.html. Accessed: Sept. 5, 2014.)

Chapter 11: The Gathering

1 Found at: www.jewishvirtuallibrary.org/jsource/biography/Herzl.html. Accessed: Aug. 4, 2014.
2 Found at: www.jewishvirtuallibrary.org/jsource/Zionism/herzlex.html. Accessed: Aug. 9, 2014.
3 Some information found at: www.jewishvirtuallibrary.org/jsource/Zionism/First_Cong_&_Basel_Program.html. Accessed: Aug. 4, 2014, and www.jewishvirtuallibrary.org/jsource/biography/Herzl.html. Accessed: Aug. 4, 2014.

Chapter 12: Dilemmas and Decisions

1 Found at: www.musicianguide.com/biographies/1608000089/Arthur-Rubinstein.html. Accessed: Oct. 20, 2014.

Chapter 13: The Life-Changing Death

1 Found at: http://arbiterrecords.org/catalog/huberman-concert-and-recital-recordings/. Accessed: Jan. 13, 2015.
2 Some information found at: www.healthgrades.com/symptoms/paralysis-symptoms. Accessed: Jan. 14, 2015.

Chapter 14: The High Price of Purpose

1 Found at: www.goodreads.com/quotes/tag/violin. Accessed: Aug. 1, 2014.
2 Some information found at: www.jewishvirtuallibrary.org/jsource/Immigration/Second_Aliyah.html, and www.jewishvirtuallibrary.org/jsource/biography/Herzl.html. Both accessed: August 10, 2014.

Chapter 15: The Beautiful Actress

1 Found at: www.huberman.info/literature/books/galafres/. Accessed: June 12, 2014.

Chapter 16: The Dresden Sanatorium

1 Found at: www.huberman.info/biography/marriage/. Accessed: Jan. 14, 2015.

Chapter 17: The Complication

1 Found at: www.huberman.info/literature/books/galafres/. Accessed: June 12, 2014.

Chapter 18: The Parting

1 Found at: www.huberman.info/literature/books/galafres/. Accessed: June 12, 2014.

2 Found at: http://en.wikipedia.org/wiki/Ernő_Dohnányi. Accessed: Aug. 14, 2014.

Chapter 19: The Golden Age of Security

1 Found at: www.goodreads.com/book/show/18877635-1913. Accessed: Oct. 7, 2014.

PART 2: WAR!

1 Found at: www.thedailybeast.com/articles/2013/06/09/before-the-fall-what-did-the-world-look-like-in-1913.html. Accessed: Aug. 12, 2014.

Chapter 20: Earthquake!

1 Found at: www.goodreads.com/quotes/tag/ww1. Accessed: Aug. 15, 2014.

2 Information found at: www.firstworldwar.com/bio/princip.htm. Accessed: Aug. 28, 2014, and www.eyewitnesstohistory.com/duke.htm. Accessed: Aug. 28, 2014, and www.history.com/this-day-in-history/archduke-franz-ferdinand-assassinated. Accessed: August 15, 2014, and www.eyewitnesstohistory.com/duke.htm. Accessed: Aug. 15, 2014.

3 To view the video of June 28, 1914, showing Archduke Franz Ferdinand and Sophie arriving at Sarajevo's town hall, shortly before the assassination, please see: www.firstworldwar.com/video/ferdinand.htm. Accessed: August 15, 2014.

Chapter 21: The Arrest

1 Found at: www.history.com/this-day-in-history/germany-and-france-declare-war-on-each-other. Accessed: Aug. 15, 2014.

2 Found at: www.firstworldwar.com/features/declarationsofwar.htm. Accessed: Sept. 15, 2014.

Chapter 22: The Scientist

1 Found at: www.ppu.org.uk/learn/infodocs/people/pp-einstein.html. Accessed: Jan. 15, 2015.

2 Found at: www.pha.jhu.edu/einstein/stuff/einstein&music.pdf. Accessed: Oct. 7, 2014.

3 Found at: www.pha.jhu.edu/einstein/stuff/einstein&music.pdf. Accessed: Oct. 7, 2014.

4 Found at: www.ppu.org.uk/learn/infodocs/people/pp-einstein.html. Accessed: Oct. 7, 2014.

Chapter 23: The World at War

1 Found at: www.history.com/this-day-in-history/germany-and-france-declare-war-on-each-other. Accessed: Aug. 15, 2014.
2 Found at: http://culture.pl/en/artist/bronislaw-huberman. Accessed: Jan. 15, 2015.
3 Found at: www.ushmm.org/wlc/en/article.php?ModuleId=10007427. Accessed: Oct. 7, 2014.
4 Found at: www.marstonrecords.com/farrar/farrar_liner.htm. Accessed: Aug. 15, 2014. (To watch Geraldine Farrar perform in *Carmen*, 1915, please see: www.diarci.com/2012/07/02/iron-wills-geraldine-farrar-emmy-destinn/. Accessed: Jan. 15, 2015.)
5 Found at: www.history.com/topics/world-war-i/lusitania. Accessed: January 15, 2015. (To watch a brief video of the Lusitania, please see: www.history.com/topics/world-war-i/lusitania. Accessed: January 15, 2015.)

Chapter 24: Discouragement and Depression

1 Found at: www.history.com/this-day-in-history/germany-and-france-declare-war-on-each-other. Accessed: Aug. 15, 2014.
2 Found at: www.history.com/topics/world-war-i/battle-of-the-somme. Accessed: Jan. 16, 2015, and www.firstworldwar.com/battles/somme.htm. Accessed: Feb. 26, 2015.

Chapter 25: The German Nurse

1 Quoted from: "The Merchant of Venice" by William Shakespeare.

Chapter 27: The Missing Months

1 Found at: www.goodreads.com/author/show/205.Robert_A_Heinlein. Accessed: Jan. 21, 2015.
2 Some information found at: www.historyplace.com/worldhistory/firstworldwar/index-1917.html. Accessed: Jan. 22, 2015.

PART 3: THE GREAT WAR ENDS

1 Found at: http://hubpages.com/hub/World-War-1-The-Cost-of-War. Accessed: December 10, 2014.
2 "Afterwards, when the First World War had killed or wounded 37 million people, ripped apart the fabric of society, uprooted oppressive regimes, and set the planet

on course for the bloodiest century in human history, they [the great powers of
Europe] all claimed, with differing degrees of insistence and self-delusion, that the
Great War was inevitable, or 'necessary,' and beyond their powers to contain or
avoid." Quote from: Paul Ham, *1913: The Eve of War*, found at: https://www
.goodreads.com/book/show/18877635-1913. Accessed: Oct. 7, 2014.

Chapter 28: The Eleventh Hour of the Eleventh Day of the Eleventh Month

1 Found at: "Vienna After War," *Poverty Bay Herald*, Vol. XLVI, Issue 14806, 9
   January 1919, page 2; http://paperspast.natlib.govt.nz/cgi-bin/paperspast?a=d&d=
   PBH19190109.2.4. Accessed: July 30, 2014.
2 Found at: www.fsmitha.com/h2/ch19vienna.html. Accessed: Aug. 1, 2014.
3 WW1 began as a local war between Austria-Hungary and Serbia in 1914. It grew
   into a war involving thirty-two countries. The Allies included Britain, France,
   Russia, Italy, and the United States. These countries fought against the Central
   Powers: Germany, Austria-Hungary, the Ottoman Empire, and Bulgaria. Found
   at: http://aenet.esuhsd.org/citizenship_lessons/connie/wwI_q.html. Accessed:
   Dec. 7, 2014.

Chapter 29: The Boy in the Brown Jacket

1 Found at: http://en.thinkexist.com/reference/quotes_about_children_and_war/.
   Accessed: Jan. 16, 2015.

Chapter 30: The Theft

1 Found at: www.history.com/this-day-in-history/world-war-i-comes-to-an-end.
   Accessed: Sept. 4, 2014.

Chapter 31: The Treaty

1 Found at: www.goodreads.com/quotes/tag/ww1. Accessed: Sept. 4, 2014.
2 Some information found at: www.historylearningsite.co.uk/treaty_of_versailles
   .htm. Accessed: Sept. 5, 2014, and www.history.com/topics/world-war-i/treaty-of-
   versailles. Accessed: Sept. 5, 2014, and www.history.com/this-day-in-history/
   keynes-predicts-economic-chaos. Accessed: Sept. 5, 2014, and www.pbs.org/
   marieantoinette/life/mirrors.html. Sept. 5, 2014, and https://uahsibhistory
   .wikispaces.com/Social+and+Economic+Changes+in+France+WWI-1929.
   Accessed: Sept. 5, 2014.
3 Found at: http://history1900s.about.com/cs/swastika/a/swastikahistory.htm.
   Accessed: Aug. 1, 2014.
4 Some information/quote found at: www.fsmitha.com/h2/ch13adolf4.htm.
   Accessed: Aug. 1, 2014.

5 Found at: www.ushmm.org/wlc/en/article.php?ModuleId=10007431. Accessed: Aug. 1, 2014.

6 Found at: www.fsmitha.com/h2/ch13adolf5.htm. Accessed: Aug. 1, 2014.

7 Found at: http://history1900s.about.com/cs/swastika/a/swastikahistory.htm. Accessed: Aug. 1, 2014.

Chapter 32: The Rabble-Rouser and the New German Party

1 Found at: https://archive.org/stream/AdolfHitlerCollectionOfSpeeches19221945/ Adolf%20Hitler%20-%20Collection%20of%20Speeches%201922-1945#page/ n39/mode/2up. Quote found at: www.fsmitha.com/h2/ch13adolf7.htm. Accessed: Aug. 1, 2014.

Chapter 33: The Decision

1 A reporter for the *Journal of the American Medical Association*. Found at: https:// virus.stanford.edu/uda/. Accessed: Jan. 17, 2015.

2 Information found at: www.felbridge.org.uk/index.php?p=2_110. Accessed: Aug. 1, 2014.

3 Some information found at: www.hubermans.net/mordechai_huberman_Family/ mordechai_huberman_family.htm. Accessed: July 27, 2014.

4 Some information found at: www.paneuropa.org/gb_int/geschichte.html. Accessed: Oct. 29, 2014.

5 Some information found at: http://en.wikipedia.org/wiki/Paneuropean_Union. Accessed: Oct. 29, 2014.

Chapter 34: A Fanatic's Promises

1 Quoted from: www.nizkor.org/hweb/people/h/hitler-adolf/hitler-1922.html. Accessed: Oct. 27, 2014.

2 Found at: www.historylearningsite.co.uk/adolf_hitler_1918_to_1924.htm. Accessed: Oct. 27, 2014.

3 Found at: www.nizkor.org/hweb/people/h/hitler-adolf/hitler-1922.html. Accessed: Oct. 27, 2014.

4 Some information found at: http://en.wikipedia.org/wiki/Mein_Kampf. Accessed: Oct. 28, 2014. (To view Hitler's Socialist Party assemble, and to hear his attitude about Germany's Jews, please see: www.youtube.com/watch?v=d0OtwfYahyg. Accessed: Dec. 14, 2014.)

   (*Mein Kampf* will later become the "bible" of the Nazi Party, a free copy given to every newlywed German couple. Found at: www.history.com/topics/world-war-ii/ nazi-party. Accessed: July 13, 2014.)

Chapter 35: Sojourn in the States

1 Found at: www.huberman.info/literature/pan_europa/living_age/. Accessed: Oct. 27, 2014.
2 Found at: www.huberman.info/literature/pan_europa/living_age/. Accessed: Oct. 27, 2014.

Chapter 36: The Movement

1. Found at: www.huberman.info/literature/pan_europa/living_age/. Accessed: Oct. 27, 2014.
2 Some information/quotes found at: www.ppu.org.uk/learn/infodocs/people/ pp-einstein.html. Accessed: Sept. 10, 2014.
3 Found at: www.jewishvirtuallibrary.org/jsource/Immigration/First_Aliyah.html. Accessed: Sept. 10, 2014.

Chapter 37: Of Conductors and Crashes

1 Found at: www.furtwangler.net/man.html. Accessed: Oct. 28, 2014. (This is a statement he made to Dietrich Fischer-Dieskau.)
2 Some information found at: www.violinist.com/blog/doritstraus/20101/10805/. Accessed: Dec. 15, 2014.
3 In 1925, Huberman published the pamphlet "My Road to Pan-Europe." In 1932, he wrote the book *Vaterland Europa*.
4 Quoted from: www.historylearningsite.co.uk/Jews_Nazi_Germany.htm. Accessed: Oct. 28, 2014.

PART 4: THE BEGINNING OF TRANSFORMATION

Chapter 38: The Trip to Palestine

1 In 1929, the World Zionist Organization, and leaders of world Jewry, establish the Jewish Agency for Israel, becoming the official representative of the Jewish people to their governing British administration, and shouldering responsibility for promoting, protecting, and building the Jewish national homeland settlements in Palestine. But the small band of Jews, already living in Palestine, complain to the League of Nations about the lack of protection Britain provides. Found at: www1 .jafi.org.il/mission/history.htm. Accessed: Oct. 29, 2014.
2 Some information found at: http://zionism-israel.com/Palestine_Massacre_riots_ of_1929.htm. Accessed: Oct. 29, 2014.

Chapter 39: The Rehearsal

1 Found at: www.historylearningsite.co.uk/adolf_hitler.htm. Accessed: Oct. 26, 2014.

2 Some information found at: www.historylearningsite.co.uk/adolf_hitler.htm. Accessed: Oct. 26, 2014.

3 On August 4, 1930, during the whirlwind of the summer's concert season, Siegfried suffers a massive heart attack, collapses, and dies. Winifred, his wife of fourteen years, eagerly assumes the leadership of the Bayreuth Festivals. Found at: http://siegfriedwagner.com/en/siegfried-wagner.html. Accessed: Nov. 10, 2014.

4 Found at: www.wagneropera.net/RW-Performers/Arturo-Toscanini.htm. Accessed: Oct. 28, 2014.

5 Found at: www.fsmitha.com/h2/ch16.htm. Accessed: Oct. 28, 2014.

Chapter 40: The Second Trip to Palestine

1 Found at: www.surrealistmovement-usa.org/pages/news_toscanini.html. Accessed: Jan. 20, 2015.

2 Found at: http://archives.chicagotribune.com/1931/06/15/page/26/article/friend-declares-toscanini-was-ambush-victim. Accessed: Nov. 10, 2014.

3 Some information found at: http://orelfoundation.org/index.php/journal/journalArticle/the_147aryanization148_of_italian_musical_life/. Accessed: Oct. 28, 2014, and www.newspapers.com/clip/633339/toscanini_beaten_1931/. Accessed: Nov. 10, 2014, and http://archives.chicagotribune.com/1931/06/15/page/26/article/friend-declares-toscanini-was-ambush-victim. Accessed: Nov. 10, 2014.

Chapter 41: The Deal

1 Found at: www.jewishvirtuallibrary.org/jsource/Holocaust/goebbels.html. Accessed: July 13, 2014.

2 Found at: www.jewishvirtuallibrary.org/jsource/Holocaust/goebbels.html. Accessed: July 13, 2014.

3 Found at: www.classicalnotes.net/features/furtwangler.html. Accessed: Nov. 8, 2014.

4 Found at: http://germanhistorydocs.ghi-dc.org/sub_document.cfm?document_id=1574. Accessed: Oct. 30, 2014, and http://en.wikipedia.org/wiki/Wilhelm_Furtwängler. Accessed: Oct. 30, 2014.

5 Found at: http://holocaustmusic.ort.org/politics-and-propaganda/third-reich/reichskulturkammer/furtwngler-wilhelm/. Accessed: Oct. 30, 2014.

6 Found at: www.classicalnotes.net/features/furtwangler.html. Accessed: Nov. 8, 2014.

Chapter 42: The Madman Comes to Power

1 Quoted from: www.nizkor.org/hweb/people/h/hitler-adolf/hitler-1922.html. Accessed: Oct. 27, 2014.

2 Only 540,000 Jews resided in Germany at the start of 1933—about one percent of the total German population. Within a year thirty-seven thousand had emigrated. Information found at: *Music in Exile: Émigré Composers of the 1930s* (Canada: Museum of Jewish Heritage and the Royal Conservatory of Music, nd), p. 20.

3 Found at: http://germanhistorydocs.ghi-dc.org/sub_document.cfm?document_id=3940. Accessed: Oct. 29, 2014.

4 Found at: www.jewishvirtuallibrary.org/jsource/Holocaust/goebbels.html. Accessed: July 13, 2014.

5 Found at: www.historylearningsite.co.uk/Nazi_Germany_dictatorship.htm. Accessed: Oct. 29, 2014.

6 Found at: www.historylearningsite.co.uk/Nazi_Germany_dictatorship.htm. Accessed: Oct. 29, 2014.

7 Found at: www.myjewishlearning.com/history/Modern_History/1914 1948/ The_Holocaust/Early_Stages_of_Prosecution.shtml. Accessed: Oct. 29, 2014.

8 Some information found at: *Music in Exile: Émigré Composers of the 1930s* (Canada: Museum of Jewish Heritage and the Royal Conservatory of Music, nd), p. 20.

Chapter 43: The Primacy of Richard Wagner

1 Quoted from: *Music in Exile: Émigré Composers of the 1930s* (Canada: Museum of Jewish Heritage and the Royal Conservatory of Music, nd), p. 19.

2 Wahnfried is the Wagner family's estate where Hitler makes his second home.

3 Information from: *Music in Exile: Émigré Composers of the 1930s* (Canada: Museum of Jewish Heritage and the Royal Conservatory of Music, nd), p. 19.

4 To read the full contents of Toscanini's letter to Hitler, please see: www.surrealist-movement-usa.org/pages/news_toscanini.html. Accessed: January 20, 2015. (Please scroll to bottom of page.)

5 Found at: http://books.google.com/books?id=0MFx0rA4tdgC&pg=PA276&lpg=PA276&dq=Richard+Strauss+and+Bayreuth+1933&source=bl&ots=AFg3S8Ygqf&sig=NLoJAAuFKEuACQY8S235K4d4nz0&hl=en&sa=X&ei=FPBgVOyWKMWmgwS7pITIAw&ved=0CCYQ6AEwAw#v=onepage&q=Richard%20Strauss%20and%20Bayreuth%201933&f=false. Accessed: Jan. 20, 2015.

6 Found at: http://jewishcurrents.org/wp-content/uploads/2014/08/Toscanini-Huberman-and-the-Jews-by-David-Platt-3.82.pdf. Accessed: Jan. 20, 2015.

7 Quote/information found at: www.wagneropera.net/RW-Performers/Richard-Strauss.htm. Accessed: Nov. 10, 2014, and http://books.google.com/books?id=0MFx0rA4tdgC&pg=PA276&lpg=PA276&dq=Richard+Strauss+and+Bayreuth+1933&source=bl&ots=AFg3S8Ygqf&sig=NLoJAAuFKEuACQY8S235K4d4nz0&hl=e

n&sa=X&ei=FPBgVOyWKMWmgwS7pITIAw&ved=0CCYQ6AEwAw#v=onepa
ge&q=Richard%20Strauss%20and%20Bayreuth%201933&f=false. Accessed:
Nov. 10, 2014.

8 Found at: http://books.google.com/books?id=0MFx0rA4tdgC&pg=PA276&lpg=P
A276&dq=Richard+Strauss+and+Bayreuth+1933&source=bl&ots=AFg3S8Ygqf&s
ig=NLoJAAuFKEuACQY8S235K4d4nz0&hl=en&sa=X&ei=FPBgVOyWKMW
mgwS7pITIAw&ved=0CCYQ6AEwAw#v=onepage&q=Richard%20Strauss%20
and%20Bayreuth%201933&f=false. Accessed: Nov. 10, 2014.

Chapter 44: Creation of the Kulturbund Deutscher Juden

1 Found at: www.jewish-theatre.com/visitor/article_display.aspx?articleID=3681.
Accessed: Jan. 20, 2015.
2 To hear Richard Strauss conduct Richard Wagner's *Parsifal*, Act III, at the 1933
Bayreuth Festival, please see: www.youtube.com/watch?v=s6kPiXuoPoI. Accessed:
Dec. 31, 2014.
3 Found at: http://holocaustmusic.ort.org/politics-and-propaganda/third-reich/
the-berlin-jdischer/. Accessed: Oct. 29, 2014.
4 Found at: http://holocaustmusic.ort.org/politics-and-propaganda/third-reich/
the-berlin-jdischer/. Accessed: Oct. 29, 2014.
5 Some information found at: http://holocaustmusic.ort.org/politics-and-propa
ganda/third-reich/the-berlin-jdischer/singer-kurt/. Accessed: Oct. 29, 2014.
6 Found at: www.datesandevents.org/people-timelines/26-albert-einstein-timeline
.htm. Accessed: Oct. 30, 2014, and www.einstein-website.de/z_biography/
princeton-e.html. Accessed: Oct. 30, 2014.
7 Found at: www.einstein-website.de/z_biography/princeton-e.html. Accessed:
Oct. 30, 2014.

Chapter 45: Hitler's Propaganda Minister

1 Found at: www.jewishvirtuallibrary.org/jsource/Holocaust/goebbels.html.
Accessed: Oct. 30, 2014.
2 Found at: www.historyplace.com/worldwar2/hitleryouth/. Accessed:
Oct. 30, 2014.
3 Found at: http://net-abbey.org/hitler-as-god.htm. Accessed: Oct. 30, 2014.
4 Found at: www.jewishvirtuallibrary.org/jsource/Holocaust/goebbels.html.
Accessed: Oct. 30, 2014.

Chapter 46: The Invitation

1 Found at: www.huberman.info/biography/palestine/. Accessed: March 3, 2015.
2 To read Huberman's entire letter to Furtwängler, please see this site: www
.huberman.info/literature/articles/nazi_germany/. Accessed: Dec. 31, 2014.

3 Found at: http://en.wikipedia.org/wiki/Wilhelm_Furtwängler. Accessed: Oct. 30, 2014.

4 Found at: http://holocaustmusic.ort.org/politics-and-propaganda/third-reich/reichskulturkammer/furtwngler-wilhelm/. Accessed: Oct. 30, 2014.

5 Found at: http://germanhistorydocs.ghi-dc.org/sub_document.cfm?document_id=1574. Accessed: Oct. 30, 2014.

Chapter 47: The Publication

1 Found at: www.huberman.info/criticism/flesch/. Accessed: Jan. 22, 2015.

Chapter 48: The Castle in Vienna

1 Some information found at: www.britannica.com/EBchecked/topic/168274/Engelbert-Dollfuss. Accessed: Nov. 23, 2014.

2 Information/Pelley quote found at: *Music in Exile, Émigré Composers of the 1930s* (Canada: Museum of Jewish Heritage and the Royal Conservatory of Music, 2009, nd), pp. 20, 30.

3 Some information found at: www.historyplace.com/worldwar2/holocaust/timeline.html. Accessed: Nov. 23, 2014.

Chapter 50: Mysticism in Palestine

1 Found at: http://forward.com/articles/195265/israel-philharmonic-celebrates—years-of-harmony/?p=all. Accessed: Dec. 19, 2014.

Chapter 51: The Decision

1 Quoted from: http://jewishcurrents.org/wp-content/uploads/2014/08/Toscanini-Huberman-and-the-Jews-by-David-Platt-3.82.pdf. Accessed: Dec. 31, 2014.

Chapter 52: The Magnificent Obsession

1 "[Huberman] recognized as erroneous his former conviction that artists exercise their art only for art's sake. The real artist, he said, does not however create art for art's sake as an end in itself . . . he creates art for men, to bring them joy, to ennoble them, to make them forget their worries." Found at: www.huberman.info/literature/pan_europa/goetz/. Accessed: March 6, 2015.

Chapter 53: The Lawless Years

1 Much of the information about Dr. Judah Magnes found at: http://ohsmemorial.com/OHS/articles/1894-magnes.htm. Accessed: Dec. 1, 2014.

Chapter 54: Germany's New Laws

1 Found at: www.jewishvirtuallibrary.org/jsource/Holocaust/nurlaws.html. Accessed: Oct. 29, 2014.
2 Some information found at: www.jewishvirtuallibrary.org/jsource/Holocaust/ HitleronNuremburg.html. Accessed: Dec. 1, 2014, and www.jewishvirtuallibrary .org/jsource/Holocaust/nurlawtoc.html. Accessed: Dec. 1, 2014, and www .jewishvirtuallibrary.org/jsource/Holocaust/nurmlaw2.html. Accessed: Dec. 1, 2014.
3 Found at: www.myjewishlearning.com/history/Modern_History/1914-1948/ The_Holocaust/Early_Stages_of_Prosecution.shtml. Accessed: Oct. 29, 2014.

Chapter 55: Realizing the Obstacles

1 Found at: www.fsmitha.com/h2/ch17jeru3.htm. Accessed: Dec. 5, 2014.
2 Found at: www.jewishvirtuallibrary.org/jsource/History/mandate.html. Accessed: Dec. 5, 2014.

Chapter 56: The Need for Immediacy

1 Found at: http://dancutlermedicalart.com/AlbertEinstein'sZionism/06Einstein'sZi onism1930-1939.htm. Accessed: Dec. 7, 2014.
2 Ibid.

Chapter 57: Recruitment

1 Found at: http://dancutlermedicalart.com/AlbertEinstein'sZionism/06Einstein'sZi onism1930-1939.htm. Accessed: Dec. 7, 2014.
2 Found at: www.jewish-theatre.com/visitor/article_display.aspx?articleID=3681, and http://books.google.com/books?id=jptpQLKExKoC&pg=PA255&lpg=PA255 &dq=how+many+Kulturbund+subscribers+in+1936&source=bl&ots=L1yxLsu8SJ &sig=GK1Uj_zDtKToQ8FPCpAYyVt8OxI&hl=en&sa=X&ei=7SiHVIipKcuWN uq4gOAN&ved=0CCAQ6AEwAw#v=onepage&q=how%20many%20Kultur- bund%20subscribers%20in%201936&f=false. Both accessed: Dec. 8, 2014.

Chapter 59: Time Is Running Out!

1 Found at: www.historylearningsite.co.uk/italy_and_germany_1936_to_1940.htm. Accessed: Dec. 18, 2014.
2 Found at: www.huberman.info/biography/palestine/. Accessed: March 3, 2015.

Chapter 61: The Manager

1 *South African Jewish Times*, "Introduction to a Great Musician," Friday, April 12, 1940.

Chapter 62: The Maestro

1 Found at: www.wsj.com/articles/SB10001424127887324619504579030741903019 418. Accessed: Feb. 2, 2015.

Chapter 63: In the Meantime

1 Found at: Hermann Rauschning, *Gesprache mit Hitler* (Zurich, 1940), p. 81.

Chapter 64: The Maestro Responds

1 Found at: http://jewishcurrents.org/wp-content/uploads/2014/08/Toscanini-Huberman-and-the-Jews-by-David-Platt-3.82.pdf. Accessed: Dec. 31, 2014.

Chapter 65: The Letter of Protest

1 Written by B. Huberman on Feb. 25, 2014, (published in the *Manchester Guardian*, on March 7, 1936), np.

Chapter 66: The Announcement in the *New York Times*

1 Found at: http://holocaustmusic.ort.org/politics-and-propaganda/third-reich/schoenberg-arnold/. Accessed: Dec. 15, 2014.

Chapter 67: The Concert at Carnegie Hall

1 Found at: www.brainyquote.com/quotes/keywords/carnegie_hall.html. Accessed: Dec. 16, 2014.
2 Found at: www.huberman.info/literature/articles/violin_stolen/. Accessed: Dec. 24, 2014.

Chapter 68: Mourning the Loss

1 Found at: www.joshuabell.com/story-his-violin. Accessed: Dec. 18, 2014.
2 Found at: http://jstandard.com/index.php/content/print/19441/. Accessed: Dec. 15, 2014.

Chapter 69: Einstein's Idea

1 Found at: Jehoash Hirshberg, *Music in the Jewish Community of Palestine: 1880–1948* (Oxford: Clarendon Paperbacks, 1995), p. 124.
2 Some information found at: http://www.historylearningsite.co.uk/Rhineland_1936.htm. Accessed: Feb. 2, 2015.
3 Quote from: http://www.historylearningsite.co.uk/Rhineland_1936.htm. Accessed: Dec. 18, 2014.

Chapter 70: The Dinner

1 Found at: http://dancutlermedicalart.com/AlbertEinstein'sZionism/06Einstein'sZionism1930-1939.htm. Accessed: Dec. 21, 2014.
2 Ibid.
3 Ibid.

Chapter 71: A Fitting Home

1 Found at: Simon, Heinrich. *Palestine Listens to Its Orchestra: Personal Reminiscences* (New York: H. K. Advertising, 1939), np.

PART 5: CATASTROPHE!

1 Bronislaw Huberman, given in a speech, New York City, Dec. 9, 1934.

Chapter 72: The Untimely Death of the Dream

1 Found at: www.jewishvirtuallibrary.org/jsource/History/riots29.html. Accessed: Feb. 4, 2015.
2 Eighty Jews were murdered by terrorist acts during the labor strike, and a total of 415 Jewish deaths were recorded during the whole 1936–1939 Arab Revolt period. The toll on the Arabs was estimated to be roughly 5,000 dead, 15,000 wounded, and 5,600 imprisoned. Found at: www.jewishvirtuallibrary.org/jsource/History/riots36.html. Accessed: Feb. 3, 2015.

Chapter 73: Effort and Sacrifice

1 Found at: www.britannica.com/EBchecked/topic/972375/Berlin-1936-Olympic-Games. Accessed: Feb. 4, 2015, and www.ushmm.org/wlc/en/article.php?ModuleId=10005680. Accessed: Feb. 4, 2015.
2 Quoted from: www.historyplace.com/worldwar2/triumph/tr-olympics.htm. Accessed: Dec. 11, 2014.
3 To view Hitler, and the 1936 Opening Ceremony of the Berlin Olympics, please see: www.youtube.com/watch?v=GePNydI9gX4. Accessed: Dec. 10, 2014.
4 Found at: www.scrapbookpages.com/Sachsenhausen/introduction.html. Accessed: Feb. 7, 2015.
5 Found at: www.jewishvirtuallibrary.org/jsource/Holocaust/olympics.html. Accessed: Feb. 4, 2015.
6 Some information found at: www.olympic.org/content/results-and-medalists/gamesandsportsummary/?sport=31728&games=1936%2f1&event=. Accessed: Dec. 14, 2014.

Chapter 74: The Message

1 Bronislaw Huberman, *The Reform Advocate*, May 29, 1936, np. (*The Reform Advocate*, founded on February 20, 1891, Chicago, IL: Bloch & Newman Publishing Company.) Some information found at: www.jewishencyclopedia.com/articles/12633-reform-advocate. Accessed: March 3, 2015.

2 Found at: www.lonelyplanet.com/israel-and-the-palestinian-territories/weather. Accessed: Feb. 8, 2015.

PART 6: THE DREAM COMES TRUE!

Chapter 75: The Rehearsals

1 Found at: www.huberman.info/literature/articles/nazi_germany/. Accessed: Dec. 31, 2014.

2 During the period between Feb. 1934 and the first concert of the orchestra on Dec. 26, 1936, Huberman played 225 concerts, with additional orchestra and chamber music rehearsals in ninety-three towns in twenty-three countries—donating the money to the orchestra.

3 Some information found at: http://blogs.forward.com/the-arty-semite/159616/duesseldorf-will-replace-mendelssohn-statue/. Accessed: Dec. 11, 2014, and Simon Wynberg, *Music in Exile: Émigré Composers of the 1930s* (Canada: Museum of Jewish Heritage and the Royal Conservatory of Music, nd), p. 14, and http://www.mendelssohn-preis.de/eng/about/about.html. Accessed: Dec. 11, 2014.

Chapter 76: Troubles and Tickets

1 Found at: Jehoash Hirshberg, *Music in the Jewish Community of Palestine: 1880–1948* (Oxford, Clarendon Paperbacks, 1995), p. 130.

Chapter 77: Toscanini Fever!

1 The testimony of Thelma Yellin, the Palestine Symphony's inaugural cellist.

Chapter 78: The Birth of the Palestine Symphony

1 Found at: http://temposenzatempo.blogspot.com/2010/11/horn-section-of-israel-philharmonic.html. Accessed: Dec. 11, 2014.

2 Found at: http://jewishcurrents.org/wp-content/uploads/2014/08/Toscanini-Huberman-and-the-Jews-by-David-Platt-3.82.pdf. Accessed: March 8, 2015.

3 Other dignitaries seated in the audience were: Signora Toscanini, the District Commissioner and Mrs. Crosbie, the Mayor and Mrs. Rokach, the Deputy Mayor and Mrs. Hos, Mr. and Mrs. Tolkowsky. Dr. and Mrs. Weizmann, Mr. and Mrs.

Ben-Gurion, Mr. and Mrs. Shertok, Lt.-Col. and Mrs. Kisch, Mr. and Mrs. Bentwitch, Mr. and Mrs. Edwin Samuel, Brigd.-General Carr and members of the staff of the Second Division, Mr. and Mrs. Jacobs, Miss Landau, Mr. Horowitz, Mr. Leonard Stein, Mr. and Mrs. Hoofien, Dr. and Mrs. Ferguson, Mr. and Mrs. Lees, Mr. and Mrs. M. Chelouche, Ahron de Menasce, Major and Mrs. Foley, Mr. and Mrs. Rubin, Mrs. Arlosoroff, Dr. Kaufmann, Mr. Victor Konn, Mr. and Mrs. A. Epstein, Mr. and Mrs. Kuppermann, Messrs. Komerov and Shimshi.

Epilogue: The Rest of the Story

1 Goetz's quote found at: www.huberman.info/literature/pan_europa/goetz/. Accessed: March 6, 2015.

2 Found at: http://dancutlermedicalart.com/AlbertEinstein'sZionism/06Einstein'sZionism1930-1939.htm. Accessed: March 6, 2015.

3 Quote found at: www.ipo.co.il/eng/About/History/.aspx. Accessed: Feb. 27, 2015.

4 Found at: www.jewishvirtuallibrary.org/jsource/Society_&_Culture/symph1.html. Accessed: Feb. 28, 2015, and www.ipo.co.il/eng/About/History/.aspx. Accessed: Feb. 28, 2015.

5 Found at: www.washingtonpost.com/entertainment/music/orchestra-of-exiles-a-reminder-of-how-artists-can-rise-to-meet-a-moral-challenge/2013/01/03/cbda3e50-5050-11e2-950a-7863a013264b_story.html. Accessed: March 6, 2015.

6 Found at: www.huberman.info/biography/palestine/. Accessed: March 4, 2015.

7 Found at: www.huberman.info/biography/palestine/. Accessed: March 4, 2015. Some information found at: www.huberman.info/biography/liberation/. Accessed: Feb. 28, 2015, and Ida Ibbeken and Tzvi Avni, *An Orchestra Is Born* (Israel: the Central Music Library in Israel and the Israel Philharmonic Orchestra, 1969), p. 87.

8 Quoted from: Josh Aronson, *Orchestra of Exiles* script, p. 39.

9 Found at: http://arbiterrecords.org/catalog/huberman-concert-and-recital-recordings/. Accessed: March 6, 2015.

10 Quoted from: Josh Aronson, *Orchestra of Exiles* script, p. 23.

11 Found at: www.joshuabell.com/story-his-violin. Accessed: Feb. 28, 2015.

12 Quoted from: Josh Aronson, *Orchestra of Exiles* script, p. 23.

13 To view the videos, please see: https://www.youtube.com/watch?v=BJhZ0J3bIYc.

14 Found at: www.denmarkarts.org/behind-the-music-erno-dohnanyi/. Accessed: Feb. 28, 2015.

15 Information found at: http://pl.net/~holsem/huberman/bio/marriage.htm. Accessed: Feb. 28, 2015, and http://books.google.com/books?id=9pWtDbd_7woC&pg=PA6&lpg=PA6&dq=Elsa+Galafres&source=bl&ots=qeHD1ijsFS&sig=fbtjWuXw-EPU7KxlfeH-6rLAvjI&hl=en&sa=X&ei=Dh6G

U8vcGK_NsQSToIDACA&ved=0CEYQ6AEwCA#v=onepage&q=Elsa%20
Galafres&f=false. Accessed: Feb. 28, 2015.

16 Found at: www.joachim-dietze.de/pdf/dohnanyi_aa.pdf. Accessed: Feb. 28, 2015.

17 Found at: www.hubermans.net/mordechai_huberman_Family/mordechai_huber
man_family.htm. Accessed: Feb. 28, 2015.

18 Quote found at: www.surrealistmovement-usa.org/pages/news_toscanini.html.
Accessed: Jan. 20, 2015.

19 Quoted from: Josh Aronson, *Orchestra of Exiles* script, p. 37.

20 Information found at: www.naxos.com/person/Arturo_Toscanini_26518/26518
.htm. Accessed: February 28, 2015, and www.bach-cantatas.com/Bio/Toscanini-
Arturo.htm. Accessed: Feb. 28, 2015. (Note: To view video: "Final Respects Paid
to Maestro Arturo Toscanini," 1957, please see: www.britishpathe.com/video/
final-respects-paid-to-maestro-arturo-toscanini/query/queues.)

21 Information found at: http://einstein.biz/biography.php. Accessed: Feb. 28, 2015,
and www.biography.com/people/albert-einstein-9285408. Accessed: Feb. 28, 2015.
(Note: To view a fascinating video on the life and work of Albert Einstein, please
see: www.biography.com/people/albert-einstein-9285408.)

22 Some information found at: www.allmusic.com/artist/william-steinberg-
mn0000693807/biography. Accessed: Feb. 27, 2015, and www.britannica.com/
EBchecked/topic/564990/William-Steinberg. Accessed: Feb. 27, 2015.

23 Found at: www.ipo.co.il/eng/About/History/.aspx. Accessed: Feb. 28, 2015, and
www.nytimes.com/learning/general/onthisday/bday/0128.html. Accessed:
Feb. 28, 2015.

24 Found at: www.independent.co.uk/news/obituaries/lorand-fenyves-6168744.html.
Accessed: Feb. 28, 2015.

25 Quoted from: Josh Aronson, *Orchestra of Exiles* script, p. 17.

26 Ibid., p. 16.

27 Ibid., p. 19.

28 Found at: www.violinist.com/blog/doritstraus/20101/10805/. Accessed: Feb. 27,
2015, and http://art-crime.blogspot.com/2012/10/arca-lecturer-dorit-straus-on-
how.html. Accessed: Feb. 27, 2015.

29 Found at: www.axa-art-usa.com/news-events/detail/detail/axa-art-americas-corpo
ration-elects-noted-fine-art-insurance-industry-expert-dorit-straus-to-its-boa.html.
Accessed: Feb. 28, 2015.

30 Quoted from: Josh Aronson, *Orchestra of Exiles* script, p. 38.

31 Found at: www.catholicherald.co.uk/commentandblogs/2014/02/07/another-
jewish-historian-concludes-that-the-latest-research-erases-the-image-of-a-pius-xii-
indifferent-to-the-fate-of-the-jews/. Accessed: Feb. 27, 2015.

32 Information about Gideon Toeplitz found at: www.adweek.com/fishbowldc/
roll-call-scribes-father-dies-in-israel/54648. Accessed: Feb. 27, 2015. Information

on Uri Toeplitz, found at: www.leo-kestenberg.com/music-educator/info_
commentaries_ang.cfm?cfgsection=multimediadokumentation&cfgsoussection=zei
tzeugen&id=215&section=commentary. Accessed: Feb. 27, 2015, and http://www
.zoominfo.com/p/Uri-Toeplitz/165262474. Accessed: Feb. 27, 2015, and www.geni
.com/people/Dr-Uri-Toeplitz/6000000023513379440. Accessed: Feb. 27, 2015.

33 Found at: www.jewishvirtuallibrary.org/jsource/biography/ben_gurion.html.
Accessed: Feb. 27, 2015.

34 Found at: www.jewishvirtuallibrary.org/jsource/biography/Dizengoff
.html. Accessed: Feb. 27, 2015.

35 Found at: www.jewishvirtuallibrary.org/jsource/biography/weizmann.html.
Accessed: Feb. 27, 2015.

36 Quoted from: Josh Aronson, *Orchestra of Exiles* script, p. 21.

37 Found at: http://holocaustmusic.ort.org/politics-and-propaganda/third-reich/
the-berlin-jdischer/singer-kurt/. Accessed: Feb. 28, 2015, and quoted from: Josh
Aronson, *Orchestra of Exiles* script, p. 21.

38 Found at: www.britannica.com/EBchecked/topic/222722/Wilhelm-Furtwangler.
Accessed: Feb. 28, 2015.

39 Found at: www.classicalnotes.net/features/furtwangler.html. Accessed:
Feb. 27, 2015.

40 Information found at: www.jewishvirtuallibrary.org/jsource/Holocaust/hitler_
timeline.html. Accessed: Feb. 28, 2015, and www.biography.com/people/adolf-
hitler-9340144. Accessed: Feb. 28, 2015. (Note: To learn more about Hitler,
and to see a video about his life, please see: www.biography.com/people/adolf-
hitler-9340144.)

41 Found at: www.dw.de/hitlers-unearthed-music-collection-yields-surprising-
finds/a-2722872. Accessed: March 15, 2015.

42 Some information found at: www.history.ucsb.edu/faculty/marcuse/classes/33d/
projects/naziwomen/winifred.htm and www.fpp.co.uk/Hitler/Wagner/Hamann1
.html. Accessed: Jan. 8, 2015.

43 Some information found at: www.jewishvirtuallibrary.org/jsource/Holocaust/
olympics.html. Accessed: Dec. 11, 2014. (Note: To view Hitler and the 1936
Opening Ceremony of the Berlin Olympics, please see: www.youtube.com/
watch?v=GePNydI9gX4. Accessed: Dec. 10, 2014.)

44 Found at: www.biography.com/people/joseph-goebbels-9313998#the-nazi-party.
Accessed: Feb. 28, 2015.

45 Found at: www.wzo.org.il/mount-herzl and at: http://www.herzl.org/english/
Article.aspx?Item=492&. Accessed: Aug. 10, 2014.

46 Found at: www.history.com/topics/world-war-ii/world-war-ii-history. Accessed:
Feb. 28, 2015. (Note: To view videos and learn more WWII history, please see:
www.history.com/topics/world-war-ii/world-war-ii-history.)

47 Found at: www.sothebys.com/en/search-results.html?keyword=Brahms. Accessed: Aug. 8, 2014.

48 Some information found at: http://blogs.forward.com/the-arty-semite/159616/duesseldorf-will-replace-mendelssohn-statue/. Accessed: Dec. 11, 2014.

Appendix: Original Orchestra Members Listed in 1936–37 Opening Concert:

1 Found at: www.pbs.org/wnet/orchestra-of-exiles/origins-map/. Accessed: Feb. 28, 2015.

INDEX